THE ROCK OF
OUR SALVATION

The Rock of
Our Salvation

William Plumer

CountedFaithful

THE ROCK OF OUR SALVATION
First published in 1867
This edition © Counted Faithful, 2018

COUNTED FAITHFUL
2 Drakewood Road
London SW16 5DT

Website: http://www.countedfaithful.org

ISBN
Book: 978-1-78872-142-4
ePub: 978-1-78872-143-1
Kindle: 978-1-78872-144-8

Contents

Contents

1
Christ All-in-All

WHEN I was a youth, in the bond of iniquity and in the gall of bitterness, I fell into distress concerning my soul. I feared I should be lost for ever. Being in the company of two Christian ladies, one of them kindly expressed the wish that my impressions might not be transient. This I understood. The other expressed the hope that Christ might be to me All-in-all. To me, whose heart was covered with a veil of unbelief, her words were as the speech of a barbarian. Yet they made an impression. From them I learned that some persons knew a secret hidden from me; and I longed to learn what it was. I hope I have gained some insight into it, and I propose to present some of the views I have obtained.

The great central truth of the religion of sinners relates to the person, character, work, sufferings, offices, and glory of Jesus Christ. These are vital in Christianity. As one is sound or corrupt here, so is he substantially right or wrong in the main. Both now and in the last day, the great question in determining character and destiny is the same: "What think ye of Christ?"

On this subject the controversy is old. It goes back to the first two men ever born. Cain and Abel split on this point. In the immediate family of Adam the strife began, and it has never ceased. In the days of Moses the hardest thing to be borne in the profession of the true religion was "the reproach of Christ." When Messiah was born, the strife was resumed with more warmth than ever. The wise men brought their gifts of gold, frankincense, and myrrh, but when Herod heard of his birth, he was troubled, and all Jerusalem with him, and he sought the young child to destroy him. And when Christ became a public teacher, some said, He is a good man; others, He deceiveth the people. One party worshipped him; the other crucified him. Even when he was on the cross, the spectators were divided – some looking on with unutterable grief; others wagging their heads and deriding him. In fact, the very thieves who died with him were not of one mind; one reviling him, the other calling him Lord. On the day of Pentecost the controversy was renewed with great vigour, and with great advantage to the cause of truth; and it has been kept up ever since. All the friends of God have at heart been on one side, and all his enemies substantially on the other – if not openly, yet secretly; if not by profession, yet in practice. For centuries since then a large portion of all the heresies that have arisen have related to the person or work of Christ. Infidelity is most bitter against Christ, while piety feeds upon the truth of which he is the sum. Many scoff and more refuse; while some admire and adore. Some obey; others cry, 'We will not have this man to reign over us.' In no age has malice against Christ been more envenomed than in the present.

Jesus Christ is a wonderful, a glorious person. To look away from self and one's own works to Christ, is to lay hold on eternal life. Safety consists in fleeing to him and abiding in him. When he is in the ascendant, the night flees away, and the morning comes – a morning without clouds. His names and titles are as important as they are significant. Every one of them is as ointment poured forth. His lips drop as the honeycomb; honey and milk are under his tongue, and the smell of his garments is like the smell of Lebanon. His people sit under his shadow with great delight, and his fruit is sweet to their taste. To them he is altogether lovely.

He is their Advocate, the angel of the covenant, the author and finisher of faith. He is as the apple-tree among the trees of the wood; the Alpha and the Omega; the Beloved, the Shepherd and Bishop of souls, the bread of life, the righteous Branch, the bridegroom, the brightness of the Father's glory, and the express image of his person. He is a bundle of myrrh.

To his saints he is and is owned to be Creator, captain, counsellor, covenant, cornerstone, a covert from the tempest, and the chiefest among ten thousand. He is to them as the Dew, the door into the fold, a daysman, a day-star, a deliverer, a diadem, and the desire of all nations, ranks, and generations of pious men.

In their eyes he is the Elect, Emmanuel, the everlasting Father and eternal life. He is a Fountain of living waters to thirsty souls, of joy to troubled souls, of life to dying souls. He is the foundation on which his people of all ages safely build their hopes of heaven. He is the father of eternity, the fir-tree under whose shadow the saints rejoice, the first and the last, the first fruits of the greatest harvest ever gathered, the first-born among many brethren and the first-begotten from the dead.

To his chosen he is as the most fine Gold, a guide, a governor, a glorious Lord, God, the true God, God over all blessed for ever. He is the Head of the church, the health, the hope, the husband, the heritage, the habitation of his people. He is the horn of their salvation. He rides upon the heavens by his name Jah. He is the Jehovah, the inheritance, Judge and King of his saints. He is their light, their life, their Lord, their leader, their lawgiver, their atoning lamb, the lily of the valley, the lion of the tribe of Judah.

He is the Man Christ Jesus, the master, the mediator, the messenger of the covenant, the minister of the true sanctuary, which the Lord pitched and not man. He is the mighty God of Isaiah, the Michael of Daniel, the Melchizedek of David and of Paul, the bright and morning star of John, and the Messiah of all the prophets.

He is the Only-begotten of the Father, full of grace and truth. He is at once the root and the offspring of David. He is the Peace, the prince, the priest, the prophet, the potentate, the purifier, the propitiation for our sins, the physician of souls, the plant of renown, the power of God unto salvation, the Passover of all saints. He is a polished shaft in the quiver of God.

He is the Rock, the refuge, the ruler, the ransom, the refiner, the Redeemer, the righteousness and the resurrection of all that walk in white. He is the rose of Sharon. He is the Seed of the woman, the seed of Abraham, the seed of David, the stem of Jesse, the Son of God, the Son of man, the shield, the strength, the surety, the Shiloh, the sacrifice, the sanctuary, the salvation, the sanctification, and the sun of righteousness to all believers.

He is that holy Thing that was born of Mary. He is the truth, the treasure, the teacher, the temple, the tree of life, the great testator of his church. He is the Way, the well of salvation, the Word of God, the wisdom of God, the faithful witness. He is the Wonderful.

His person is one; his natures are two. He is both human and divine, finite and infinite, created and uncreated. He was before Abraham, though not born for ages after that patriarch slept with his fathers. He was dead, and behold he is alive for evermore.

On earth he had not where to lay his head; yet he disposes of all diadems. By him kings rule and princes decree justice. He has the arm of a God, and the heart of a brother. To him all tongues shall confess and all knees bow; yet learned he obedience by the things which he suffered. None loves like him, none pities like him, none saves like him.

It is not surprising that such a person lives and reigns in the hearts of his people. No marvel that the virgins love him, and the saints praise him, and the martyrs die for him, and the confessors are not ashamed of him, and the sorrowing sigh for him, and the penitent lie at his cross and pour out their tears before him, and the humble trust in him, and the believing lay fast hold of him and will not let him go. His frown shakes the frame of universal nature, his smile gives life, his presence converts dungeons into palaces, his blood cleanses from all sin, his righteousness is the white robe of the redeemed.

If men would be safe, or wise, or holy, or happy, or useful, or strong, or victorious; let them look to Jesus, let them look to none else, let them walk in him, abide in him, glory in him, and count as loss all things besides. You may look at the law till the spirit of bondage overwhelms you with terrors and torments. You may go about to establish your own righteousness till you can boast, and sin, and perish like a Pharisee. You may weep till the fountain of your tears has gone dry, you may have all gifts, understand all mysteries, bestow all your goods to feed the poor, and yield your body to be burned; but all these things will not atone for sin, will do nothing toward regaining the lost favour of God, will not make you meet for the inheritance of the saints in light. "None but Christ, none but Christ, none but Christ," has been the cry of the faithful witnesses of all ages when truth has triumphed, when oracles were struck dumb, when sinners were converted, when saints shouted for joy, when the Word of God mightily grew and prevailed.

True piety begins, continues, and is perfected, by our union with Christ. We are cleansed through his blood, we are clothed in his righteousness, we are purified by his Spirit. We meet the demands of the law of this day of grace when we walk as he walked, and have the same mind that was in him. In proportion as men are truly pious, they make him the foundation and the top-stone, the sum and substance, and centre of all their hopes and rejoicings before God. He is accepted and believed on in the world, not merely because there is no other Saviour, but because his way of saving sinners precisely suits their case, and because it brings glory to God in the highest. The true believer not only trusts in Christ, but makes his boast in him. He not only makes mention of him; he admits none into comparison with him. To all the ends, parts, and purposes of salvation, Christ stands alone. There is none like him, there is none with him, there is none before him, there is none after him, there is none beside him. He had no predecessor; he has, and shall have, no successor. He has no vicegerent; he has no assistant; he wears an undivided crown, and wields a perfect sovereignty over an undivided kingdom. If God's people exalt him above all others, so does his holy and eternal Father. If they crown him Lord of all, God also hath highly exalted him, and given him a name that is above every name. If they surpassingly admire and extol him, there is cause for this preference. It is a holy, reasonable thing, to fall before him and cry, My Lord and my God. If he is the delight of the sons of men, he is also the delight of his Father. Listen to the voice from the excellent glory: "This is my beloved Son, in whom I am well pleased."

We sadly err when we begin in the spirit and end in the flesh; when we regard Christ as the Author, but not as the Finisher, of our faith. A legal spirit is the bane of piety. It is as great a foe to holy comfort as it is to gospel grace. Through the law believers are dead to the law, that they may live unto God. This is the evangelical plan. Here is the secret of growing conformity to God. Here is power, here is life, here is wisdom. We are complete in him.

In the wars of opinion, the greatest contests ever known have been on the question whether Christ is the sole and sufficient cause of salvation to men. Strange that any who have God's Word should be at a loss on this subject. The language of Scripture could not be more clear: "Christ is the end of the law for righteousness to every one that believeth." (*Romans 10:4*). This is the sum of inspired teachings on the subject. This doctrine is quite beyond the suggestion of human wit, but wholly accordant with right reason. The gospel is not the progeny of human wisdom, but it is the proper remedy for human woes. The heart of man is strongly wedded to a plan that will not abase pride nor silence boasting. Although in regeneration folly is so far cured that the soul reclines upon Jesus, yet even the converted sometimes fall into sad declensions, and lose their clear and lively apprehensions of the one way of salvation provided by God. Then follow darkness, dejection, and strange perplexities. They are then "bewitched" and "obey not the truth."

Christ is our life; severed from him, we are withered branches. It is only when Christ is clearly seen and cordially embraced that our peace is like a river, and our righteousness like the waves of the sea. The entire Christian race is run by pressing towards the mark for the prize of the high calling of God in Christ Jesus. All the acts of faith are the fruit of the Spirit; the object of them all is the person of the Lord Jesus Christ; the warrant of them all is the promise of God, the offer of the gospel: and while they utterly renounce self, they bring Christ into the soul, the hope of glory.

Oh that men would learn that mount Sinai is far from Jerusalem, and that Calvary is hard by it. The nearer we are to the law as a covenant of life, the further we are from Christ, from deliverance. The hosts of saints who have finished their course and gone home to God all found in themselves sin, guilt, folly, misery, and helplessness; while in him were hid all the treasures of wisdom, grace, and glory. Hear their sayings:

John Brown of Haddington said: "The command is, 'Owe no man any thing.' What a mercy that there is no such precept as this, Owe a Saviour nothing; or even this, Study to owe him as little as possible. Oh what a mercy that my admission into eternal life does not depend on my ability for anything; but as a poor sinner, will win in leaning on Christ as the Lord my righteousness; on Christ, made of God unto me righteousness, sanctification, and redemption. I have nothing to sink my spirits but my sins; and these need not sink me either, since the great God is my Saviour."

M'Cheyne said: "Live within sight of Calvary, and you will live in sight of glory."

When dying, Dr Nevins said: "I recommend Christ to you; I have nothing else to recommend."

Well was it said of old, "It is better to die with Christ than to reign with Caesar."

John says, "The testimony of Jesus is the spirit of prophecy." (*Revelation 19:10*).

Peter says, "To Him gave all the prophets witness." (*Acts 10:43*).

Paul says, "God forbid that I should glory, save in the cross of our Lord Jesus Christ." (*Galatians 6:14*).

This subject suggests a few remarks to two classes of persons:

1. To Christians. In choosing Christ, you acted wisely. Exquisite suffering for him is better than exquisite enjoyment with the world. It is better to be a prisoner for him than a prince without him. To die in Christ is to fall asleep in Jesus, and be for ever with the Lord. Hold fast your profession of his name. Stick to him, stand up for him, live unto him, look to him, be ready to die for him, let your desires centre in him, let your motives to holy living be drawn from him, let your sorrows be sanctified by him. Let your joys be heightened, chastened, sweetened by him. Keep to him alone. We are as much bound to believe that there is but one Mediator as that there is but one God. (*1 Timothy 2:5*). None else can do us any good. Devotion to Christ cannot be excessive. Many love, and serve, and trust, and praise him too little; but whoever loved, or served, or trusted, or praised him too much? "There is no love of duty where there is no love to Christ."

2. To such as have not fled to Christ, and are yet in their sins. Will you not embrace the Saviour? If Christ shall not be taken as your surety, you must pay your own debt. Despise not his cross. It is the life of men. By wicked men it was designed to be, and is still esteemed, the seal of infamy, the badge of ignominy. Christ crucified was to the Jews a stumbling-block, and to the Greeks foolishness. But see to it that you follow not their wicked ways. Come to Christ; he died for our sins; he offered himself without spot to God, a ransom for many, a sweet-smelling savour. Cast yourselves upon him. Believe in him, and the law has no more penal demands against you; believe in him, and God will accept you in the Beloved; believe in him, and your right to the tree of life is at once complete; believe in him, and the sting of death is extracted; believe in him, and you shall have part in the first resurrection; believe in him, and you shall have boldness in the Day of Judgment. But reject him a little longer, and

your heart will be harder than it is now; reject him a little longer, and the call to light and life will reach you no more; reject him a little longer, and the day of grace will be gone for ever; reject him a little longer, and you will awake to shame and everlasting contempt. "There is a fearful chasm in the heart that has no love for Christ."

2
The Divinity of Christ

THE design of this chapter is to state and prove the doctrine of the true, proper, and supreme divinity of the Lord Jesus Christ. His Godhead is true, not fictitious; it is proper, not figurative; it is supreme, not merely super-angelic. None is divine in a higher sense than the Saviour of lost men. The proofs of this truth are various, multi-form, and abundant.

I. The names of God are, in Scripture, given to Jesus Christ. One apostle says of him, "This is the true God, and eternal life." (*1 John 5:20*). Speaking of the Israelites, another apostle says, "Of whom as concerning the flesh Christ came, who is over all, God blessed for ever." (*Romans 9:5*). In both Testaments he is called Immanuel, which means God with us. (*Isaiah 7:14; Matthew 1:23*). Speaking of him, Paul says: "God was manifest in the flesh." (*1 Timothy 3:16*). The evangelical prophet calls him the "mighty God, the everlasting Father." (*Isaiah 9:6*). Peter says, "He is Lord of all." (*Acts 10:36*). Paul says, He is "the Lord of glory." (*1 Corinthians 2:8*). Both Isaiah and Joel call him by the awful and incommunicable name, *Jehovah*. (*Isaiah 6:5; Joel 2:32*. Compare *John 12:41; Romans 10:13*). The Bible styles our Saviour, God, the true God, God blessed for ever, Lord of all, Lord of glory, God with us, Jehovah, Lord of hosts. This language is used by prophets and apostles at periods long separated and on occasions very diverse; some before his birth, others at his birth, and others after his ascension to glory. Surely God's Word thus teaches that he is divine.

Lord Jesus, thou God over all, thou Jehovah of hosts, be thou our Friend. Bless and help each one of us. Be unto us a horn of salvation.

II. Divine attributes are also ascribed to him. *Eternity* is one of his perfections: "In the beginning was the Word." (*John 1:1*). John the Baptist was born six months before our Lord, yet of our Saviour he says, "He was before me." (*John 1:15*). In prophecy, Christ gives this account of himself: "The Lord possessed me in the beginning of his way, before his works of old. I was set up from everlasting, from the beginning, or ever the earth was." (*Proverbs 8:22, 23*). When on earth, he asserted his own eternity and self-existence: "Before Abraham was, I am." (*John 8:58*). More than sixty years after his ascension from Olivet, and within eight verses of the close of the New Testament, Jesus says of himself, "I am Alpha and Omega, the beginning and the end, the first and the last." (*Revelation 22:13*). He who is himself the Alpha, the first, the beginning, must be self-existent, independent, and eternal. Surely he who can truly thus speak of himself is divine.

O thou eternal Son of God, thou Father of eternity, remember that we are of yesterday and are crushed before the moth. Bring us, in the fulness of thy grace, to behold thy glory, which thou hadst with thy Father before the world was.

Omnipresence is another attribute of God claimed by Christ: "Where two or three are gathered together in my name, there am I in the midst of them." (*Matthew 18:20*). Christ could not thus meet all the little groups of his worshippers in all parts of the world, unless he were omnipresent. He claims the same perfection when he says to his disciples, "Lo, I am with you alway, even unto the end of the world." (*Matthew 28:20*). If this promise conveys any natural and obvious sense, it is one that, beyond a doubt, implies the omnipresence, and therefore the divinity, of Jesus Christ.

Blessed Saviour, who art everywhere present, preside in all our solemn assemblies, large and small. Walk thou in the midst of the golden candlesticks. Be thou unto us for a little sanctuary.

Omniscience is another attribute of God belonging to Christ. Peter said, "Lord, thou knowest all things." (*John 21:17*). By his omniscience, Jesus declared Judas a devil, even when he was unsuspected by any of his intimate friends. By his omniscience, he convinced Nathanael of his Messiahship and Divinity. Two things are wholly inscrutable except to omniscience. One is, the human heart. Yet we are expressly informed that, even in his humiliation, Jesus "knew all men, and needed not that any should testify of man, for he knew what was in man." (*John 2:24, 25*). And when for three-score years the Son of man had been in glory he said, "All the churches shall know that I am he which searcheth the heart." (*Revelation 2:23*). The other thing unsearchable except to God only, is the Divine nature. Yet Jesus declares that he is master of that awful mystery: "As the Father knoweth me, even so know I the Father." (*John 10:15*). Surely he who thus knows the unsearchable God is himself God.

Lord Jesus, search us, and know our hearts, try us, and know our thoughts, and see if there be any wicked way in us; lead us in the way everlasting; and reveal to us the glorious mystery of God.

Immutability is another perfection belonging to God only; and by inspired men it is ascribed to Jesus Christ. Having shown that this earth and the heavens above, with all that is grand and solid in them, must pass away, the Scriptures say of Christ, "Thou art the same, and thy years shall not fail." (*Psalm 102:25-27; Hebrews 1:10-12*). The inspired author of the *Epistle to the Hebrews* declares in explicit terms that "Jesus Christ is the same yesterday, and today, and for ever." (*Hebrews 13:8*). Without profaneness, we cannot ascribe unchangeableness to any but God. Yet Paul says that Jesus is ever the same. Is he not Divine?

Blessed Saviour, we rejoice that thou art the same as when thou didst weep at the grave of Lazarus; as when thou didst pour salvation on the dying thief; as when, in ascending to glory, thou didst bless thy followers. We rejoice that thy state is changed and thy nature immutable. Oh pity and bless us. Be unto us a sure foundation, a munition of rocks.

Beyond all doubt, *omnipotence* is an attribute of God only. We cannot reason with one who persistently contends that almightiness is the property of man or angel. But God's Word abundantly teaches that Jesus Christ is omnipotent. Surely he who in his own name raises the dead and subjects the universe to his power is almighty. Paul says Jesus does both these things: "Our conversation is in heaven; from whence also we look for the Saviour, the Lord Jesus Christ: who shall change our vile body, that it may be fashioned like unto his glorious body, according to the working whereby he is able even to subdue all things unto himself." (*Philippians 3:20, 21*). Surely such energy is omnipotent. In *Revelation 1:8*, Christ thus reveals himself: "I am Alpha and Omega, the beginning and the ending, saith the Lord; which is, and which was, and which is to come, the Almighty." Nor did Jesus acquire omnipotence by his ascension to glory. Indeed, almightiness cannot be acquired, else a creature might become God. But even in his humiliation Jesus said, "What things soever the Father doeth, these also doeth the Son likewise ... As the Father raiseth up the dead, and quickeneth them; even so the Son quickeneth whom he will." (*John 5:19, 21*). Jesus could do none of these things, if his power could be resisted. But irresistible power is omnipotent power, is divine power, and so Christ is divine.

O thou which art, and which wast, and which art to come, the Almighty, cover us in the hollow of thy hand. If our hold on thee is feeble, let thy hold on us be the grasp of omnipotence. Go forth conquering and to conquer, till all the earth owns thee Lord of all.

III. Those things which can be done by none but God are done by Jesus Christ, and therefore he is God. Such is the work of creation: "All things were made by him; and without him was not any thing made that was made," (*John 1:3*). "By him were all things created, that are in heaven, and that are in earth, visible and invisible, whether they be thrones, or dominions, or principalities, or powers: all things were created by him and for him." (*Colossians 1:16*). If by creation the Father is shown to be truly God, by creation also we establish the divinity of the Son.

Glorious Redeemer, we all were made by thee and for thee. We own thy perfect and sovereign right to us and over us. All we have and are, in soul or body, belongs to thee. Nor can anything dissolve the ties that bind us to thee for ever.

Jesus Christ also upholds, preserves, and governs the worlds which he has made. Isaiah says: "The government shall be upon his shoulder." (*Isaiah 9:6*). Paul says: "To the Son he [the Father] saith, Thy throne, O God, is for ever and ever." (*Hebrews 1:8*). In one place the same apostle says, he "upholdeth all things by the word of his power." (*Hebrews 1:3*). In another he says: "By him all things consist." (*Colossians 1:17*). Indeed his care and superintendence of all things is a necessity; for Paul says: "He must reign, till he hath put all things under his feet." (*1 Corinthians 15:25*). Thus all creatures, from the smallest insect that is seen by the microscope up to the archangel that worships and ministers before the eternal throne; all events, from the falling of a hair of the head to the wasting of nations by famine, pestilence, and war; all rule and authority, from that of a petty official to that of thrones and principalities in heaven; the material universe, from the least particle that floats in the sunbeam to the grandest system of worlds that roll in immensity – all hang dependent on his powerful providence; and if one link in the chain of that dependence were broken, they would all rush headlong to destruction. He always has governed this world; and he shall ever hold the sceptre over it, till his last foe shall be vanquished, and his last hidden one made victorious.

Lord Jesus, who upholdest all things by the word of thy power, bear us up, bear us on, bear us through, giving us the victory over death, and hell, and all the powers of darkness.

Again, redemption is more glorious than creation or providence; and Jesus Christ is the sole author of redemption. I never heard of anyone who believed in redemption by the Lord, who did not ascribe it to the Son. He alone was fit for this great work. Beveridge says: "Man can suffer, but he cannot satisfy; God can satisfy, but he cannot suffer; but Christ, being both God and man, can both suffer and satisfy too, and so is perfectly fit both to suffer for man and to make satisfaction unto God. And thus Christ, having assumed my nature into his person, and so satisfied Divine justice for my sins, I am received into grace and favour with the Most High God."

Two things the Scriptures make very clear. One is, that Christ has redeemed us from the curse of the law – that salvation is by his blood and righteousness. The other is, that for this redemption Christ is entitled to the warmest love and the highest honours, and that he actually receives both from all the redeemed. The Author of one's eternal salvation cannot be inferior to the Author of one's earthly existence, and so ought to be honoured and adored, because he is Divine.

Lord Jesus, who hast died the just for the unjust, set thy love on us, wash us from our sins in thy most precious blood, and make us kings and priests unto God.

Moreover, when Christ was on earth, he claimed and exercised the power of pardoning men's iniquities. "Man, thy sins are forgiven thee," – *Luke 5:20* – were his brief and solemn words of superhuman authority. He himself tells us that he thus spoke that we "might know that the Son of man hath power on earth to forgive sins." (*Matthew 9:6*). In fact, Christ is exalted a Prince and a Saviour to this very end, that he may grant repentance and remission of sins unto Israel. Verily he is God.

Lord Jesus, spread the skirt of thy bloody garment over our souls, and grant us repentance and remission of sins, and we shall be saved.

Nor is this all. Jesus Christ shall raise the dead. God says, in *Deuteronomy 32:39*, "I kill, and I make alive." In *Revelation 1:18*, the Lord Christ says, "I have the keys of hell and of death." Raising the dead is an act of almighty power, and so no creature can do it. Yet Paul says, "In Christ shall all be made alive." (*1 Corinthians 15:22*). When on earth, more than once Jesus gave life to the dead. He spake, and was obeyed, like a God: "Lazarus, come forth." He said, "This is the will of him that sent me, that every one which seeth the Son, and believeth on him, may have everlasting life: and I will raise him up at the last day." (*John 6:40*). Nay more, he even raised his own body from the dead: "I lay down my life, that I might take it again." "Destroy this temple, and in three days I will raise it up." (*John 2:19; 10:18*). Truly this is the Son of the Highest, and may fitly count it no robbery to be equal with God.

Kind Redeemer, we cheerfully follow thee into the grave, in hope of a glorious resurrection. We would not live always. In the last day raise us up, and make our vile bodies like unto thy glorious body. Give us part in the first resurrection.

In like manner shall Jesus Christ judge the quick and the dead at his coming. He expressly says that the Father hath given the Son "authority to execute judgment also, because he is the Son of man." (*John 5:27*). In the same chapter he says: "The Father judgeth no man, but hath committed all judgment unto the Son." (*John 5:22*). The great tribunal before which we must all stand is "the judgment-seat of Christ." (*Romans 14:10*). In *Revelation 1:7*, John says, "Behold he cometh with clouds; and every eye shall see him, and they also which pierced him: and all kindreds of the earth shall wail because of him." If Divine perfections are required for anything, it is for deciding on the destinies of men and angels; yet the unerring God has committed this judgment into the hands of Christ. He must, therefore, be God.

Lord Jesus, when thou comest in thy glory, with all thy holy angels, and the heavens shall flee away at thy presence, by thy mercy let us have boldness in the Day of Judgment.

And as Jesus made, and governs, and shall judge the world, so shall he destroy these heavens and this earth. So says inspiration: "Thou, Lord, in the beginning hast laid the foundation of the earth; and the heavens are the works of thine hands: they shall perish … as a vesture shalt thou fold them up, and they shall be changed." (*Hebrews 1:10-12*). Who can do this, and do it with the ease with which man folds up a garment and lays it aside, but God only? Yet Jesus Christ shall do this very thing. Surely he is divine.

Jesus, our Lord and our God, when thou shalt dissolve the frame of all sublunary things, remember and spare us according to the riches of thy grace in glory.

IV. The Bible has done more to root out idolatry than all other books. It declares that idolaters shall have their part in the lake of fire. Yet this same holy book authorises the highest acts of worship to be offered to Christ. Faith in him is as much required as faith in the Father: "Ye believe in God, believe also in me." (*John 14:1*). We are required in both Testaments to embrace him and trust in him on pain of perdition: "Kiss the Son, lest he be angry, and ye perish from the way when his wrath is kindled but a little. Blessed are all they that put their trust in him." (*Psalm 2:12*). "He that believeth not the Son shall not see life; but the wrath of God abideth on him." (*John 3:36*). The Scriptures never require of us to rely on man. On the contrary, they say, "Cursed is he that trusteth in man." (*Jeremiah 17:5*). But they also say: "There shall be a Root of Jesse, and he that shall rise to reign over the Gentiles; in Him shall the Gentiles trust." (*Romans 15:12*). Yea, more: "At the name of Jesus every knee shall bow, of things in heaven, and things in earth, and things under the earth." (*Philippians 2:10*). And all this is by God's command; for "when he bringeth in the First-begotten into the world, he saith, And let all the angels of God worship him." (*Hebrews 1:6*). Before he was born, his mother's cousin Elisabeth by the Holy Ghost called him; "My Lord." (*Luke 1:43*). After his resurrection, Thomas adoringly said, "My Lord and my God." (*John 20:28*). The first Christian martyr worshipped him, crying,

"Lord Jesus, receive my spirit." (*Acts 7:59*). That Jesus receives the highest worship offered in heaven the Scriptures clearly assert: "And I beheld, and I heard the voice of many angels round about the throne and the beasts and the elders: and the number of them was ten thousand times ten thousand, and thousands of thousands; saying with a loud voice, Worthy is the Lamb that was slain to receive power, and riches, and wisdom, and strength, and honour, and glory, and blessing. And every creature which is in heaven, and on the earth, and under the earth, and such as are in the sea, and all that are in them, heard I saying, Blessing, and honour, and glory, and power, be unto him that sitteth upon the throne, and unto the Lamb for ever and ever." (*Revelation 5:11-13*). No part of God's Word speaks of a higher degree or more complete universality of solemn worship than is here said to have been offered to the Son. Verily he is divine. He is God. He has supreme divinity. There is no idolatry in heaven, yet Jesus is worshipped there.

O thou Lamb of God, grant us this one favour – to worship thee with true devotion here below, and after this life to unite with the heavenly throng in ascribing to thee blessing, and honour, and power, and glory, and salvation.

The foregoing is but an outline of the argument on this glorious theme. The Bible is full of it. Sometimes we have nearly whole chapters devoted to this weighty matter. Such are the eighth chapter of *Proverbs* and the first chapter of the *Epistle to the Hebrews*. Many considerable portions of several books of the Bible are given to establish the same truth. The *Gospel of John* is evidently written chiefly for the same purpose. The very first verse may be taken as a text of the whole: "In the beginning was the Word, and the Word was with God, and the Word was God." Time would fail us to dwell on each of the proofs of our Lord's divinity found in this gospel.

Indeed, we may with Melville say: "There is no such book of contradictions as the Bible, if there be no person who was both human and divine. Nothing but such a combination will make sense of the Bible, or rescue it from maintaining a vast mass of inconsistencies. Some may think that it would simplify the Christian theology to remove from it the mystery that two natures coalesced in the one person of Christ; but as the divinity of our Lord is the foundation of our hope, so is it the key to the Bible. We acknowledge, reverently, a great mystery, but not the thousandth part as great as the whole Bible becomes on the supposition that Christ was only man."

*   *   *

1. If Jesus Christ is divine, he may safely be trusted with our whole case. He will betray no interest committed to him. He invites all to come. He welcomes all who come. He is all-sufficient. He is chosen, called, and ordained of God, to this very work of saving lost men who seek a refuge in him. A pious man once said: "If I did not know my Saviour to be God, I should this night lie down in despair: the Scripture could in this case convey no comfort to my mind." But He is divine, and we may safely rest the whole weight of our salvation on his almighty arm, and trust our most complicated affairs to the solution of his infinite wisdom.

2. Faith in the Lord Jesus Christ is a most reasonable duty. "He that hath the Son hath life; and he that hath not the Son of God hath not life." (*1 John 5:12*). If we fail here we fail utterly, for there is salvation in no other. He is the Rock. All hopes not built on him must for ever perish. Jesus is set for the rise and the fall of many. He will be to us a rock of salvation or a stone of stumbling; the shadow of a great rock in a weary land, or a rock of offence to the unbelieving. I have long since ceased to marvel that Jehovah has laid such stress on this doctrine. In their measure the pious do the same. They all cling to it as their last hope. Oh that every man would ask God to give him faith, saving faith; for "no man can say that Jesus is the Lord, but by the Holy Ghost." (*1 Corinthians 12:3*).

3. Will you have this Lord Jesus for your Saviour? Will you bow your head, and take his yoke upon you? If you confess and forsake your sins, he is faithful and just to forgive your sins, and to cleanse you from all iniquity. Will you have him? You need him. You need him now. You need him urgently. You need him to help you live. You will need him to help you die. You will need his grace and mercy for ever.

3
The Sonship of Christ

THE Scriptures say much of the Son of God. Many scores of times is the Saviour called the Son, the Son of the Blessed, the Son of the Highest, or the Son of God. Very often too have we the corresponding term, Father, expressing the relations of the first person of the Godhead to the second.

The Sonship of Christ is one of the glorious mysteries of our religion. Angels are, indeed, sometimes called the sons of God. Thus, in the only reliable history of the origin of our world, we are told that at the creation "the morning stars sang together, and all the sons of God shouted for joy." (*Job 38:7*). Because Adam came into existence without any created instrumentality, but directly from the hand of God, he is called the son of God. (*Luke 3:38*). And because all believers are, by the Holy Spirit, renewed into the image of the Most High, and are adopted into the heavenly family, they are called the sons of God. (*Romans 8:14; 1 John 3:1*). But the whole tenor of the argument in the early part of the *Epistle to the Hebrews* goes to show that Jesus Christ is the Son of the Father in a sense far higher than can be claimed for any mere creature. He is pre-eminently God's own Son, (*Romans 8:32*); and God's dear Son, (*Colossians 1:13*); and God is pre-eminently his Father, (*John 5:18*).

Some have maintained that Christ was the Son of God only in the sense that he was conceived by the power of the Holy Ghost in the womb of the Virgin Mary. In proof, they cite *Luke 1:35:* "The Holy Ghost shall come upon thee, and the power of the Highest shall overshadow thee: therefore also that holy thing which shall be born of thee shall be called the Son of God." Should we admit that this passage teaches that Christ's human nature was so derived from the Holy Spirit as to make it proper to call him the Son of God, this would not show that he was in no higher sense begotten of the Father. Nor would this express his relation to the Father. But the passage fairly admits of another construction, namely, that he who is thus miraculously brought into the world is thereby infallibly proven to be the Son of God in the highest sense ever claimed.

It has also been maintained by some that Christ's designation to office constituted his Sonship. In proof, they cite *John 10:36:* "Say ye of him, whom the Father hath sanctified, and sent into the world, Thou blasphemest, because I said, I am the Son of God?" But, like the preceding, this passage may fairly refer to the proof, and not to the cause or nature of his Sonship with God. One text says, "The Son of God is come." Another says, "God sent forth his Son," (*Galatians 4:4*). He did not become the Son of God by coming or by being sent, but being the Son of God, he was sent and is come. Many other texts afford similar proof.

Others have said that Christ is called the Son of God only because he rose from the dead. For proof they cite *Acts 13:33:* "God hath fulfilled the promise unto us, in that he hath raised up Jesus again; as it is also written in the second psalm, Thou art my Son, this day have I begotten thee." But this passage receives its clear exposition from *Romans 1:4*, where the apostle says that Jesus Christ our Lord was "declared [defined, marked out as by a boundary, determined, that is, beyond doubt proven] to be the Son of God with power, according to the Spirit of holiness, by the resurrection from the dead." In other words, Christ's resurrection for ever settled in all fair minds the question of his Sonship with God.

Others have said that Christ was called the Son of God simply because he is heir of all things. In proof, they cite *Hebrews 1:3-5:* "He sat down on the right hand of the Majesty on high; being made so much better than the angels, as he hath by inheritance obtained a more excellent name than they. For unto which of the angels said he at any time, Thou art my Son, this day have I begotten thee?" But heirship comes from Sonship; not Sonship from heirship: "If children, then heirs." (*Romans 8:17*). The fact that Christ is heir of all things is irrefragable proof that he is the Son of God. But Christ's Sonship is more than all these.

I. He is the Son of the Father in a higher and more glorious sense. In the preceding chapter, it has been shown that he existed long ages before he became incarnate; that he was possessed of all divine attributes; that he was uncreated, and justly claimed supreme divinity. This Sonship of our Lord clearly implies that he has the same nature with the Father; and so, as the Scriptures say, He was begotten of the Father. When we say that Christ is by nature the Son of God, we mean that the Father communicates to him his being and perfections. He himself says, "All things that the Father hath are mine." (*John 16:15*). "As the Father hath life in himself, so hath he given to the Son to have life in himself." (*John 5:26*). Indeed, "the communication of the Divine essence by the Father is the generation of the Son." In nature, the Father and the Son are perfectly the same. Nor did the Father ever communicate by generation his divine essence to any other; so that Jesus Christ is properly called God's only Son, and his *only begotten* Son. This generation of the Son is entirely peculiar to himself, and is the foundation of all the holy worship offered to the Redeemer in heaven and earth, of all saving confidence reposed in the efficacy of his blood-shedding and intercession, and of the all-controlling gratitude felt towards him for his amazing condescension in coming into the world and dying for our salvation.

II. The Sonship of Christ is real, not imaginary; and proper, not figurative. It is the foundation of the everlasting relation between the Father and the Son, and not merely the mode of our conceiving of the Divine subsistence. Christ is as truly and properly the Son of God as Abel was the son of Adam; that is, his nature is as truly the nature of his Father as the nature of any man is that of his parent. Adam "begat a son in his own likeness, after his image." (*Genesis 5:3*). So, by his generation, Jesus Christ is "the brightness of his Father's glory, and the express image of his person." Every other name and title of our Lord has a delightful fitness and significancy. Why should that of Son of God be an exception? He is called Jesus, because he shall save his people from their sins. Who deserves the name of Saviour as he does? He is called Christ, because the Spirit was wonderfully poured upon him. If Aaron's anointing filled his presence with sweet perfume, the anointing of Christ fills heaven and earth with an odour of a sweet smell. He is called Lord and Master, because he has perfect sovereignty over us. None ever so worthily wore a crown or swayed a sceptre. He is called Wonderful, for his person, his birth, his life, his works, his doctrines, his death, his resurrection, his glory, all entitle him to that appellation. He is called Counsellor, for none deals so prudently. (*Isaiah 52:13*). His wisdom and plans will yet destroy every dark plot of iniquity. He himself says, "Counsel is mine, and sound wisdom: I am understanding; I have strength." (*Proverbs 8:14*). The Spirit of counsel and might rests upon him. (*Isaiah 11:2*). Speaking of the man whose name is The Branch, the prophet says: "He shall build the temple of the Lord, and the counsel of peace shall be between them both:" that is, between Jehovah and the Branch, between the Father and the Son. (*Zechariah 6:12, 13*). So that he is the Counsellor of God. He is also the Counsellor of all men who believe in him. He is the true light, the infallible teacher of all the saints. He is called Redeemer. None half so fitly bears that title. Others bought back captives with such corruptible things as silver and gold; he redeems through his most precious blood. They redeem from temporal, he from eternal woe. He is the Christ, and Jesus Christ is the Son of God, and Jesus Christ the Son of God is the Saviour of lost men; but all this only shows that our Lord has many and excellent names and titles, as he has also many crowns on his head. He is called Jehovah, because he is self-existent, independent, eternal, and unchangeable. He is called God, because the fulness of the Godhead dwells in him bodily. He is called the Son of God, because he is the only begotten of the Father, full of grace and truth. His "names and titles, which are more than two hundred in number, include everything which is great or glorious, amiable or excellent, in the estimation of mankind." (Payson). He has no empty titles, no insignificant names. There is none like him.

III. The Sonship of Christ is eternal. This is clearly taught: "He is before all things." (*Colossians 1:17*). "He made the worlds." (*Hebrews 1:2*). Of course he existed before them. There never was a point in duration when the Son was not. Some have argued against the eternity of the filiation of our Redeemer from the phrase, "This day have I begotten thee." But Owen well says, "'Today' being spoken of God, of him who is eternal, to whom all time is so present as that nothing is properly yesterday nor today, does not denote necessarily such a proportion of time as is intimated; but it is expressive of an act eternally present, nor past, nor future." Addison Alexander says, "This profound sense of the passage is no more excluded by the phrase 'this day,' implying something recent, than the universality of Christ's dominion is excluded by the local reference to Zion. The point of time, like the point of space, is the centre of an infinite circle."

IV. Of course the Sonship of Christ implies much more than Mediatorship. It is eminently fitting that the Mediator between God and man should be the Son of God and the Son of Man; but Sonship is not Mediatorship, any more than Messiahship is Sonship. The Word did not become God's Son, but being God's Son, he became God's Anointed by receiving the Spirit without measure.

V. The filiation of Christ is, and ought to be freely admitted to be, ineffable. When, as "the angel of the Lord," the Son of God appeared to Manoah, that holy man said unto him, "What is thy name? ... And the angel of the Lord said unto him, Why askest thou thus after my name, seeing it is secret?" (*Judges 13:17, 18*). Payson says: "It was doubtless the eternal Word, who is frequently called the Angel of the Covenant, that appeared on that occasion. The name which is here given him, signifies secret, mysterious, wonderful; and in each of these senses it may properly be ascribed to Christ." Christ himself says: "No man knoweth who the Son is, but the Father." (*Luke 10:22*). The Sonship is ineffable, because the Divine nature is incomprehensible. Divinity is essentially inscrutable. So the Scriptures everywhere declare: "Canst thou by searching find out God? canst thou find out the Almighty unto perfection? It is as high as heaven; what canst thou do? deeper than hell; what canst thou know? The measure thereof is longer than the earth, and broader than the sea." (*Job 11:7-9*). Another Scripture declares the incomprehensibility of the nature both of the Father and of the Son: "Who hath ascended up into heaven, or descended? who hath gathered the wind in his fists? who hath bound the waters in a garment? who hath established all the ends of the earth? what is his name, and what is his son's name, if thou canst tell?" (*Proverbs 30:4*). God, indeed, has revealed himself to us in a trinity of persons. He has said that the relation between the first and second of these persons is best expressed in our language by the terms Father and Son. But we must not strain such terms to make them imply all that we understand by them when used to denote human relationships. Among men, a father exists before his son; but God the Father is eternal, and God the Son is eternal. The great idea conveyed by the word Father is, that he is the fountain of the divinity. So, when we use the words begat and begotten in this connection, the meaning is, that we cannot better express the manner in which the Father communicates the divine nature to the Son than by the use of these terms.

At this point it is convenient to give a statement of the doctrine of Christ's Sonship in several orthodox Confessions. This may prevent mistake, and show how steadfast has been the faith of God's people on this point.

The Apostles' Creed says, "I believe in God the Father Almighty, Maker of heaven and earth; and in Jesus Christ his only Son, our Lord."

The Creed as given by Irenaeus has it, "I believe in one Christ Jesus, the Son of God, who was incarnate for our salvation."

The Nicene Creed (properly so called) says, "We believe in one Lord Jesus Christ, the Son of God, begotten of the Father, the only-begotten, that is, of the substance of the Father, God of God, Light of Light, very God of very God, begotten, not made, of one substance with the Father."

The Athanasian Creed says, "The Catholic faith is this: That we worship one God in Trinity, and Trinity in Unity … The Son is of the Father alone; not made, nor created, but begotten."

The Confession of Wirtemberg says, "We believe and confess that the Son of God, our Lord Jesus Christ, begotten of his eternal Father, is true and eternal God."

The Confession of Belgia says, "We believe that Jesus Christ, in respect of his divine nature, is the only Son of God, begotten from everlasting, not made or created, (for then he should be a creature,) but of the same essence with the Father and co-eternal with him."

The Confession of Saxony says, "The Son of God our Lord Jesus Christ, who is the image of the eternal Father, is appointed our Mediator, Reconciler, Redeemer, Justifier, and Saviour."

The Augsburg Confession teaches, "that the Word, that is, the Son of God, took unto him man's nature in the womb of the blessed Virgin Mary."

In further support of this doctrine, consider the following:

1. It is clear that the Jews expected their Messiah to be the Son of God. Nathanael was an Israelite indeed, and he said to Christ, "Rabbi, thou art the Son of God; thou art the King of Israel." Martha too said to him: "I believe that thou art the Christ, the Son of God, which should come into the world." The high-priest said to Jesus, "I adjure thee by the living God, that thou tell us whether thou be the Christ, the Son of God." (*John 1:49; 11:27; Matthew 26:63*). Where did they all get the impression that Messiah should be the Son of God, if their prophets did not so teach them?

2. From many Scriptures it appears reasonable to infer that the Spirit of God designed to teach us Christ's Sonship with God. You remember that famous confession of Peter: "We believe and are sure that thou art that Christ, the Son of the living God." (*John 6:69*). John expressly informs us that he wrote his gospel "that we might believe that Jesus is the Christ, the Son of God." (*John 20:31*). Again he says: "These things have I written unto you that believe on the name of the Son of God; that ye may know that ye have eternal life, and that ye may believe on the name of the Son of God." (*1 John 5:13*).

3. On two occasions Christ received from God the Father glorious testimony to his Sonship. "Jesus, when he was baptised, went up straightway out of the water: and lo, the heavens were opened unto him, and he saw the Spirit of God descending like a dove, and lighting upon him: and lo, a voice from heaven, saying, This is my beloved Son, in whom I am well pleased." (*Matthew 3:16, 17*). The other occasion was that of his transfiguration, when a voice out of the cloud, called by Peter the "excellent glory," said, "This is my beloved Son, in whom I am well pleased; hear ye him." (*Matthew 17:5*).

4. The Scriptures lay great stress on this doctrine. In fact they assert, in plain terms, that the belief of it is essential to the formation and establishment of Christian character. "Who is he that overcometh the world, but he that believeth that Jesus is the Son of God?" (*1 John 5:5*). The Ethiopian treasurer made the confession of his faith in these simple words: "I believe that Jesus Christ is the Son of God." Upon this profession he was baptised. And John says expressly: "Whosoever denieth the Son, the same hath not the Father." (*1 John 2:23*).

5. It is admitted that the term "Word" is applied to Christ in reference to his existence before his incarnation, and without reference to

his office as Mediator. Yet John uses the term "Word" and the term "Only-begotten of the Father" as interchangeable terms: "The Word was made flesh, and dwelt among us, (and we beheld his glory, the glory as of the only-begotten of the Father,) full of grace and truth." (*John 1:14*). The glory of the Word and the glory of the only-begotten of the Father is the same.

6. The ordinance of Baptism is administered "in the name of the Father, and of the Son, and of the Holy Ghost." All who believe the doctrine of the Trinity admit that *Father* and *Holy Spirit* designate divine persons. Surely the term *Son* does the same.

7. The Scriptures expressly state that the only-begotten Son, who is in the bosom of the Father, he hath declared him; that is, the only-begotten Son who has an eternal and infinite intimacy with the divine nature has revealed him.

8. The glory of the priesthood of Christ arises chiefly from his filiation with God. So the apostle sets it forth; He maketh the Son a High Priest; "We have a great High Priest, Jesus the Son of God." (*Hebrews 4:14; 7:28*). The *greatness* of our High Priest clearly results from his being the Son of God.

9. If Christ was the Word before he was made flesh, he was the Son before he was manifested to destroy the works of the devil. (*John 1:1, 14; 1 John 3:8*). Surely this is fair reasoning.

10. Fuller says: "It is the proper deity of Christ which gives *efficacy* to his sufferings: 'by *himself* he purges our sins.' (*Hebrews 1:3*). But this efficacy is ascribed to his being 'the Son of God:' 'The blood of Jesus Christ, his Son, cleanseth us from all sin.' His being the Son of God therefore amounts to the same thing as his being a divine person." Yea, more; it shows how he is divine, namely, by an eternal generation.

The inferences from this discussion are many and important. The doctrine is full of rich consolation. Our Redeemer not only has glorious power and exaltation, but he has them because, being the Son of God, he learned obedience by the things which he suffered. (*Hebrews 5:8*). Our Advocate has by nature a right to equality with God; and, being full of love and kindness, he is sure to manage the cause of all his people so as to secure their final salvation.

4

The Incarnation of Christ

WHEN we say, The Son of God became incarnate, we mean to say that he became the Son of man, taking to himself human nature entire. In the Apostles' Creed this doctrine is thus expressed: "He was conceived by the power of the Holy Ghost, and born of the Virgin Mary." The Athanasian Creed says: "He is not only perfect God, but perfect man, of a reasonable soul and human flesh subsisting." The Westminster Assembly thus teach: "The Son of God, the second person of the Trinity, being very and eternal God, of one substance and equal with the Father, did, when the fulness of time was come, take upon him man's nature, with all the essential properties and infirmities thereof, yet without sin; being conceived by the power of the Holy Ghost, in the womb of the Virgin Mary, of her substance. So that two whole, perfect, and distinct natures, the Godhead and the manhood, were inseparably joined together in one person, without conversion, composition, or confusion. Which person is very God and very man, yet one Christ, the only Mediator between God and man."

Respecting Christ's human nature, many wild and dangerous opinions have been held; but these need not now be formally refuted. The proof of the true doctrine will be sufficient.

The union of Christ's natures was formed, not by his humanity seeking to be affianced to divinity. This would have been presumptuous aspiring. But his Godhead sought union with manhood. This was infinite love and condescension. Christ's human nature never existed separately, or otherwise than in union with his divinity. From his conception this union was complete. The pre-existent divine nature took to itself human nature. Christ's human nature never had a personal subsistence by itself. So that Christ did not assume a human person, but human nature. "His person is not a compound person; the personality belongs to his Godhead, and the human nature subsists in it by a peculiar dispensation. The assumption of our nature made no change in his person; it added nothing to it; and the only difference is, that the same person who was possessed of divinity has now taken humanity." So that things done or suffered in either nature are ascribed to the one person, Christ Jesus. The properties of each nature are, and will ever continue to be, entire and distinct. Divinity cannot be subject to any change. Humanity cannot cease to be humanity – cannot become divinity. The Creator cannot cease to be Creator. The creature cannot cease to be a creature.

This union of the two natures in Christ is not without some similitude in ourselves. In his constitution man has two substances, one a soul, the other a body; one spiritual and immortal, the other material and perishable. By their union, one of these substances is not changed into the other. They remain distinct even when united. Yet a man is one person, and not two persons. When we say, He is sad, all know we refer to his soul. When we say, He is muscular, all know we speak of his body. Yet in both cases we speak of the same person. So Christ's person is one, and not two. When he spake of himself he said, *I, mine, me*. When his apostles spake of him, they said, he, his, him. When we address him, we say, *thou thine, thee. (Acts 1:24)*. The Scriptures also use singular nouns respecting him, and call him a Prophet, a Priest, a King, a Shepherd, a Redeemer. The union of his natures could not be more perfect. It is personal, perpetual, indissoluble.

The Scriptures say Christ was *"made of a woman."* Human beings have come into the world in four ways. The first man, the very fountain of human nature, had neither father nor mother. Neither man nor woman was the instrument of his existence. The first woman had neither father nor mother, yet she derived her nature from Adam, but in no sense from a woman. Since the first pair, every mere man has had both father and mother. Yet none have denied that all these had human nature entire. Jesus Christ had a mother, but no father according to the flesh; even as in his divine nature he had a Father only. He was made of a woman.

To be our Saviour, it behoved Christ to have a human nature. His incarnation was fitting and necessary.

It was meet that the nature which had brought our ruin should bring our deliverance.

It was fit that the nature which had sinned should make reparation for our wrongs, and so should die.

This earth, which is the abode of men, not of God or of angels, was the proper theatre for the display of the grace, and mercy, and justice, and power, manifested in the life and death of Jesus Christ. He that was rich thus became poor, that we through his poverty might be rich. (*2 Corinthians 8:9*). In some respects, this was the most amazing step in our Lord's humiliation. It is more surprising that a prince should marry a shepherdess than that, having made her queen, he should nobly protect and richly endow her, or even die in her defence.

Christ was "*made under the law.*" As to his divine nature, he could in no sense be under the law. He was the Lawgiver. He was God; and God cannot live and act under rules fit for the government of creatures. If the Saviour was to live under the law as a rule of life, and set us an example in all things, he must do it in a finite nature, and as his mission was to us, most fitly in our nature.

Besides, Divinity cannot suffer, cannot die. But by his incarnation, Jesus was made "lower than the angels, for the suffering of death."

Thus he was made under the law in the two senses of being voluntarily subject to its precept, being thus bound to fulfil all righteousness; and being voluntarily made under the penalty of the law, that he might taste of death for every man. He even obeyed the law of religious rites under which he lived. In his infancy he was circumcised. In his manhood he was baptised. He perfectly, personally, perpetually kept the whole moral law. He never sinned once, even by omission. And he freely placed himself, and lived and died, under the curse of the very law which he perfectly obeyed during his whole life. Edwards says: "The meritoriousness of Christ's obedience depends on the perfection of it. If it had failed in any instance, it could not have been meritorious; for imperfect obedience is not accepted as any obedience at all in the sight of the law of works, to which Christ was subject. That is not accepted as obedience to a law that does not fully answer it."

The efficacy of Christ's death depended on his dying in the place and stead of sinners, who were under the curse of the law. If he did not bear the curse for us, we shall surely be obliged to bear it ourselves. Let us consider a few distinct propositions:

I. Prophecy required that Christ should assume human nature. It said he should be of "the seed of Abraham" and of "the seed of David." (*Genesis 12:3, 7; 17:7, 8; Galatians 3:16; 2 Samuel 7:12; John 7:42; Acts 13:23; Romans 1:3; 2 Timothy 2:8*). Other predictions required that he should "at the latter day stand upon the earth," (*Job 19:25*); that he should have a body, (*Psalm 40:6;* and *Hebrews 10:5*); that he should hang upon his mother's breasts, (*Psalm 22:9*); and that his body should be dead, (*Isaiah 26:19*).

Yet still more clearly, the very first gospel ever preached, even in Eden, foretold that he should have a human nature, and that derived from his mother: "The seed of the woman shall bruise the serpent's head." (*Genesis 3:15*); and later: "Behold, a virgin shall conceive, and bear a Son, and shall call his name Immanuel." (*Isaiah 7:14*). So that the Scriptures would not have been fulfilled if Christ had not had a human nature – a human nature derived from his mother alone. In prophetic vision, Daniel called him the *Son of man. (Daniel 7:13*).

II. These predictions have been fulfilled. The whole history of our Lord upon earth proves it. God has "sent forth his Son, made of a woman." In the New Testament he is often called a *man.* In the gospels alone he is more than seventy times called the *Son of man.* More than sixty times he gives this appellation to himself. The year of his ascension Stephen saw him glorified, and called him the *Son of man.* Sixty years later John did the same. The gospel of Matthew is styled "The book of the generation of Jesus Christ, the Son of David, the Son of Abraham." John says: "The Word was made flesh, and dwelt among us." (*John 1:14*). Paul says: "He took on him the seed of Abraham." (*Hebrews 2:16*). In *1 John 1:1-3*, John expressly says that by three senses, hearing, sight, and touch, he and the other apostles had satisfied themselves of his incarnation.

Jesus Christ had all that is necessary to constitute human nature entire. He himself said, "Behold my hands and my feet, that it is I myself: handle me, and see; for a spirit hath not flesh and bones, as ye see me have." (*Luke 24:39*). Christ had a soul. He said, "My soul is exceeding sorrowful unto death." (*Mark 14:34*). He had a spirit:

"In that hour Jesus rejoiced in spirit." (*Luke 10:21*). "When he had cried with a loud voice, he yielded up the ghost." (*Matthew 27:50*). Jesus Christ had a will: "Father, not as I will, but as thou wilt." (*Matthew 26:39;* See also *Matthew 27:34; John 7:1*). Jesus Christ had the affections of a man. He rejoiced. (*Luke 10:21*). He wept. (*John 11:35*). He was grieved. (*Mark 3:5*). He had hopes, even in his early infancy. (*Psalm 22:9*). He had natural affection for kindred spirits. We are told that he loved Mary, and Martha, and Lazarus, and John, and the rich young ruler. In some places his soul and body are mentioned together: "The child Jesus grew, and waxed strong in spirit, filled with wisdom." (*Luke 2:40*). He performed bodily acts. He walked, he rode, he ate, he drank, he sailed, he slept, he rested. He was not indeed subject to mortal diseases. (*Psalm 91:5-8*). But he had the general infirmities of our nature. He hungered. (*Matthew 4:2*). He thirsted. (*John 19:28*). He was wearied. (*John 4:6*). He was greatly, pained. (*Luke 12:50*). He was tempted. (*Hebrews 2:18*). He endured unparalleled agony. (*Luke 22:44*). He died, as all admit. He had no moral infirmity. He was without sin. (*Hebrews 4:15*).

III. The incarnation of Christ is something entirely beyond human comprehension. It is an ineffable mystery. The Scriptures say, "Without controversy great is the mystery of godliness: God was manifest in the flesh." (*1 Timothy 3:16*). How could it be otherwise? The Father of eternity became an infant of days. "Though all things were created by him, he was placed on a level with his own creatures." He, whom the heaven of heavens could not contain, was laid in a manger. The eternal Word and the child Jesus were one person. Possessed of infinite blessedness, the Son of God is united with the man of sorrows. Himself in both natures spotlessly holy, he consents to be treated, tormented, punished, as a sinner. He made all things, yet was made flesh. He governed all things, yet was subject to his parents. He opened his hand and satisfied the desire of every living thing, yet fasted forty days himself. All the infinite perfections of God and all the innocent infirmities of man meet in the God-man, Christ Jesus. There is no greater gulf than that which separates created and uncreated. Yet the Son of God passes it all, and takes our nature into indissoluble union with divinity. This union could not be more intimate. Soul and body may be separated for a season. When Christ himself died, his soul went to Paradise, while his body lay in the sepulchre of Joseph. But the union of his human and divine natures was not dissolved by death. Paul calls the blood shed by him the blood of God. (*Acts 20:28*). So close was this union that we fitly speak of our Lord as a *divine sufferer.* When he was on earth, he spoke of himself as "the Son of man which is in heaven." (*John 3:13*). We ascribe to the person of our Saviour whatever belonged to either of his natures, or was done in either of them. His incarnation is a mystery in itself. Basil says, "He was conceived not of the substance, but by the power of the Holy Ghost; not by his generation, but by his appointment and benediction." His incarnation is a mystery of love. It expresses infinite benevolence. It is also "the wisdom of God in a mystery," – a mystery of power, of truth, and of grace. It is the mystery of mysteries, because it is "the mystery of God." We are not required to divest it of inscrutableness, but we are required to embrace it, and rejoice in it. It is a fundamental doctrine, the belief of which is essential to salvation: "Every spirit that confesseth that Jesus Christ is come in the flesh is of God: and every spirit that confesseth not that Jesus Christ is come in the flesh is not of God." (*1 John 4:2, 3*).

IV. The Son of God did not become man at the giving of the first gospel promise, but more than four thousand years after it. He took our nature "when the fulness of time was come." This phrase designates:

1. The time set in the counsels of God. Jesus Christ was born no sooner and no later than the purpose of God had determined. (*Acts 4:28*).

2. The time fixed in prophecy, which is but the revealed purpose of God. The seventy weeks of Daniel had expired. The second temple was soon to fall.

3. The state of the Jewish nation was such to render Christ's appearance at that time very seasonable. The tabernacle of David had fallen very low, was cleft with breaches, and was lying in ruins, for Herod the Great, now king over Judea, was not a descendant of the royal Psalmist, but was an Idumean. Now was the fit time to build up the throne of David. (*Amos 9:11; Acts 15:16*).

4. Many things in the general state of the world rendered this a fit time for Christ's coming.

It had been fully demonstrated by the experience of many powerful and civilised nations, that the world by wisdom could never come to know God. Letters, arts, science, civilisation, philosophy, commerce, and experience had shown that they were all powerless to save men from polytheism, or to teach them the true nature of God.

Consequently, human misery was unabated. Men multiplied their sorrows by hastening after another God than Jehovah. The world had long been oppressed with its woes. The cry of its wailings was very loud.

At Christ's birth the earth was populous – much more so than it had commonly been at any previous period. So that his coming was likely to be known to many and to produce an impression on vast multitudes.

When Christ came the Greek was the polite language of the world, and the Latin was the popular language of multitudes in many lands, so that both what was spoken and what was written was likely to be widely and rapidly diffused.

At the birth of Christ, the Roman empire, the greatest and most terrible monarchy the world ever saw, was in its strength. It was the *iron* dynasty of all ages. It was peculiarly fitting that in the height of its dominion the stone cut out of the mountain without hands should break in pieces this immense and cruel power, and the God of heaven set up a kingdom which shall never be destroyed. (*Daniel 2:42-45*). By words of peace and grace, by deeds of love and mercy, by meekness and holiness, by patience and martyrdom, this gigantic tyranny was wholly changed in less than three centuries after our Lord's crucifixion.

Christ was the Prince of peace, and it was seemly that he should come when war was not raging. When he was born the temple of Janus was shut – a thing that had not occurred for centuries till about that time. This was a sign that peace everywhere prevailed.

> "Nor war nor battle-sound
>   Was heard the world around;
>   No hostile chiefs to furious combat ran;
>   But peaceful was the night,
>   In which the Prince of Light
>   His reign of grace upon the earth began."

The Jews were at this time very widely dispersed over the world. Though they often visited the holy city, yet they went everywhere. So that any change effected in Judea was likely soon to be known in all the chief cities of the world. On the day of Pentecost there were Jews, devout men of every nation under heaven at Jerusalem, and on their conversion and dispersion they went everywhere preaching the word of the gospel. (*Acts 2:5-11; 8:4*).

Christ was born when the spirit of persecution was not raging violently in the world generally, so that his doctrine was less likely to be fiercely assailed for a season than if it had been propagated a century or two earlier or later.

No period could be conceived so little adapted to the exhibition of a *false,* and so well calculated to put to the test the merits of a *true* religion.

Thus did Christ become incarnate "in the fulness of time," that is, at the right time, at the fittest time possible.

V. The incarnation of Christ was the greatest event that ever happened. The birth of a prince often sends a thrill of joy through an empire, yet he may prove a shame and a curse to the nation and the world; but the birth of Christ brought inestimable blessings to Jews and Gentiles, and shall do so for ever. No ancient monarchy lives, even in history, to *bless* mankind; but the birth and kingdom of Christ are, and ever shall be, gladsome truths. The hopes of virtuous millions hang upon them. The joys of saints and angels are kindled by them. "The creation of the world was a very great thing, but not so great as the incarnation of Christ. It was a great thing for God to make the creature, but not so great as for the Creator to become a creature." Christ's incarnation was the confirmation of all that had been said and done in preceding ages to encourage the hopes of penitent men. It fulfilled the glorious pledges of redemption. It opened boundless and amazing prospects of enlargement and glory to God's people and to their Redeemer. Some of its effects were immediate and some remote. Some related to angels and some to men; some to Jews and some to Gentiles. The wise men who came from the east to worship Christ were Gentiles, and were representative men. Christ's personal ministry was a blessing to several Gentiles, and the only men converted in sight of his cross were pretty certainly Gentiles.

These things were assurances of the fulfilment of all God had promised respecting heathen nations. These conversions were first-fruits of the great harvest to be gathered in all lands. The immediate effect of Christ's birth on the pious Jews was most happy. To Simeon and Anna, and such lovely specimens of genuine godliness, the event gave joy unspeakable. Those who hated God and all his messengers, of course wondered and perished. The effect on angels was amazing. They felt new joys in heaven. One of their number announced the event to the shepherds, and "suddenly there was with him a multitude of the heavenly host praising God, and saying, Glory to God in the highest, and on earth peace, good-will toward men." Previous to the birth of Christ for about four hundred and twenty years, God's Spirit, as a Spirit of inspiration, had been quite withheld from men. But about the time of his appearance, there are recorded no less than eleven instances in which men and women received the Holy Ghost as a spirit of prophecy.

The effect of Christ's incarnation on fallen angels was great. Their power began at once to dwindle. They cried out, "Why hast thou come to torment us before the time?" The Lord himself said: "I saw Satan's kingdom fall like lightning from heaven." It is credibly stated that the Delphic oracle ceased to give its usual responses, and when asked the reason, replied, "There is a Hebrew boy who is king of the gods, who has commanded me to leave this house, and be gone to hell, and therefore you are to expect no more answers." And Porphyry says: "Since Jesus began to be worshipped, no man has received any public help or benefit of the gods."

From the day that Christ was born to this hour, all the desirable changes which have taken place in the world, either in persons or communities, have been in consequence of his incarnation and of his glorious progress in setting up his kingdom. So shall it ever be. His kingdom is constantly enlarging. His diadem is more and more glorious. Every soul saved is a new jewel in his crown.

Of Christ's incarnation Robert Hall says: "The epoch will arrive when this world will be thought of as nothing but as it has furnished a stage for 'the manifestation of the Son of God;' when his birth, his death, his resurrection from the dead, his ascension to glory, and his second appearance, events inseparably connected, will concentrate within themselves all the interest of history; when war and peace, and pestilence and famine, and plenty and want, and life and death, will have spent their force, and leave nothing but the result of Christ's manifestation upon earth."

VI. The person of Christ as now constituted remains perpetual. The bond of union between his divine and human natures is indissoluble. As he was from his conception, so he continues to be, "God and man, in two distinct natures and one person, for ever." The *same* Lamb that was slain is now in the midst of the throne. (*Revelation 5:6*). The *same* Jesus that ascended from Olivet shall come again. The progress of duration shall neither change his natures nor his person, his character nor his readiness to save. He is able; he is willing.

*   *   *

1. Let none be offended at the mystery of the incarnation. If we cannot comprehend, let us adore. No fact is more plainly asserted or more amply proved. Let us receive and rest upon it. He who has no heart to praise the incarnate mystery, has none of the spirit of heaven. What a shame it is that the song of angels announcing Christ's birth "has never been answered by a general shout of gratitude from earth. Only a few faint voices from the low places of the earth have responded to the loud concert of angels." O that must be a bad heart which loves not the Saviour. Many hear of his love with hearts colder than marble. Such hearts cannot be right in the sight of God. No heart is good that loves not goodness incarnate. If Christ's incarnation has its mysteriousness, it yet is the only doctrine that enables us to unlock every text of Scripture relating to his person. It admits that, as God, he made the worlds; as a child, he grew in stature; as a man, he was sorrowful; as Mediator and in a low condition, he said, "The Father is greater than I;" and as God-man, he stands between Jehovah and us. Let us humbly and piously receive this doctrine; for as the Athanasian Creed says, "It is necessary to everlasting salvation, that we believe rightly the incarnation of Jesus Christ."

2. Salvation is clearly and wholly of the Lord. The devising of the scheme is as clearly divine as the execution and application. Human wit, and wisdom, and strength, and merit are nothing in such a work. "Boasting is excluded by the law of faith." We are nothing; we

can do nothing; we deserve nothing. Our Lord has won the crown, and he shall wear it. It is his of right; it shall be his in fact.

3. Let us give God his own time. He knows what is best. He took four thousand years to prepare the way for the coming of the Redeemer. With the Lord one day is as a thousand years, and a thousand years as one day. We are no judges of what is best or wisest. There is as much wisdom in saying, "When thou wilt," as in saying, "What thou wilt," or "How thou wilt."

4. If any ask, Are we bound to celebrate the birth of Christ on any given day of the year? the answer is, God has given no such command, and he is sole Lawgiver in his church. There is no proof that for centuries the primitive church had any such observance. When such a day was at length observed, many churches fixed on the sixth day of January. Many learned men contend that Christ was born in October. Some think he was born in May. It seems certain that the Roman emperor would not require women as well as men to take long journeys in the depths of winter, and that shepherds would not then be watching their flocks in the open air. (Compare *Matthew 24:20* and *Mark 13:18*). But if any man observe a day in honour of our Lord's nativity, let him keep it unto the Lord. "One man esteemeth one day above another: another esteemeth every day alike. Let every man be fully persuaded in his own mind." (*Romans 14:5*). It is, however, a significant fact, that God has concealed from us any positive knowledge of the day, the month, and even the year of our Saviour's birth.

5
The Messiahship of Jesus

IN the English Bible we have the word Messiah, or Messias, four times; twice in *Daniel*, and twice in *John*. But in the original Scriptures we have the word forty times. It is commonly translated, and often points to the Saviour. In the New Testament we have the word *Christ* more than five hundred and sixty times. Both Messiah and Christ signify *anointed*.

Jesus Christ was but once anointed with material oil, and that not by an official, but by a woman; not to his office, but to his burial.

Jesus Christ was anointed to office by superabundant influences of the Holy Spirit, who is the oil of gladness indeed. (*Psalm 45:7; Hebrews 1:9; Matthew 3:16; Luke 4:1, 14, 16*). The Father gave not the Spirit by measure unto him. (*John 3:34*).

That the Jews and others expected a great deliverer, called by the prophets Messiah, cannot be denied. The woman of Samaria, ignorant as she was, said, "I know that Messias cometh." (*John 4:25*). Luke says, "The people were in expectation, and all men mused in their hearts of John, whether he were the Christ, or not." (*Luke 3:15*). Indeed, there is evidence that the ancients generally expected a great deliverer to arise.

In inquiring into the Messiahship of Jesus of Nazareth; the Jewish Scriptures are taken for truth. We believe all that is written in the law, and in the Psalms, and in the prophets. Besides, it is clear that if Jesus is not the promised deliverer, then the Messiah has not yet appeared. Jews and Christians alike reject all the pretenders who have arisen from the time of the Emperor Adrian to the year 1666, when Sabatai Sevi for a while deceived some. Nor is there any dispute between Jews and Christians as to the need of Messiah. We all, in words at least, confess that we are undone without him. Nor is there any doubt that for some cause great calamities have overtaken the Jews. They admit it. Rabbi David Levi speaks of the facts of "the exact accomplishment of every event foretold by Moses as affording such clear and unequivocal proofs of divine inspiration as to strike the deist and infidel dumb." He says: "I am free to assert, no nation ever suffered the like during a period of almost eighteen hundred years ... The punishments which Moses denounced against the Jews have been exactly fulfilled in every particular." Nor is there any dispute as to whether Jesus of Nazareth lived, and taught, and died on the cross. Jews and Christians, Mohammedans and Infidels are alike agreed on this point. This chapter is an argument for the Messiahship of the great teacher of Nazareth.

The first question to be considered is:

I. Has the time fixed by prophecy for the coming of the Messiah already passed?

The correct answer is, It has. The arguments are clear and decisive.

On his deathbed Jacob uttered this prediction: "The sceptre shall not depart from Judah, nor a lawgiver from between his feet, until Shiloh come: and to him shall the gathering of the people be." (*Genesis 49:10*). The word here rendered *sceptre* is used in that sense by no less than six prophets. (*Numbers 24:17; Psalm 45:6; Isaiah 14:5; Ezekiel 19:11, 14; Amos 1:5, 8; Zechariah 10:11*); and *sceptre* in this clause corresponds with *lawgiver* in the next. The Septuagint gives it this sense, and so do ancient Jewish interpreters and the Chaldee Paraphrase. That *Shiloh* points to the Messiah is also admitted by the three Chaldee paraphrasts, the Jewish Talmud, and all later Jews; and that the word signifies Saviour, or Peacemaker, or Sufferer, of the Son, or the Sent, has the consent of nearly all the best scholars. Nor can we get any good sense from the passage unless we admit that *Shiloh* means Messiah. "To him shall the gathering of the people be," is a phrase like that of Isaiah predicting the same person: "He shall stand for an ensign of the people." (*Isaiah 11:10*). That the sceptre or political power did continue with Judah until the birth of Jesus of Nazareth is evident; for though Herod was not of that tribe, but was an Idumean, yet the Jewish senate did never swear fealty to him until after the birth of Christ. But in the days of Titus, about the year AD 70, all show and form of political power forsook the Jews. From that time they had not the smallest remnant of dominion. But their father and prophet Jacob said their power should last till Messias should come. Therefore the time for the coming of Messias is already past.

The same thing might be argued from *Psalm 40:6-8:* "Sacrifice and offering thou didst not desire; mine ears hast thou opened: burnt-offering and sin-offering hast thou not required. Then said I, Lo, I come: in the volume of the book it is written of me, I delight to do thy will, O my God." The blood of bulls and goats never did expiate the sins of men. Even as types, they were to be wholly abolished after the coming of Christ. Here then we have the prediction that the legal sacrifices shall be abolished when He that is to come, the Messiah, shall do the work so pleasing to God. It is now many centuries since any Jewish priest offered a bloody sacrifice. When God would wholly reject sacrifices, Messiah was to do his will. Sacrifices have ceased, and where is Messiah, if Jesus of Nazareth is not he?

Another prophecy fixing the time for the coming and death of Messiah is found in *Daniel 9:24-27:* "Seventy weeks are determined upon thy people and upon thy holy city, to finish the transgression, and to make an end of sins, and to make reconciliation for iniquity, and to bring in everlasting righteousness, and to seal up the vision and prophecy, and to anoint the Most Holy. Know therefore and understand, that from the going forth of the commandment to restore and to build Jerusalem unto the Messiah the Prince shall be seven weeks, and threescore and two weeks: the street shall be built again, and the wall, even in troublous times. And after threescore and two weeks shall Messiah be cut off, but not for himself: and the people of the prince that shall come shall destroy the city and the sanctuary; and the end thereof shall be with a flood, and unto the end of the war desolations are determined. And he shall confirm the covenant with many for one week: and in the midst of the week he shall cause the sacrifice and the oblation to cease, and for the overspreading of abominations he shall make it desolate, even until the consummation, and that determined shall be poured upon the desolate."

The rule by which time is here counted is doubtless that given by Ezekiel (*Ezekiel 4:6*): "I have appointed thee each day for a year;" so that by seventy weeks we are to understand four hundred and ninety years. This is the longest time we have any reason for giving to the computation of the seventy weeks.

These weeks were to date from "the going forth of the commandment to restore and to build" Jerusalem. There were four decrees respecting the return of the Jews from Babylon. One was issued in the first year of Cyrus. (*Ezra 1:1-4*). The next came out in the second year of Darius. (*Ezra 6:1-12*). The third was in the seventh year of Artaxerxes. (*Ezra 7:11-26*). The fourth and last was in the twentieth year of Artaxerxes. (*Nehemiah 2:1*). The first two edicts speak of rebuilding the temple only. But the prophecy requires that the decree should relate to the rebuilding of the city, its walls and streets. So, counting from the last two decrees, we have "seventy weeks of *solar* years from one of them, and as many weeks of *lunar* years from the other" till the death of Christ. But count as we may, the seventy weeks of Daniel must have expired more than eighteen hundred years ago.

More than this, the prophecy says Messiah was to be cut off before the overflowing desolation befell the holy city. All history declares that Jesus was crucified more than thirty-three years before the armies of Rome laid waste Jerusalem. Surely the time for the coming of Messiah is past, and Jesus of Nazareth came neither too soon nor too late to meet the demands of prophecy in this respect.

I adduce but one other passage to show that Messiah has come: "Thus saith the Lord of hosts; Yet once, it is a little while, and I will shake the heavens, and the earth, and the sea, and the dry land; and I will shake all nations, and the Desire of all nations shall come: and I will fill this house with glory, saith the Lord of hosts ... The glory of this latter house shall be greater than of the former, saith the Lord of hosts." (*Haggai 2:6-9*). By this sure word, Messiah, "the Desire of all nations," was to appear during the time of the second temple, here called "this latter house." It is also evident, as none will deny, that the second temple was destroyed by the Romans. Not one stone was left upon another. Messiah, therefore, must have come. This passage also teaches that the glory of the second temple should excel the glory of the first. This promised glory did not consist in the superior magnificence of the structure, "for many of the priests and Levites and chief of the fathers, who were ancient men, that had seen the first house, when the foundation of this house was laid before their eyes, wept with a loud voice," says an eye-witness,

Ezra. (*Ezra 3:12*). Indeed, in the very chapter containing the prophecy, Haggai has these words, "Who is left among you that saw this house in her first glory? and how do ye see it now? is it not in your eyes in comparison of it as nothing?" (*Haggai 2:3*). So that the second temple was inferior to the first; and yet the second house was to have a glory surpassing the glory of the first. What was it?

Nor was the second temple equal, much less superior to the first in its appendages. For it is admitted that the first temple had, and that the second temple lacked, the holy fire, which came from heaven, the spirit of prophecy, the ark of the covenant, the Shekinah and the Urim and Thummim. In the eyes of Jews these were grand things. But they were not found in the second temple, and they were in the first. The promised superior glory of the latter house must have been that in it Messiah, "the Desire of all nations," was to appear. Malachi says: "The Lord, whom ye seek, shall suddenly come to his temple, even the messenger of the covenant, whom ye delight in." (*Malachi 3:1*). This key unlocks the mystery. Simeon told us what this glory was, when "he came by the Spirit into the temple: and when the parents brought in the child Jesus, to do for him after the custom of the law, he took him up in his arms and blessed God, and said, Lord, now lettest thou thy servant depart in peace, according to thy word, for mine eyes have seen thy salvation, which thou hast prepared before the face of all people; a light to lighten the Gentiles, and the glory of thy people Israel." (*Luke 2:27-32*). Thus it has been shown by four prophecies uttered during a period of eleven hundred and sixty-nine years, the first 1689 BC, the second, 1020 BC, the third 538 BC, and the fourth 520 BC, that the time for the coming of the Messiah is already past.

The second question to be considered is,

II. Does Jesus of Nazareth meet the demands of prophecy respecting the Messiah?

Surely he does. Messiah was to be a lineal descendant of David. He was to be "a root of Jesse," "a rod out of the stem of Jesse." (*Isaiah 11:1, 10*). The first words of the first gospel are: "The book of the generation of Jesus Christ, the son of David," and then his genealogy is traced from Abraham through David. The scribes said that the promised "Christ is the son of David." When our Lord said, "What think ye of Christ? whose son is he? They say unto him, The son of David." (*Matthew 22:42*). When men saw his miracles, they said, "Is not this the son of David?" The blind men so saluted him. (*Luke 18:38*). The hosanna of the multitude was "to the son of David." (*Matthew 21:9, 15*). Indeed, before Jesus was born, the genealogy of Mary the mother of Jesus, and of Joseph her husband, were determined by the very process of law by which the lands of Judea were held, and this under the decree of the Roman emperor. Jesus meets this requirement of prophecy. He is the lineal descendant of David. None of the false Christs have given the slightest evidence that they were descended from David. Should any arise hereafter, they can never show their descent from David, for the genealogical tables of his family and of his tribe are confessedly irrecoverably lost. No man even pretends to have them in possession.

The prophets further said that Messiah should be born in Bethlehem of Judea. So the chief priests and scribes informed Herod, correctly quoting *Micah 5:2* in proof: "Thou Bethlehem, in the land of Juda, art not the least among the princes of Juda." (*Matthew 2:4-6*). Now it is a matter of common notoriety that "Jesus was born in Bethlehem of Judea." (*Matthew 2:1*). Truly, God governs all things. Just before the birth of Jesus, his mother and her betrothed husband were required by an imperial edict to repair to Bethlehem, some distance from their usual residence, there to be duly registered, "because they were of the house and lineage of David," and there to us was born "in the city of David a Saviour, which is Christ the Lord." (*Luke 2:4, 11*). None of the false Christs either proved or claimed that they had been born in Bethlehem.

Prophecy required that Messiah should be born in a miraculous manner: "The Lord himself shall give you a sign; Behold, a virgin shall conceive, and bear a son, and shall call his name Immanuel," which being interpreted is "God with us." (*Isaiah 7:14*). That Jesus was thus born the angel declared at the time of his conception; that he was thus born was admitted by the husband of his mother, who fully vindicated the purity and innocence of his wife: that he was thus born God and angels and men have borne witness. No one else was ever thus born.

Jesus and none else endured all the suffering which prophecy decreed to Messiah. He had no form nor comeliness, and when we saw him there was no beauty that we should desire him. He was despised and rejected of men, a man of sorrows, and acquainted with grief; we hid our faces from him; we esteemed him not. His visage was so marred more than any man, and his form more than the sons of men. He made himself of no reputation. He took upon him the form of a servant. Prophecy said: "They weighed for my price thirty pieces of silver." (*Zechariah 11:12*). The chief priests covenanted with Judas "for thirty pieces of silver." (*Matthew 26:15*). The Psalmist predicted: "They pierced my hands and my feet." (*Psalm 22:16*). Isaiah said: "He was wounded." (*Isaiah 53:5*). Zechariah said: "They shall look on me whom they have pierced." (*Zechariah 12:10*). We all know how his hands and his feet were pierced by the nails, how the soldiers pierced his side, and how Jesus himself afterwards showed the print of the nails. In *Psalm 22:7, 8*, we read, "They shall laugh him to scorn, and shake their heads, saying, He trusted on the Lord that he would deliver him: let him deliver him, seeing he delighted in him." In *Matthew 27:39, 43*, we read, "They that passed by reviled him, wagging their heads, and saying, He trusted in God; let him deliver him now, if he will have him: for he said, I am the Son of God." Isaiah says, "He was numbered with the transgressors." Mark says, "He was crucified between two thieves." The prophet says, "In my thirst they gave me vinegar to drink." His biographers tell us how "Jesus, that the Scripture might be fulfilled, said, I thirst, and they took a sponge and filled it with vinegar, and put it on a reed, and gave it him to drink." The prophets said, "They part my garments among them, and cast lots upon my vesture." In the gospels we learn how the soldiers "took his garments, and made four parts, to every soldier a part, and also his coat: now the coat was without seam, woven from the top throughout. They said therefore among themselves, Let us not rend it, but cast lots for it, whose it shall be." Isaiah and Daniel foretold that he should be cut off. No living man denies that Jesus died a violent death.

Isaiah said he should be "brought as a lamb to the slaughter, and as a sheep before her shearers is dumb, so he opened not his mouth." All history tells how meekly, and silently, and patiently he endured. "When he suffered, he threatened not."

Prophecy foretold that he should triumphantly enter Jerusalem riding upon a young ass. In this way did he meekly enter the holy city, weeping over its impending ruin. Indeed, time would fail us to tell how, according to prophecy, not a bone of him was broken, how he died with the wicked, how he made his grave with the rich, how he never saw corruption, how according to the prophecy, he is sitting at the right hand of God, to the intent that "all the house of Israel might know assuredly, that God hath made that same Jesus whom they crucified both Lord and Christ."

Look at another matter. By the prophet Amos God says: "Surely the Lord God will do nothing, but he revealeth his secret unto his servants the prophets" (*Amos 3:7*). It cannot be denied that Jesus of Nazareth has done more to change the opinions and practices of mankind than Cyrus, and Alexander the Great, and the Roman empire. Yet, if he is not the Messiah, the Old Testament is silent concerning him. No man or set of men have ever changed the opinions of enlightened nations as Jesus did. Yet, if he is not the Messiah, God never showed his prophets anything concerning him. Can it be believed that God has never by any prophet said a word to warn mankind against him, or to invite them to receive him? – him whose coming has done more to revolutionise men's opinions, to mollify asperities, to diffuse virtue and happiness among the most enlightened nations, than any other hundred men that ever lived.

*   *   *

1. Let Christians greatly rejoice in the abundant evidence of the divine mission of Jesus. In embracing his doctrine we are not following cunningly devised fables. O no! Jesus was truth itself.

2. If in Jesus of Nazareth we have found the Messiah, have we embraced him? Such a Deliverer is not to be put off with civilities and compliments. We may say, Lord, Lord; but we must do more. We must take his yoke upon us. We must do his will. We must embrace him, and rely on him. We must by the Holy Ghost call him Lord. Have you in your heart received him! An American errorist has written a book in which he calls him the "Magnificent Jesus." He is far more than that. The temple at Jerusalem was magnificent. The temple of Diana was magnificent. Jesus is the Messiah, the Saviour of lost men, the Son of God. He is to be obeyed and loved, adored and embraced. God has set forth his Son as an object of religious

faith. Will you receive him as such? Without faith in him we cannot be saved. He himself said: "If ye believe not that I am he, ye shall die in your sins." (*John 8:24*).

3. If we ourselves have found Jesus the Messiah, let us, like Andrew, tell our brother the good news and bring him to Jesus. There is none like Jesus. There is none with Jesus. There is none besides Jesus. He is the Son of God. He can save, and he alone. Oh that you would embrace him and then persuade others to do so too. You will soon need his help. A great master of logic has recently left the world. When one of the clergy spoke of his fortitude in looking death in the face, he said: "Talk not to me of fortitude; it is my faith in Christ that gives me grace and strength."

4. Pray for the Jews. God can open their eyes. None else can. It is affecting to hear them on this point. Dr Raphall, formerly of England, now of New York, says: "While I and the Jews of the present day protest against being identified with the zealots who were concerned in the proceedings against Jesus of Nazareth, we are far from reviling his character or deriding his precepts, which are, indeed, for the most part, the precepts of Moses and the prophets. You have heard me style him the 'Great Teacher of Nazareth,' for that designation I and the Jews take to be his due."

The Late Mordecai M Noah also said: "I did not term Jesus of Nazareth an impostor. I had never considered him such. The impostor generally aims at temporal power, attempts to subsidise the rich and weak believer, and draws around him followers of influence whom he can control. Jesus was free from fanaticism: his was a quiet, subdued, retiring faith; he mingled with the poor, he communed with the wretched, avoided the rich, rebuked the vain-glorious. In the calm of the evening he sought shelter in the secluded groves of Olivet, or wandered pensively on the shores of Galilee. He sincerely believed in his mission; he courted no one, flattered no one; in his political denunciations he was pointed and severe; in his religion calm and subdued. These are not the characteristics of an impostor; but, admitting that we give a different interpretation to his mission, when one hundred and fifty million believe in his divinity, and we see around us abundant evidence of the happiness, good faith, mild government, and liberal feelings which spring from his religion, what right has anyone to call him an impostor? That religion which is calculated to make mankind great and happy cannot be a false one."

PRAYER: O God, bring the children of Abraham to embrace Jesus Christ; and to us and to all that dwell in this land give hearts to receive thy Son, to believe on his name, to own him as our Saviour; so that all the blessings of the covenant of grace may come on us and overtake us; that we may be blessed in the city and in the field; that thy blessing may rest on the fruit of our body, and on the fruit of our ground, and the fruit of our cattle, and the increase of our kine, and the flocks of our sheep; that thy blessing may rest on our basket and on our store; that we may be blessed when we come in and blessed when we go out; and that they who come out against us one way may flee before us seven ways. Oh that all the land and world may soon avouch the Lord Jehovah to be their God, his Son Jesus Christ to be their Saviour; his Holy Spirit to be their Sanctifier, Comforter and Guide; and unto the King eternal, immortal, and invisible, the only wise God our Saviour, be glory, and honour, dominion and power, now and for ever. Amen.

6
Christ the Mediator

THE word Mediator is not found in the English version of the Old Testament. There we find the word *daysman* in very much the same sense, (*Job 9:33*). In that place the Septuagint version employs the word rendered in the New Testament *mediator*. A daysman was an umpire and a reconciler. In the New Testament the word mediator is found six times. Once it points to Moses: "The law was ordained by angels in the hand of a mediator." (*Galatians 3:19*). Moses was a messenger to make known God's will to Israel, and to present the requests of the people to God. Once the word *mediator* is clearly used in a general sense, and refers to no particular person. "A mediator is not a mediator of one, but God is one." (*Galatians 3:20*). The meaning of this verse is, doubtless, that a mediator cannot act where there are no parties, and that he must act for both parties. As God is one, he needed not to be reconciled to himself. Mediation comes in between God and those estranged from him. In all other cases, the word plainly refers to Christ. Thus he is said to be "The Mediator of a better covenant," and "The Mediator of the New Testament." (*Hebrews 8:6; 9:15*). In *Hebrews 12:24* we are said to have come "to Jesus the Mediator of the new covenant." We also have the word in *1 Timothy 2:5:* "There is one God, and one Mediator between God and men, the man Christ Jesus." Boston says, "Mediator properly signifies a midsman, that travels betwixt two persons who are at variance, to reconcile them." Owen says, "Christ's mediation consists in his being the middle person between God and us." In the Gaelic version, the word for mediator is "go-between."

Jesus Christ is Mediator not typically, but properly; not partially, but completely; not merely as a messenger from God to us, and as one presenting our requests to God, but as one who has removed all obstacles to friendly intercourse between God and man, and brings together in holy fellowship the offended Judge of all the earth and offending sinners.

The doctrine of mediation is no novelty. It has great antiquity. Job foresaw the day when the Redeemer should be manifest. Indeed to Him gave all the prophets witness. Even some of the heathen had a faint idea of mediation. Plato says, "God does not mingle in familiar intercourse with mortals, but all intercourse and conversation with him are maintained by means of demons," or spirits. Ever since the fall, men have been afraid of the Divine presence. I find no Scripture for the opinion that, "although man had remained immaculately innocent, yet his condition would have been too mean for him to approach to God without a mediator." On the contrary, our first parents had delightful communion with the Lord God until they sinned against him. We know of nothing in the nature of God or of man to hinder their intercourse until iniquity separated between them. God's tender mercies are over all his works. He stoops to the meanest worm. Infinite condescension is one of the glories of his nature. Christ's mediation fairly presupposes man's sinfulness and alienation from God. Where there is no controversy, there is no room for mediation. If persons are already at one, they need no reconciliation. If God loves and approves man's course and character, and if man loves and approves of God's ways, perfections and government, there is nothing to keep them from mutual delight. There is then no contest between them; nothing to be settled; no room for mediation. Dick says: "The necessity of the mediation of Christ arises from the existence of sin, which, being contrary to the nature and will of God, renders those who have committed it obnoxious to his displeasure."

Where there are parties entirely alienated, another, the equal and friend of both, may interpose, and tender his kind offices, and do whatever he is able to do honourably to reconcile the contestants. A mediator is different from a petitioner. From his dignity, he has a right to be heard with respect and candour. By his divinity, Christ was equal with God; by his humanity, he was equal with man. He was so much the friend of God, that he was willing to die for the glory of divine justice. He was so much the friend of man, that he was willing to lay down his life for human redemption.

The doctrine of mediation is that which chiefly distinguishes genuine Christianity from a system of pure deism. Let us consider this subject:

I. The advantages of mediation as a method of reconciling God and man are many.

1. It is very humbling to man, the sinner, the wrong-doer. It says to him, You are unworthy and unfit to come into the presence of God. You can neither justify nor excuse your wicked conduct. You are rejected. God will not even treat with you in your own name. He utterly abhors all your works, all your pleas, all your merits. You are condemned. You are vile.

2. A system of mediation is more honourable to God than any other mode of reconciliation could be. It shows that he is infinitely just and holy; so that he cannot look upon sin, or have any close, friendly intercourse with sinners, except through a third party – one in whom he is well-pleased.

3. Mediation marks sin as very base, deserving all the woes and wrath denounced against it. Though God is the Maker of our bodies and the Father of our spirits, yet so unspeakably does he detest sin and count it a horrible thing, that he refuses not only communion, but even conference, with the offender, except through the Son of his love.

4. A system of mediation marks sin as a public offence, demanding a public satisfaction and reparation. It is no private wrong that can be secretly repaired or adjusted. In accepting Christ as Mediator, every sinner confesses, before angels and men, that he has insulted and injured the government of God, and done what in him lay to disturb the order and harmony of the universe.

II. Let us consider Christ's fitness for the work of mediation.

1. His person is wonderfully and admirably constituted. He is at once "God manifest in the flesh" and "the man Christ Jesus." (*1 Timothy 3:16; 2:5*). As a daysman, he can lay his hand upon both God and us. He knows God's rights. He knows our sins. By his divine nature, he has zeal for the divine glory. By his human nature, he has

sympathy with us. He has all that is perfect and infinite in God, and all that is amiable and excellent in man. He will not betray God's interest, because it is the glory of his Godhead. He will not betray our interest, because it is the crown of his manhood. He has the confidence of God and of all right-minded men. He is in sympathy with Jehovah on the throne, and with man in his misery. He knows what God demands, and what man requires. God has no claims that Christ does not hold to be just. Man has no real wants that Christ is not ready to supply. From his very nature, he must vindicate the laws and government of God, and at the same time hold forth the cup of salvation to us poor sinners. He can so present our cause and nature to God that he will not turn away from us with loathing. And he can so present to us the glorious perfections of God as to show us their infinite amiability. By his divine nature, it is no robbery for him to assert equality with God. God has never denied him anything: "Him the Father heareth always." His claims to be heard are never questioned in heaven. For the honour of God he has poured out his blood, infinitely more precious than the blood of all the pious martyrs. And if man can be brought to hearken to terms of peace at all, surely it will be by Jesus Christ. He is so loving, he died so freely, he speaks so kindly, his grace is so rich, and his ways are so condescending, that if we will not hear him we will hear no one. By his human nature he is capable of suffering, and in his human nature he did actually suffer the penalty of the law; and being without sin himself, he was a spotless sacrifice to Divine justice. By his divine nature, which took the human into indissoluble union with itself, infinite merit attached to all Christ did and suffered. As the Father, by reason of Christ's holiness, found no fault in him, so we, by reason of his love and gentleness, are not repelled from him. There is no more approachable being in the universe than Jesus Christ. If God is his Father, we are his brethren. As man he suffered; as God he satisfied. His divinity gives unshaken stability to his mediation, as well as infinite worth to his humiliation.

2. Jesus Christ was chosen of God to this very office. The Father calls him "mine elect, in whom my soul delighteth." (*Isaiah 42:1*). He is "chosen of God, and precious." (*1 Peter 2:4*). Not by any arrogance, but by Divine appointment, he is the first-born among many brethren. All he said and all he did by the commandment of

his Father: "As the Father gave me commandment, even so I do." (*John 14:31*. Compare *John 10:18*). God never entrusted the work of mediation between him and sinners to another, though he appointed some men as types and shadows of Christ, who alone was to do this work. God is in Christ – God is in none but Christ – reconciling the world to himself. Christ is our peace.

3. To the full work of Mediator Jesus Christ not only brought ample qualifications and a divine commission, but he has met with entire acceptance from God. In every way possible God has declared his confidence in Christ, and his approval of his undertaking. Before his incarnation, in anticipation of what he was yet to do, God poured out his Spirit on many souls, granted them pardon, acceptance, and renewal, and at death received them to glory. When Christ was on earth, and before his death, God expressed his approval of him by a voice from heaven, by amazing miracles, and by leading some truly to love him, and to forsake all and follow him. God further expressed approval of Christ by raising him from the dead, by giving him a glorious admission into heaven, and a seat with himself on his throne. God has further and wondrously expressed approbation of Christ's mediation by making the preaching of Christ crucified the power of God unto salvation – the salvation of millions, many of whom were sunk in almost unparalleled guilt, and shame, and ignorance, and misery, till they heard and believed the gospel.

4. In suffering and dying for us Jesus Christ needed not to subject himself to humiliation but for a time. He lived on earth over thirty years. Thenceforward his whole person partakes of incomparable bliss. Since his ascension into heaven he has no pains, no sorrows, no bitterness of soul. His short conflict was followed by eternal triumph; his brief agony by eternal joy. The lower he sunk on earth, the higher he rises in glory. What a blessed truth is this! How could his people be happy if they thought he was still a sufferer?

Of course Christ is a far better mediator than Moses. (*2 Corinthians 3:9*). The mediation of the former was temporary; that of the latter everlasting. This is the last dispensation. "There remaineth no more sacrifice for sins." (*Hebrews 10:26*). We may not expect "the bringing in of a better hope." The mediation of Moses was typical; that of Christ was real. Moses laid many burdensome rites on the people; Christ appointed a very simple worship. The tendency of the law, through sin, was unto death; through faith the gospel gives life. (*Hebrews 9:13, 14*). The former was the ministration of death; the latter is the ministration of the Spirit. The mediation of Moses prepared men for the gospel; that of Christ prepares men for glory. Christ excels Moses in that he is the Mediator of a better covenant established upon better promises. (*Hebrews 8:6*). Christ is more kind and compassionate than Moses. Both refused a crown; but Jesus wore a crown of thorns and hung on the cross. Moses was a servant, but Jesus Christ was a Son. Both the authority and energy of Moses were limited; but Jesus raised the dead and performed countless miracles in his own name, and all power in heaven and earth is given unto him. Moses did a good work; but Christ a far better work. The law was given by Moses; but grace and truth came by Jesus Christ.

III. Let us look at some of the great and happy effects of Christ's mediation.

1. Through it, and through it only, do we obtain correct and sufficient knowledge of the divine nature. Like Moses, good men cry, "Show me thy glory." Like the disciples, they say, "Show us the Father, and it sufficeth us." We do greatly desire to have before us some representation of God; and as all idols and images made or conceived by man are no representation of him, but a horrible dishonour to him, it is with delight that we find Christ the image of God, the express image of his person. (*2 Corinthians 4:4; Colossians 1:15; Hebrews 1:3*). So that now to know God, and Jesus Christ, whom he hath sent, is eternal life. (*John 17:3*). No man can see God's face and live. No man hath seen God at any time. The only begotten Son, who is in the bosom of the Father, he hath declared him. Now, if we would know what is the nature of God, let us look at it through the veil of Christ's flesh. He himself says: "I and my Father are one." "I am in the Father, and the Father in me;" and in yet stronger terms, "He that hath seen me hath seen the Father."

2. It is only by and through the mediation of Christ that we can indulge any hope of reconciliation with God. We cannot answer for one of a thousand of our offences. We are justly condemned. God rightly counts us "reprobate silver." The single sin of not loving God with all our heart, and mind, and soul, and strength, is enough to blot out every hope of heaven. But our iniquities have risen up like

the mountains. They are more than the hairs of our heads. And the guilt of every sin is greater than any man ever saw the guilt of any sin to be. Surely there is no hope left us that we shall ever see God's face in peace, unless it be by Christ's mediation. How sweet are his precious words: "I am the door;" "I am the way, the truth, and the life: no man cometh to the Father, but by me."

3. Through the mediation of Christ, and through it alone, are our hearts brought into such a state that we admire and delight in God. The Holy Spirit is the Spirit of Christ. Christ promised to send that Spirit for the conversion and purification of men's hearts. So that now, us "that were sometime alienated and enemies in our mind by wicked works, hath he reconciled." (*Colossians 1:21*). Christ's Spirit by the gospel slays our enmity. Thus Christ is "made unto us sanctification." By the cross of Christ we are crucified unto the world, and the world unto us. All grace, all saving virtue comes to us through the mediation of Christ. Owen says: "God communicates nothing in a way of grace unto any, but in and by the person of Christ as the mediator and head of the church." (*John 1:18*). "The head of every man is Christ: and the head of Christ is God." (*1 Corinthians 11:3*).

4. Through the mediation of Christ, and not otherwise, can men be brought into the society and fellowship of angels. When the believer is exploring the counsels of love and the glories of redemption, as he goes deep into these unfathomable mines, he finds a bright cherub or a burning seraph in the same region of exulting inquiry, and, asking what they do here, he is told that they have divine permission to "look into these things." Angels hymned the birth of Christ. Angels rejoice at the conversion of sinners and the progress of Christ's kingdom. Though Christ is not the Saviour of angels, yet by virtue of his great merit and dignity he has become Lord of angels. They serve and worship and obey him. They are his ministers. God has "set him at his own right hand in the heavenly places, far above all principality, and power, and might, and dominion, and every name that is named, not only in this world, but also in that which is to come: and hath put all things under his feet, and given him to be the head over all things to the church." (*Ephesians 1:20-22*). Thus saints and angels constitute the one family named in heaven and earth. Thus "in the dispensation of the fulness of times" he shall "gather together in

one all things in Christ, both which are in heaven, and which are on earth." (*Ephesians 1:10*). The apostasy severed us from God and from one another. By creation angels belonged to another order of beings. The work of Christ brings us to love God and one another, and gives to angels and men a common Lord, the God-man, Jesus Christ.

5. The mediation of Christ, in an unparalleled manner, makes known the wisdom of God. That this is so is admitted by all good men, who never cease to admire the wonderful plan of salvation. That this is so is declared in Scripture. Paul says the whole scheme and mystery of salvation is, "to the intent that now unto the principalities and powers in heavenly places might be known by the church the manifold wisdom of God." (*Ephesians 3:10*). The scheme of Christ's mediation is God's chief work. As poet, painter, sculptor, and architect, Michelangelo accomplished many admirable things; but above all the rest his monument is St Peter's at Rome. So God has filled the heavens and the earth, the sea and the dry land with wonders; but above all his other works the plan of salvation by Jesus Christ is God's monument, displaying his infinite skill and wisdom.

6. It is only through the mediation of Christ that the divine government has consistency, and the divine attributes have harmony, in the salvation of our race. "A God all mercy is a God unjust." A God all justice could not forgive a sinner. In the cross we see mercy infinite and justice inflexible kissing each other. Truth, which cannot swerve, here meets peace which cannot be broken. Righteousness, which is the stability of God's throne, by Christ's mediation issues in blessings unparalleled to the rebellious.

7. Through the mediation of Christ, and through it alone, can an enlightened conscience ever find relief. But the blood of the covenant can hush the perturbations of the most agonised soul. It gave peace to the penitent thief on the cross, and to the penitent murderers of Christ. It quieted the conscience of even Saul of Tarsus, when he relied upon it.

8. By the mediation of Christ, man recovers communion with God, lost by the fall. This is a wonderful result; "Now in Christ Jesus ye who sometimes were far off are made nigh by the blood of Christ." (*Ephesians 2:13*). So that, with the last surviving apostle, all Christians may unite in the exultant exclamation, "Truly our fellowship is with

the Father, and with his Son Jesus Christ." (*1 John 1:3*). Bringing man into the fellowship of angels was very glorious, but it was as nothing compared with his restoration to communion with God.

IV. Christ is sole Mediator. So says the Scripture: "There is one God, and one Mediator between God and men, the man Christ Jesus." (*1 Timothy 2:5*). One such Mediator is enough. The Word of God speaks of no more. The necessities of man demand no more. By Scripture we are as clearly shut up to the faith of one Mediator as to the belief of one God. If it is an offence to the heavenly Majesty to believe in many gods, it cannot be pleasing to the Most High that we should hold the doctrine of many mediators. "We do shockingly insult the Lord Jesus Christ and his Father when we bring in a great rabble of mediators and intercessors. Christ only, and Christ alone, is worthy of the Daysman's crown. To mention another is theft and robbery. (*John 10:1*).

V. We should greatly rejoice in Christ, the one Mediator. He is our life and our light. Let us make him our joy and our song. We cannot praise him too much. We shall never laud him enough. He is the admiration of all heaven. He ought to be the delights of the sons of men.

> "Were the whole realm of nature mine,
> That were a present far too small;
> Love so amazing, so divine,
> Demands my soul, my life, my all."

VI. As Mediator, Christ holds and executes the offices of Prophet, Priest, and King. This method of stating his work is not a human invention. It is clearly and often taught in the Scriptures. It is based in the nature of things. It is really a useful mode of presenting truth. Christ does the full work of a Mediator.

*   *   *

Controversies between two parties are of three kinds:

1. Such as are founded in mere mistake, both parties being innocent and honest, neither intending any harm. In this case, all that is wanted is light, explanation. But God is not mistaken respecting

us. He understands our case perfectly. He is not misinformed. He is under no misapprehensions respecting us. He has no prejudices against us. And although we are willingly mistaken respecting God in many particulars, and have wicked prejudices against him, it is because we hate the light; for when we know him, we glorify him not, nor like to retain him in our knowledge; our carnal mind is enmity against him. The controversy between God and us cannot be settled by mere explanation. Jehovah's conduct needs none; ours admits of none.

2. In the second kind of controversy, both parties are to be blamed – both have done wrong. In human strifes this is often the case. One wrong leads to another. Before adjustment, oft-times, both parties are censurable. But God has done us good, and not evil, all our days. He has never wronged us. Even when he has afflicted us, he has punished us less than our iniquities deserved. He has brought no false accusation against us. He has mercifully spared us, when he might justly have cut us down. He has done all things well. We have destroyed ourselves. He is holy, just, and good. In this fearful controversy we cannot blame him.

3. The only other kind of controversy between two parties is, where all the blame is on one side. This is the character of our controversy with God. We have sinned against him, not he against us. We are all wrong; we are wholly wrong; we are terribly wrong. Our iniquities have separated between us and God. He is righteous; we are unjust. He is holy; we are vile. He can do without us; without him we are undone. Let us say all this, and confess the whole truth. Let us joyfully accept the mediation of Jesus Christ. This way of reconciliation is as safe for us as it is honourable to God. This is the only method of ending the fearful contest. Reject this, and nothing remains but an eternal overthrow.

And the sooner we make peace with God the better. There is no time to be lost. Now is the day of salvation. Awake, O sleeper, and call upon thy God.

The responsibility of living under the gospel is great in proportion to its incalculable advantages. (*Hebrews 2:1-4; 10:28-30*).

7
Christ a Prophet

THE prophetical office of Christ claims solemn attention. The life of men's souls is involved in it. The necessity of some great teacher to enlighten mankind was confessed by the heathen as well as by the Jews. Socrates said: "You may resign all hope of reforming the manners of men, unless it please God to send some person to instruct you." Plato said: "Whatever is set right in the present ill state of the world can be done only by the interposition of God." Cicero, speaking of the philosophers, said: "Do you think that those precepts of morality had any influence, except in a very few instances, upon the men who speculated, wrote, and disputed concerning them? No; who is there of all the philosophers whose mind and manners were conformed to the dictates of right reason? Who of them ever made his philosophy the law and rule of his life, and not merely an occasion of displaying his own ingenuity? On the contrary, many of them have been slaves to the vilest lusts." How the pious Jews longed, and waited, and prayed for the coming of a great prophet is declared in many Scriptures.

Let us consider this subject:

I. Among the ancients and moderns, civilised and rude, the office of prophet has been held in high esteem. In this agree Jews, Christians, Mohammedans, and pagans. The evangelical prophet expressed the popular sentiment of his countrymen and the common sense of mankind when, in the same list, he enrolled the prophet with the mighty man, and the man of war, and the judge, and the prudent, and the ancient, and the captain, and the honourable man, and the counsellor, and the eloquent orator. (*Isaiah 3:2, 3*). Such men are the stay and the staff of a people. Among them all, none were more important, or were charged with more weighty duties, than the prophets.

II. But what is the office of a prophet? The word prophet comes to us from the Greek, where its literal signification is a foreteller. The Hebrews had two words for a prophet. One was from their word to *see.* It was in use a long time in the early history of that people. So we read in *1 Samuel 9:9*: "Beforetime in Israel, when a man went to inquire of God, thus he spake, Come, and let us go to the seer: for he that is now called a Prophet was beforetime called a Seer." The other word for a prophet signifies primarily to *boil up* or *pour forth*, as a fountain; then to pour forth words like those who speak with fervour of mind, or under divine inspiration. Then it came to signify a prophet, one who spake in the name of God, or in the place of God. Proof is not wanting in the Scriptures themselves that the word designates one who speaks eloquently or beautifully. God said to Moses, "Aaron thy brother shall be thy prophet." This is God's answer to Moses, who had objected to his mission on the ground that he was "of uncircumcised lips." The Greek word *prophet* is by Paul himself applied to a heathen poet, (*Titus 1:12*), either because the poet had written eloquently, or because he was held in high esteem as a teacher. In the New Testament the word *prophesy* has at least in one case the sense of edifying the church by preaching. "The gift of prophecy included that of prophetic foresight, but it included more. The prophet was inspired to reveal the will of God, to act as an organ of communication between God and man. The subject of the revelations thus conveyed was not, and could not be, restricted to the future. It embraced the past and present, and extended to those absolute and universal truths which have no relation to time." A prophet then is an inspired, and so an infallible teacher, able to tell the past or the future, authorised to speak for God and by his authority, not merely as an expounder of truths already revealed, but to teach truths before unknown or forgotten by mankind. In this full and broad sense, Jesus Christ was a prophet.

III. The fundamental passage on which we found the doctrine of Christ's prophetical office is *Deuteronomy 18:15-19:* "The Lord thy

God will raise up unto thee a Prophet from the midst of thee, of thy brethren, like unto me; unto him ye shall hearken; according to all that thou desiredst of the Lord thy God in Horeb in the day of the assembly, saying, Let me not hear again the voice of the Lord my God, neither let me see this great fire any more, that I die not. And the Lord said unto me, They have well spoken that which they have spoken. I will raise them up a Prophet from among their brethren, like unto thee, and will put my words in his mouth; and he shall speak unto them all that I shall command him. And it shall come to pass, that whosoever will not hearken unto my words which he shall speak in my name, I will require it of him." This prophecy is quoted by Peter in his address to the people in Jerusalem after the cure of the lame man. (*Acts 3:22, 23*). It is also cited by Stephen, in his pungent address to the Jews who were about to stone him to death. (*Acts 7:37*). In this prediction several things claim attention.

1. It is a *promise* made to the people on the occasion of their asking that God would not again speak to them in so awful a manner as he had done. God was not angry at them for this request, but approved of their words. The prediction is full of kindness. It is a gracious engagement to give them a teacher whose presence should not be terrible to them.

2. We have the best evidence that this prediction is not fulfilled, unless Jesus of Nazareth was the promised teacher. The last chapter of *Deuteronomy* was evidently not written by Moses, for it tells of things done after his death. It was probably written by different hands. Some, perhaps not without reason, ascribe it to Ezra, who compiled the canon of the Old Testament more than nine hundred years after the death of Moses. Its precise date we are not able to give; but it declares that up to that time there had not arisen in Israel a prophet like unto Moses. (*Deuteronomy 34:10*). Nay more, no prophet like Moses had, in the belief of the Jews, arisen till the time of John the Baptist; for they asked him, "Art thou that prophet? And he answered, No." (*John 1:21, 25*). So when they saw the miracles Jesus did, they said, "This is of a truth that Prophet that should come into the world." (*John 6:14*). Again: "Many of the people … said, Of a truth this is the prophet." (*John 7:40*). Jews do not pretend any more than Christians that "that prophet" has arisen since the coming of Jesus of Nazareth. He has not as yet come at all, unless Jesus be he.

3. The great prophet that was to come was to be raised up from the midst of Israel, and to be one of their brethren. Jesus Christ was, as descended from his mother, a Jew. No one denies this.

4. The promised prophet was to be like unto Moses. In the following particulars Moses was a striking type of Christ:

Moses was hardly born when his life was sought by bloody men. No sooner was the birth of Jesus known, than Herod sought the young child to destroy him.

Moses brought God's people out of the house of bondage. Jesus Christ delivers God's people from a worse than Egyptian bondage.

Moses was faithful in all his house. So Jesus was faithful to Him that appointed him. (*Hebrews 3:2*). Each of them spake the will of God in honesty and sincerity.

Moses was a mediator between God and his ancient people. He is expressly so called in *Galatians 3:19:* "The law was ordained by angels in the hands of a mediator." Moses received the mind of God and bore it to the people; and he heard the wishes of the people, and bore them to God. Nor did anyone but Moses perform this office to the Jews. So now Christ is our one and sole Mediator. "For there is one God, and one Mediator between God and men, the man Christ Jesus." (*1 Timothy 2:5*).

Moses was very intimate with God: "The Lord spake unto Moses face to face, as a man speaketh unto his friend." (*Exodus 33:11*). "The Lord knew Moses face to face." So Christ was in the beginning with God. "No man hath seen God at any time, the only begotten Son, which is in the bosom of the Father, he hath declared him." (*John 1:18*).

Beyond all others before Christ, Moses attested his doctrine and commission by signs and wonders, both in the land of Egypt and in the sight of all Israel. (*Deuteronomy 34:11, 12*). So Jesus Christ has filled the world with the renown of his stupendous miracles. Even when he was on earth, many who were not his disciples said, "When Christ cometh, will he do more miracles than these which this man hath done?" (*John 7:31*). Jesus called on his enemies to "believe the works" which he wrought. (*John 10:38*). Indeed, our Saviour's miracles were not only amazing in kind; they were countless in number. Having told us much of Christ, John says: "There are also many other things which Jesus did, the which, if they should be written every one, I suppose that even the world itself could not contain the books that should be written." (*John 21:25*). So Cleopas said that "Jesus of Nazareth was a prophet mighty in deed and word before God and all the people." (*Luke 24:19*).

Moses introduced a new state of things, setting aside the patriarchal dispensation. So Jesus Christ introduced a new dispensation in the place of the Mosaic. Now we have the gospel instead of the Sinaitic covenant.

In all these respects Moses was a striking type of Christ. Yet, as was fitting, the Antitype far excelled him. Moses was a servant. Christ was a Son. Moses was a mere man. Christ was "God manifest in the flesh." Moses was a sinner. Christ never displeased his Father. The Mosaic dispensation passed away. Christ shall never be superseded; while eternity lasts, the Lamb himself shall feed his people, and lead them to fountains of living waters. (*Revelation 7:17*).

So convincing was the evidence which Christ gave of his divine mission, that the woman of Samaria said, "I perceive that thou art a prophet." (*John 4:19*). And the blind man who was healed by him, in the midst of taunts and threats said, "He is a prophet." (*John 9:17*). So when he raised the young man of Nain, "there came a fear on all: and they glorified God, saying, That a great prophet is risen up among us." (*Luke 7:16*). And at one time multitudes of the Jewish nation, gathered at the holy city, were so affected that they said, "This is Jesus the prophet of Nazareth of Galilee." (*Matthew 21:11*). Indeed, during his ministry his miracles were confessed. Nor did anyone ever successfully impugn his teachings, or assail his claims to be *the* prophet of God.

The objections made were frivolous, such as these: "Search and look: for out of Galilee ariseth no prophet." (*John 7:52*). To this bold statement there are several fair answers. 1. Neither Moses nor any other writer of the Jewish Scriptures had said where all the prophets should be born. 2. At this very time the Jews had among their canonical books the writings of two prophets, *Jonah* and *Nahum*, both of whom were natives of Galilee. 3. Jesus did not *arise* out of Galilee, for he was born in Bethlehem of Judea. 4. Isaiah had expressly foretold, not that Messiah should be born in Galilee, but that his ministry should greatly enlighten that dark region, sometimes called Galilee of the Gentiles, because it bordered on Syria and Arabia, and because there many Gentiles dwelt with the Israelites. (Compare *Isaiah 9:1, 2,* and *Matthew 4:14-16*). 5. The cities of refuge, it is commonly admitted, were types of Christ, and one of these, Kedesh (or Kadesh) of Naphtali, was in Galilee; for Galilee included Asher, Issachar, Zebulon, and Naphtali.

Another objection has no more force. When Simon the Pharisee saw how Christ permitted the poor sinful woman to wash his feet with her tears, and to anoint him, he said, "This man, if he were a prophet, would have known who and what manner of woman this is that toucheth him: for she is a sinner." (*Luke 7:39*). But Jesus *did* know not only the woman's sinfulness, but also her penitence, and amply vindicated his conduct. Simon did not know that Jesus came into the world to save *sinners.* The mistake was all on his side.

IV. It remains to show how Jesus Christ fulfils "the office of a prophet, in revealing to the church in all ages, by his Spirit and Word, in divers ways of administration, the whole will of God, in all things concerning the edification and salvation of believers."

1. For about four thousand years Jesus Christ made known the will of God by his servants, the prophets. "At sundry times and in divers manners" he "spake in time past unto the fathers by the prophets." (*Hebrews 1:1*). So Peter also says, Of this "salvation the prophets have inquired and searched diligently, who prophesied of the grace that should come unto you: searching what, or what manner of time the Spirit of Christ which was in them did signify, when it testified beforehand the sufferings of Christ, and the glory that should follow. Unto whom it was revealed, that not unto themselves, but unto us they did minister the things, which are now reported unto you by them that have preached the gospel unto you with the Holy Ghost sent down from heaven." (*1 Peter 1:10-12*). These Scriptures bring out these truths: *a.* All the will of God was not revealed at once, but at divers times from Adam to Malachi. *b.* God's will was revealed in various ways; sometimes in dreams, sometimes in visions, sometimes by sending an angel, sometimes by an audible voice, and sometimes by the Son of God assuming a human form. *c.* But whatever the manner of the revelation, it was always by "the Spirit of Christ which was in the prophets." *d.* Much that the prophets spoke was dark to themselves, so that they found it necessary to study very carefully their own writings.

e. The burden of their messages was the sufferings of Christ and the glory that should follow. *f.* Their teachings were in their aspect chiefly prospective, relating to gospel times. *g.* The same Holy Spirit, who dictated the prophecies, gives efficacy to the preached gospel. *h.* Much that was said by the prophets, amounting in all to thirty-nine books, was put in writing, and committed to the ancient church, as the depository of the truth.

2. The prophets were followed by John the Baptist, who, for the clear light he gave and for pointing out the very man who was to save the world, was "more than a prophet." (*Matthew 11:9*). He was in a sense an evangelist. He was Christ's herald and forerunner.

3. Then came Jesus Christ himself, the Light of the world, the life of men, and the desire of all nations. God "hath in these last days spoken unto us by his Son." (*Hebrews 1:2*). Men saw him full of grace and truth. Men wondered at the gracious words that proceeded out of his mouth. And no marvel; "for it pleased the Father that in him should all fulness dwell." (*Colossians 1:19*). During his personal ministry Christ taught us the will of God in four ways. *a.* He wrought miracles in his own name and by his own power, thus showing not only that he was a teacher sent from God, but that he was himself divine. *b.* In his entire human nature he set us an example of piety and benevolence, making plain to us all our duties. Whatever Christ did as a man, we are bound to do. In obedience to parents, in submission to civil rulers, in forgiveness of injuries, in all things his example was perfect. *c.* During his personal ministry Christ uttered several remarkable predictions, which have been and shall be of eminent service to the church of God. Christ's predictions were strongly marked. *d.* Jesus Christ preached much and in a manner wholly incomparable. When the minions of cruelty were sent to arrest him, they were disarmed by his amazing discourses. When asked why they did not bring him before the chief priests and Pharisees, the only account they could give of the matter was, "Never man spake like this man." (*John 7:46*). The guilty hands lifted against him fell nerveless before his amazing words. No wonder the people were "astonished at his doctrine: for he taught them as one having authority, and not as the scribes." (*Matthew 7:28, 29*). The Word of God in his mouth was a sharp two-edged sword. (*Deuteronomy 18:18* and *Revelation 1:16*).

4. When Christ left this world and ascended up far above all heavens, "he gave some, apostles; and some, prophets; and some, evangelists; and some, pastors and teachers; for the perfecting of the saints, for the work of the ministry, for the edifying of the body of Christ." (*Ephesians 4:11-13*). This whole work of the apostles and their co-labourers was conducted under the guidance and teaching of the Holy Ghost, who both taught them and brought to their remembrance all things taught them by the Master personally. (*John 14:26*). It was given them what they should say. The same Spirit in his converting power was poured upon their hearers.

5. Jesus Christ inspired his apostles and evangelists to write for our use twenty-seven distinct books, giving a full account of his life and doctrine, and of his will in all things pertaining to life and godliness, to the end of the world.

6. It is still Christ's gracious plan to pour out his Spirit on faithful ministers in preaching his Word, and on the hearers of his Word, so that great numbers are still converted, sanctified, and built up in faith and holiness unto eternal life. In these several methods Jesus Christ carries on his great work as the prophet of God.

Let us consider a little the excellence of his work as a teacher.

1. Everything he has taught us either by himself or by his servants is *true*. In it all there is no mistake, no error, no delusion. The more it is tried, the more true it is proven to be. In a world full of falsehood and delusion, pure truth is a great matter. Now whether men jest or are serious in asking, What is truth? we can look up to God and say, "Thy word is truth." "It is truth without any admixture of error." It is the truth of God. And it all comes to us through the Spirit of Christ. Indeed, he is the Rock, out of which the river of truth has ever flowed to make glad the city of God.

2. All he has taught us is very *pure*. It cannot defile. "The words of the Lord are pure words: as silver tried in a furnace of earth, purified seven times." (*Psalm 12:6*). "The commandment of the Lord is pure, enlightening the eyes." (*Psalm 19:8*). "The law is holy, just, and good." (*Romans 7:12*). The reason why the wicked hate God's Word is that it is so holy.

3. Jesus Christ has, in ways already stated, revealed to us the *whole* will of God for our salvation. He has kept back nothing that would be

profitable to us. He says expressly: "All things that I have heard of my Father I have made known unto you." (*John 15:15; Psalm 40:9, 10; Deuteronomy 18:18*).

4. The whole will of God thus made known to us through our great Prophet is accompanied by the strongest attestations. It is confirmed by witnesses who hazarded their lives, and in most cases actually died martyrs. God has also borne witness, both with signs and wonders, and with divers miracles, and gifts of the Holy Ghost. It is confirmed by the spotless life of Christ himself, and by the holy lives of his prophets and apostles. It is confirmed to us by its converting and sanctifying power over men's souls. It is confirmed by the commanding authority it has over the human conscience. It is confirmed to us by covenant and by God's awful and unimpeachable oath.

5. The will of God, as revealed to us by our great prophet, is practicable. The doctrines can be loved and are loved by all whose hearts are right. All the precepts are just. They are obeyed sincerely by the godly. They were obeyed perfectly in our Lord's human nature, thus showing that they could be kept whenever sin did not oppose.

6. Our great prophet has made the will of God very plain. "The common people heard him gladly." He never mystified his hearers. "That which maketh manifest is light." God's Word is even a discerner of the thoughts and intents of the heart. It exposes to our view the secrets of our souls and the glorious mysteries of heavenly things. Neither Christ nor his servants handled the Word of God deceitfully. If to any the Bible is a *sealed book,* it is because of the blindness of their heart. "All the words of my mouth are in righteousness; there is nothing froward or perverse in them. They are all plain to him that understandeth, and right to them that find knowledge." (*Proverbs 8:8, 9*).

7. God's will is made known to us in the kindest, gentlest way. Our great prophet did not strive, nor cry, nor cause his voice to be heard in the streets. He held up a little child as the pattern he would have us follow. Even Moses, his servant, who was the minister of the Sinaitic covenant, was the meekest of mere men.

8. Jesus Christ teaches all his people effectually. "I will put my law in their inward parts, and write it in their hearts; and I will be their God, and they shall be my people." (*Jeremiah 31:33*). So that David

said no more than every child of God may say: "I will never forget thy precepts: for with them thou hast quickened me." (*Psalm 119:93*).

*   *   *

1. Let us not waste our life and time in gaping after some strange thing, some new doctrine, or some new revelation. Let us seek the old paths, the ways in which the prophets, and apostles, and martyrs, and confessors, and righteous men walked. There never was but one way of salvation for sinners. There is but one way now. It is taught us by Jesus Christ. Let us not, like the foolish, say, "Who shall ascend into heaven? (that is, to bring Christ down from above:) or, Who shall descend into the deep? (that is, to bring up Christ again from the dead.) But what saith it? The word is nigh thee, even in thy mouth, and in thine heart: that is, the word of faith, which we preach; that if thou shalt confess with thy mouth the Lord Jesus, and shalt believe in thy heart that God hath raised him from the dead, thou shalt be saved. For with the heart man believeth unto righteousness; and with the mouth confession is made unto salvation." (*Romans 10:6-10*).

2. The teachings of Christ as our great Prophet are not submitted to us for criticism, for speculation, for our entertainment; no. "These things have I written unto you that believe on the name of the Son of God; that ye may know that ye have eternal life." (*1 John 5:13*). "Whatsoever things were written aforetime were written for our learning, that we through patience and comfort of the Scriptures might have hope." (*Romans 15:4*). Hear the word of this salvation not as critics, but as criminals; not as theorists, but as candidates for eternity; not as idle spectators of a drama, but as those who must give account to God.

3. How very reasonable it is that such poor, ignorant, blind creatures as we are should pray for light and wisdom, and especially for the teaching of the Spirit of Christ. Of him it was promised by Christ, "He shall receive of mine, and shall show it unto you." (*John 16:14*). Other things being equal, he who prays most will learn fastest. When Daniel was to expound Nebuchadnezzar's dream, he and his friends found out the secret by prayer. (*Daniel 2:18*). Luther said: "Three things make a good theologian – meditation, temptation, and prayer." David was a prophet, yet often he cried, "Teach me

thy statutes;" "Open thou mine eyes, that I may behold wondrous things out of thy law." (*Psalm 119:12, 18, 26, 64, 68, 124, 135*).

4. Whatever we do or leave undone, let us not fail to hear and obey this great Prophet. God says we must: "Unto him shall ye hearken;" "Whosoever will not hearken unto my words which he shall speak in my name, I will require it of him." (*Deuteronomy 18:19*). This is the law under which the gospel is promulgated. Let none think to screen himself from this awful responsibility by the fact that Christ is no longer on earth. He is here by his essential presence, and he is here by his faithful ambassadors. Before he left the world, he said to his ministers: "He that heareth you heareth me; and he that despiseth you despiseth me; and he that despiseth me despiseth him that sent me." (*Luke 10:16*). The law of nations is, He that despises an ambassador insults the government that sent him. Such also is the law of the God of heaven.

8

The Priesthood of Christ

IN Scripture much is said of the offices of Christ. In particular, his priesthood is distinctly stated. One of the epistles, that to the *Hebrews*, is an inspired treatise on this subject. It is clear and simple. It discusses the chief points in a natural order, and concludes with practical inferences fairly drawn. Christ's priesthood is our theme at present. We can find no better order in which to present the matter than that suggested by Paul.

I. The first thing asserted and proved by the apostle is, that our High Priest, Jesus Christ, is *divine.* All his offices required that he should be God. None but God could be such a King as Christ is. None but God knows the things of God, or could infallibly declare them to us as the Prophet of the church. None but God could satisfy justice, and bring in everlasting righteousness sufficient for lost men. On Christ's divinity the power of his priesthood must rest. So Paul thought: and he takes up the whole of *Hebrews 1* in proving it. He uses four arguments, which to a pious mind are conclusive.

1. He says that Christ is "the brightness of the Father's glory, and the express image of his person." Then he says Christ's holy Father calls him "God:" "Thy throne, O God, is for ever and ever." (*Hebrews 1:3, 8*). Then he shows, from *Psalm 102:25, 26,* that he is called Lord. In that psalm the word Lord occurs eight times. In every instance the original word is Jehovah, the great and incommunicable name of the self-existent God.

2. Paul argues the divinity of Christ from the fact that he is Creator. He says expressly, "By him God made the worlds;" and, "Thou, Lord,

in the beginning hast laid the foundation of the earth; and the heavens are the works of thy hands." (*Hebrews 1:2, 10*). He also says: "This man was counted worthy of more glory than Moses, inasmuch as he who hath builded the house hath more honour than the house. For every house is builded by some man; but he that built all things is God." (*Hebrews 3:3, 4*).

3. The third argument for Christ's divinity here employed is, that he is the author of providence. He governs and sustains the universe. Paul says of Christ, "He upholds all things by the word of his power;" and, "Thy throne, O God, is for ever and ever." (*Hebrews 1:3, 8*). Again Paul says: God "hath appointed him heir of all things." (*Hebrews 1:2*). Well does Whitby say, "I believe it is as impossible to understand how a man should have this empire over all things in heaven and earth, and over death itself, and yet be a mere man, as it is to understand any mystery of the sacred Trinity."

4. Paul's fourth argument for the divinity of our High Priest is, that by command of his Father he is to be worshipped: "When he bringeth the first-begotten into the world, he saith, And let all the angels of God worship him." (*Hebrews 1:6*). Any one of these arguments, fairly stated, is conclusive. If Christ is fitly called God and Lord, or if he is the Creator, or if he is the author of providence, or if he is rightly worshipped, he is divine. What higher or better evidence have we that the Father is possessed of supreme divinity than that he is rightly called God and Jehovah, that he made all things, that he governs all things, and that it is proper to pay him religious worship? If we cannot prove the Son divine, neither can we prove the Father divine.

II. The second proposition of Paul respecting our High Priest is, that he is *human,* has our nature, is a man. We can conceive how our Lord might have been King in his divine nature alone. He could have ruled the world without becoming incarnate. To some extent, perhaps to a saving extent, he might have done the work of a prophet, and taught us the mind and will and nature of God, without becoming man. True, we should have very much missed his perfect example, set us in the days of his flesh. But by his Word and Spirit he might have made men wise unto salvation without his example. He did this for four thousand years, and gathered many sons to glory. But how could he have been a *priest* without a nature capable of obeying, of suffering, and of dying. Divinity cannot obey, cannot suffer, cannot die. Without a nature capable of suffering, he could make no atonement. Although Christ's humanity has at divers times and under various pretexts been denied, yet it is now seldom impugned. It is not necessary therefore to argue this matter at length. A few verses on the point will be enough. In *Hebrews 2:7* we have these words applied to him: "Thou madest him a little [or for a little while] lower than the angels." In *Hebrews 2:9,* Paul says that he "was made a little lower than the angels for the suffering of death." In *Hebrews 2:10* Paul says that it was by suffering that Jesus became a perfect Captain of salvation. Then in *Hebrews 2:14* he says: "Forasmuch then as the children are partakers of flesh and blood, he also himself took part of the same; that through death he might destroy him that had the power of death." And in *Hebrews 2:17:* "Wherefore in all things it behoved him to be made like unto his brethren, that he might be a merciful and faithful High Priest in things pertaining to God, to make reconciliation for the sins of the people." And in *Hebrews 2:18:* "For in that he himself hath suffered being tempted, he is able to succour them that are tempted."

These passages assign four distinct reasons why our Lord must be human:

1. Thus only could he be lower than the angels. 2. That he might suffer, and so atone. 3. That by death he might destroy him that had the power of death. And 4. That he might by experience learn what temptation and sorrow were, and so be a merciful High Priest.

III. Jesus Christ was duly called of God to be our High Priest. He was no bold intruder into those awful functions. Every step he took was agreeable to the counsels of God. This is to us a matter of great importance; and so we are not left in doubt upon it. In *Hebrews 5:4, 5* we read: "No man taketh this honour to himself, but he that is called of God, as was Aaron. So also Christ glorified not himself to be made an high priest; but he that said unto him, Thou art my Son, today have I begotten thee." If it can be shown that any man was ever called of God to any office, much more can it be proved that the Son was called of his Holy Father to be a High Priest.

IV. Not only ancient usage, but the law of Moses required that the high priest should be anointed. Jesus is the Messiah, the Christ, the

Lord's Anointed. Twice in God's Word, once in prophecy, and once in direct and inspired application to Christ, do we find these words: "God, thy God, hath anointed thee with the oil of gladness above thy fellows." (*Psalm 45:7; Hebrews 1:9*). In his first great sermon after his baptism and return to Nazareth, Jesus Christ clearly and unequivocally applied to himself these words of Isaiah: "The Spirit of the Lord God is upon me, because he hath anointed me to preach good tidings to the meek," etc. (Compare *Luke 4:16-22* and *Isaiah 61:1-3*). He said: "This day is this Scripture fulfilled."

V. Jesus Christ was *sent* of God into the world on the very work of a high priest. Malachi had foretold that he should be the "Messenger of the covenant;" and Paul well calls him "the *Apostle* and High Priest of our profession." (*Malachi 3:1* and *Hebrews 3:1*). In John's gospel Christ is thirty times declared to have been *sent* by his Father: "I must work the works of him that sent me;" "It is my meat to do the will of him that sent me," are examples. Indeed, Jesus said expressly that he both taught and wrought miracles that men might believe that God had sent him. (*John 11:42*). And in his days humble souls so received him; for Nicodemus said: "We know that thou art a teacher come from God."

VI. Jesus Christ was fit to be our High Priest, because he was "without sin." (*Hebrews 4:15*). He was without original sin, for he was not represented in Adam, our first parent standing only for such as descended from him by ordinary generation. So the angel who announced him to Mary called him "that *Holy Thing* which shall be born of thee." It was every way necessary that our High Priest should be holy. God could have been in no way pleased with a high priest acting, offering, or interceding for us, if like ourselves he was a sinner, tainted and vile. Nor could we, with any just sense of sin, ever have been brought to put our confidence in one who was himself guilty and rebellious. Jesus was not only not a sinner, but he was impeccable. It is with great delight that we read: "Such an High Priest became us, who is holy, harmless, undefiled, separate from sinners." (*Hebrews 7:26*). God the Father knew how vital this point was, and so he has given us the most ample satisfaction respecting it. At Christ's baptism a voice from heaven said: "This is my beloved Son, in whom I am well pleased." (*Matthew 3:17*). So on the mount of transfiguration, a voice out of the cloud said, "This is my beloved Son, in whom I am well pleased; hear ye him." (*Matthew 17:5*). John says he was "full of grace and truth." (*John 1:14*). Even the miserable trifler who sat in judgment on our Lord said: "I find no fault in this man." Nay, more; he says, "I find no fault at all;" "I find no fault in him;" "I find no fault in him." (*Luke 23:4; John 18:38; 19:4, 6*). Even infidels generally have admitted that his character was blameless. The only true thing his enemies ever said in their malice against him while on earth was, that in which we glory: "This man receiveth sinners." (*Luke 15:2*). Though not a sinner himself, he loves sinners, he pities sinners, he died for sinners, he saves sinners, he saves none but sinners, he had no other errand on earth. O blessed be God, the Lord Christ owed no obedience to the law for himself, for he was the Lawgiver. He needed not, as other high priests, daily to offer up sacrifice, first for his own sins, and then for the people's. (*Hebrews 7:27*). *We* have his merits and his blood for *our* salvation. He needed no sacrifice to make him personally a sweet savour unto God.

VII. Christ is a priest, not after the order of Aaron, but after the order of Melchizedek. Under the law, the high priest held no other office; but Melchizedek and Christ held the two offices of King and Priest. Melchizedek signifies king of righteousness; and he was also king of Salem, which is King of peace. So Jesus, by reason of his infinite super-eminence, is most fitly styled both king of righteousness and king of peace. He brought in everlasting righteousness, so that God is now as righteous as he is merciful in pardoning sin and in accepting the sinner. And Jesus is the King of peace. He is the author of all the peace between God and penitent sinners, between Jews and Gentiles. His blood speaks peace to the conscience. He is our Peace. Neither the name of Melchizedek, nor that of his parents is found in the genealogical tables of the tribe of Levi. "And it is evident that our Lord sprang out of Juda; of which tribe Moses spake nothing concerning priesthood." (*Hebrews 7:14*). Melchizedek was greater than Aaron, greater than Levi, greater than Abraham; for to him Abraham paid tithes, and from him received a blessing; "and without all contradiction the less is blessed of the better." In the whole history of Melchizedek he appeared but once; so "now once in the end of the world hath Christ appeared to put away sin by the sacrifice of himself." (*Hebrews 9:26*). And as Melchizedek, so Christ had no predecessor and no successor in office. He needed none. None was fit for such a work. Christ's work is perfect.

VIII. Jesus Christ made a suitable offering to God. "Every high priest is ordained to offer gifts and sacrifices: wherefore it is of necessity that this man have somewhat also to offer." (*Hebrews 8:3*). Accordingly Christ gave "himself for us an offering and a sacrifice to God for a sweet-smelling savour." (*Ephesians 5:2*). In order to Christ's oblation availing for us, it must be something that he had a right to offer, something that he was willing to offer, something that was itself very precious, and something that God entirely approved and highly esteemed. On each of these points the Scriptures give us the most entire satisfaction. Not a doubt is left on the mind of one who takes God's Word for his guide. Other priests offered bulls and goats and lambs; but Jesus offered himself, his entire human nature. "We are sanctified through the offering of the body of Jesus Christ once for all." (*Hebrews 10:10*). Here, as in many other places, *body* means the whole man. First he offered his corporeal nature. It was spat upon, smitten, crowned with thorns; was nailed to the cross, was thrilled with agony, was dead and buried. He also offered his soul. Even before his arrest, so terribly did the wrath of God press upon him that his sweat was as great drops of blood. He exclaimed: "My soul is exceeding sorrowful, even unto death." All this was according to prophecy, for the evangelical prophet had said, "Thou shalt make his soul an offering for sin." (*Isaiah 53:10*). His divinity was the altar, which sanctified his oblation. His whole person made the offering, or presented the gift. And his entire human nature was the sacrifice. His sacrifice was true, not fictitious; real, not imaginary; proper, not typical. His one oblation was enough. It opened the gates of heaven to all believers. God has accepted it before angels and men. Under the law of Moses no sacrifice took away *sin*. (*Hebrews 10:4*). All was type, figure, shadow of something to come. But when Christ came he slew the enmity, he took away the handwriting that was against us, he satisfied divine justice, he brought redemption. Under the law sacrifices were ordained only for sins of ignorance, sins against the law of ceremonies, and sins admitting of restitution. No provision was made for sacrifices for murder, or unbelief, or pride, or malice. Accordingly, when David found himself convicted of violating the sixth and seventh commandments, he said, "Thou desirest not sacrifice, else would I give it." But "the Lamb of God taketh away the sin of the world." "The blood of Jesus Christ, his Son, cleanseth us from all sin." So that "he has perfected for ever them that are sanctified." He has made the comers to his altar perfect, as concerning offering for sin.

IX. When the high priest under the law had shed the blood and offered the victim, he made his intercessions in this lower world, in a place made with hands; but Christ has entered "into heaven itself, now to appear in the presence of God for us." (*Hebrews 9:24*). Thus he is "made higher than the heavens." (*Hebrews 7:26*). None else was ever permitted to stand before the blazing throne in heaven and with authority plead with God. In all things Jesus has the pre-eminence. Now "if any man sin, we have an Advocate *with the Father,* Jesus Christ the righteous." (*1 John 2:1*). We know where he is and what he is doing. He "is passed into the heavens." He is at the right hand of God. He is preparing a place for his people. "He ever liveth to make intercession for us." (*Hebrews 7:25*). His blood speaketh peace. His appearance is our advocacy. The arguments he uses are the wounds he received. His intercession never fails. "Him the Father heareth always." If you would see how he prays, study *John 17*. It is remarkable, however, that the law of Moses gives no form of words to be used by the high priest in the holy of holies. So Christ's intercession may be very much in his "appearance for us." When an Athenian was about to be sentenced for crime, his worthy brother, who had terribly bled for the liberties of his country, came into court, looked at the prisoner tenderly and at the judges imploringly, at the same time lifting up the stump of an arm, as if to plead. It was enough. The argument was decisive. The prisoner went free.

X. The high priest, having fulfilled his office in the holy place, came forth and gave his benediction to Israel, saying: "The Lord bless thee, and keep thee: the Lord make his face shine upon thee, and be gracious unto thee: the Lord lift up his countenance upon thee, and give thee peace." (*Numbers 6:24-26*). "So Christ was once offered to bear the sins of many; and unto them that look for him shall he appear the second time without sin unto salvation." (*Hebrews 9:28*). O yes! He will come again, not in sadness, not with lips swollen with grief, not with his visage marred more than any man; but in his glory, and all the holy angels with him. Then shall he say, "Come, ye blessed of my Father, inherit the kingdom prepared for you from the foundation of the world." (*Matthew 25:34*). O that our ears may hear that blessed plaudit!

XI. Under the law men came into the high priest's office, and went out of it again; but Jesus Christ, "because he continueth ever, hath an unchangeable priesthood." He "ever liveth." He "is consecrated for evermore." He is made a high priest, not "after the law of a carnal commandment, but after the power of an endless life." He "is a priest for ever." (*Hebrews 7:16, 17, 24, 25, 28*). He abideth ever over the house of God. O I am glad – are not you? – that there is to be no change in the priesthood of our profession. No change is possible. None but Jesus is worthy of the office. Any change would be for the worse. We could never have another like Jesus.

$$* \quad * \quad *$$

His priesthood suggests these lessons:

1. How vain are all other sacrifices for sin. No tears, no blood, no offerings but those of Christ can avail for us. He who pleads other merits before God is a thief and a robber. (*John 10:1*). A few years ago, an archbishop of Paris was dying of wounds received in a riot. He said: "O God, I offer to thee my present bodily sufferings as an atonement for the errors of my episcopate." But the sufferings of a sinner have no merit, no efficacy to atone. Jesus only, Jesus alone has so suffered as to make reconciliation for the people.

2. In Christ we have all we need. Jesus is so excellent in person and character, and is so highly in favour with God, that if he will but manage our cause and plead for us before the throne, we cannot fail. He counts it not robbery to be equal with God, and yet he is not ashamed to call us brethren. He can lay his hand upon God and upon us. In all things he suits our case and meets our necessities. His offering was perfect. It was fully accepted of God. He was a sin-offering. He bore the sin of many. This suits us. *Sinners,* sinners *only,*

sinners *always* need expiation. The effect of Christ's oblation has been marvellous. Its wonders will never cease. It is now filling heaven with a happy throng of worshippers, and with thundering hallelujahs.

3. With Christ for our High Priest, we may exercise great boldness in prayer. Thus Paul reasons: "Let us therefore come boldly unto the throne of grace, that we may obtain mercy, and find grace to help in time of need." Again: "Having an high priest over the house of God, let us draw near with a true heart in full assurance of faith, having our hearts sprinkled from an evil conscience, and our bodies washed with pure water." (*Hebrews 4:16; 10:21, 22*).

4. In Christ's priesthood we have a sure foundation for Christian steadfastness. So Paul reasoned: "Seeing then that we have a great High Priest, that is passed into the heavens, Jesus the Son of God, let us hold fast our profession." Again: "Let us hold fast the profession of our faith without wavering; for he is faithful that promised." (*Hebrews 4:14; 10:23*). It cannot but be safe to rely on such a Redeemer, and fearlessly do our duty.

5. This doctrine is essentially connected with the whole life of faith as Paul shows at length in *Hebrews 11*.

6. This doctrine is full of comfort to the afflicted. So Paul uses it at length in *Hebrews 12*.

7. This doctrine leads the pious soul to acts of thanksgiving, as nothing else does. "By him therefore let us offer the sacrifice of praise to God continually, that is, the fruit of our lips giving thanks to his name." (*Hebrews 13:15*). The great gospel feast is that of the Eucharist.

8. The great motive to a life of benevolence is drawn from this doctrine of Christ's priesthood. So Paul uses it: "Be not forgetful to entertain strangers;" "Remember them that are in bonds, as bound with them;" "To do good and to communicate forget not: for with such sacrifices God is well pleased." (*Hebrews 13:2, 3, 16*).

9. It is at our peril that we reject the priesthood of Jesus. Yea more, we are undone if we do it. On this point Paul is urgent: "How shall we escape, if we neglect so great salvation?" "See that ye refuse not him that speaketh." "He that despised Moses' law died without mercy under two or three witnesses: of how much sorer punishment, suppose ye, shall he be thought worthy, who hath trodden underfoot the Son of God, and hath counted the blood of the covenant, wherewith

he was sanctified, an unholy thing, and hath done despite unto the Spirit of grace." (*Hebrews 2:3; 12:25; 10:28, 29*). These solemn and awful texts establish these points: 1. Neglect of Christ is refusal of his grace. 2. Persistent neglect of Christ is followed by inevitable damnation. 3. There is something worse than dying without mercy under Moses' law. 4. Sin reaches its height when we trample on the blood of Christ. 5. He who neglects Christ, does despite to the Holy Spirit. A gospel despiser is acting as foolishly as he is wickedly. O impenitent man! Your condition is indeed sad. Your worst fears are not as bad as the truth would justify. The awful sentence of a broken law is against you; your own conscience will sooner or later flash damnation in your face; even now your polluted heart often writhes in agony; your wicked life is a token of perdition. The day of your death is near at hand; there is a dreadful hell just before you, and you deserve to be cast into it. O turn, O turn, O turn to God before the door of mercy closes for ever!

9
Christ a King

THOSE who reject Christ as King have never truly received him as Prophet or Priest. His yoke and his doctrine, his rule and his rest, go together. If his love does not make us obedient to his laws, we have no interest in his merits. We are not wise unto salvation till we bow to his authority. If we are partakers of his redemption, we are certainly partakers of his holiness. We may talk of his wonderful teachings, or boast of our interest in his amazing sacrifice, but it is all in vain so long as we refuse to own him as our Leader and Commander. Wherever he comes to bless, he comes as a Conqueror. His rule is as just as it is welcome to the penitent: "For to this end Christ both died, and rose, and revived, that he might be Lord both of the dead and living." (*Romans 14:9*). No law of Christ is too strict for a believer. With a controlling power his conscience enforces, and his heart embraces every precept of his Master. The kingly office of Christ is our theme.

I. Prophecy required that Christ should be a King. So ran that great fundamental prediction made to David: "I will set up thy seed after thee ... and I will establish his kingdom ... and I will stablish the throne of his kingdom for ever. I will be his Father, and he shall be my Son." (*2 Samuel 7:12-14*). Again: "I have set my King upon my holy hill of Zion." (*Psalm 2:6*). Again: "Unto us a Child is born, unto us a Son is given: and the government shall be upon his shoulder: and his name shall be called Wonderful, Counsellor, The mighty God, The everlasting Father, The Prince of Peace. Of the increase of his government and peace there shall be no end, upon the throne of David, and upon his kingdom, to order it, and to establish it with judgment and with justice from henceforth even for ever." (*Isaiah 9:6, 7*). The great promise to Bethlehem Ephratah was: "Out of thee shall he come forth unto me that is to be Ruler in Israel." (*Micah 5:2*). So also the angel Gabriel said of him to Mary: "He shall be great, and shall be called the Son of the Highest: and the Lord God shall give unto him the throne of his father David: and he shall reign over the house of Jacob for ever; and of his kingdom there shall be no end." (*Luke 1:32, 33*). It is thus clear that prophecy required him to be a King.

II. When Jesus Christ was upon his trial before Pilate, that guilty trifler "said unto him, Art thou a king then?" And in the language commonly used in those days to affirm, he answered, "Thou sayest that I am a king." (*John 18:37*). The meaning is, Thou correctly sayest I am a king. And that all may see his solemn earnestness, he immediately adds, "To this end was I born, and for this cause came I into the world, that I should bear witness unto the truth. Every one that is of the truth heareth my voice." So that Christ's mission into this world would have been in vain, if this "*truth*" had not been received. Twenty-seven years after Christ's trial, Paul, writing to a young minister, and giving him a *charge* to be faithful, calls his attention to this awful scene in the judgment-hall, when "Jesus Christ before Pontius Pilate witnessed a good confession." (*1 Timothy 6:13*). The only thing Christ confessed on his trial before Pilate was, that he was a king and Christ. This was his "good confession." It was good, because it was true. "He sealed it with his precious blood."

III. Jesus Christ is often called Lord, Master, Governor, Ruler, Shepherd, Prince, Prince and Saviour, the great Prince, the Prince of Life, the Prince of Peace, the Prince of princes, the Prince of the kings of the earth, a King, the King, the King of kings and Lord of lords. This last title is first found in *1 Timothy 6:15, 16:* "Which in his times he shall show, who is the blessed and only Potentate, the King of kings, and Lord of lords, who only hath immortality, dwelling in the light which no man can approach unto; whom no man hath seen, nor can see: to whom be honour and power everlasting. Amen." Some apply this passage to Christ, some to the Father, and some to the Godhead without distinction of persons. For the purposes of this argument, either mode suits our object. If it refers to Christ, it settles the question of his kingly authority. If it refers to the Father, or to the Divinity without distinction of persons, then it settles the point that the highest sovereignty is thus declared. And we have the very same language, thirty-five years after, applied to Christ: "The Lamb shall overcome them: for he is Lord of lords, and King of kings;" "And he hath on his vesture and on his thigh a name written, King of kings, and Lord of lords." (*Revelation 17:14; 19:16*). Surely Jesus is a King.

IV. In the Scriptures, Jesus Christ is said to possess all the badges and tokens of a king. He has a throne: "Thy throne, O God, is for ever and ever," (*Hebrews 1:8*); "To him that overcometh will I give to sit with me in my throne," (*Revelation 3:21*). He has a crown; for we read of "the crown wherewith his mother crowned him in the day of his espousals." (*Song of Solomon 3:11*). About a thousand years later John says: "And a crown was given unto him: and he went forth conquering, and to conquer." (*Revelation 6:2*). And to show the amplitude of his kingly authority, John says: "And on his head were many crowns." (*Revelation 19:12*). Christ has a sceptre: "A sceptre of righteousness is the sceptre of thy kingdom." (*Hebrews 1:8*). Christ has a kingdom. He says to Pilate: "My kingdom is not of this world: if my kingdom were of this world, then would my servants fight, that I should not be delivered to the Jews: but now is my kingdom not from hence." (*John 18:36*). Christ has subjects. In the verse just cited he speaks of his servants. His people in heaven and earth feel honoured by being allowed to live under him, and to serve him. And at God's command all the angels of heaven have taken the oath of allegiance to him: "Let all the angels of God worship him." (*Hebrews 1:6*). He has the sword: "Gird thy sword upon thy thigh, O most Mighty, with thy glory and thy majesty." (*Psalm 45:3*). He deals with his enemies like a great King: "He shall break them with a rod of iron, and dash them in pieces like a potter's vessel." (*Psalm 2:9*). Surely he is a King.

V. But what sort of a king is Christ? Let us see.

1. He is an *everlasting* King: His "goings forth have been from of old, from everlasting." (*Micah 5:2*). He "was in the beginning with

God." (*John 1:2*). He "was set up from everlasting, from the beginning, or ever the earth was." (*Proverbs 8:23*). Nor shall he ever cease to be King: "Thy throne, O God, is for ever and ever." (*Hebrews 1:8*). The great prophet of the captivity expressly says his "kingdom is an everlasting kingdom," "which shall never be destroyed." (*Daniel 2:44; 7:27*). "His throne shall endure as the days of heaven." Glory to God for that.

2. He is a *wise* King. One of his names is Wisdom. (*Proverbs 8*). According to prophecy, he has *dealt prudently* in all things. (*Isaiah 52:13*). He has never made any mistake. He orders and establishes his kingdom with the knowledge of omniscience. He leads his people by the right way, that they may go to a city of habitation. (*Psalm 107:7*). He teaches them all in the way of wisdom; he leads them in right paths. When they go, their steps shall not be straitened; and when they run they shall not stumble.

3. He is a *just* King. He preserveth the faithful, and plentifully rewardeth the proud doer. Just and right is he. He accepteth not the person of princes, nor regardeth the rich more than the poor. "A sceptre of righteousness is the sceptre of his kingdom." (*Hebrews 1:8*). However things may seem to us, righteousness and judgment are the habitation of his throne. Our King can do no wrong. He never has done wrong to any. Much as he had set his heart on saving sinners, he would not open the gates of paradise to one of them till he had bound himself by oath and covenant to satisfy all the claims of justice, and to bring in everlasting righteousness. He will not carry one sinner to glory, trampling on the rights and government of God as he goes. When the awful scenes of the last day shall come, the heavens shall declare his righteousness, and all the people see his glory. Not a blot shall be found on his escutcheon, nor an error in his awards. Hallelujah! The Judge of all the earth will do right.

4. Christ is an *almighty* King. Nothing is too hard for him. None can resist him. He carries the keys of the invisible world; he opens, and none can shut; he shuts, and none can open. He controls all causes and all agents. He is the Lord strong and mighty, the Lord mighty in battle. Who would set the briers and thorns against him in battle? he would go through them, and burn them together. At his rebuke the pillars of heaven tremble. The hiding of his power none

can understand. He is "the Almighty." (*Revelation 1:8*). Hallelujah, for the Lord God omnipotent reigneth.

5. Jesus is a *meek, tender, merciful, condescending* King. He never breaks the bruised reed. He never quenches the smoking flax. The haughtiest monarchs he has trodden to hell; but he never trampled on a broken heart. "Rejoice greatly, O daughter of Zion; shout, O daughter of Jerusalem: behold, thy King cometh unto thee: he is just, and having salvation; lowly, and riding upon an ass." (*Zechariah 9:9*). Yes, He who commands the twenty thousand chariots of heaven, (*Psalm 68:17*), entered the holy city in the humblest manner, even when receiving a triumph decreed to him by prophecy. Yea more, he wept over the very city that was about to imbrue its hands in his blood. It was but ten days after his ascension till he sent his ministers and his Spirit to call his murderers to repentance; and in one day thousands of them were made to rejoice in his loving-kindness. Though the heaven is his throne and the earth is his footstool, yet he dwells with him that is poor and of a contrite spirit, and trembles at God's Word.

6. Jesus Christ is a King of *exhaustless resources*. He has unsearchable riches. He is heir of all things. The stars, and the sea, and the dry land are his, for he made them. He is Lord of angels. "He is Lord of all." (*Acts 10:36*). Yea, he is "the Lord of glory." (*1 Corinthians 2:8*). All power in heaven and earth is given unto him. (*Matthew 28:18*). When he promises grace and glory, we know it is sure to come. When he pledges a crown and a kingdom and a royal priesthood to the humblest of his followers, we may judge of his immense treasures and possessions. He gives even to his enemies, many a time, great wealth, and even diadems, though he respects no man's person. The earth is his, and the fulness thereof.

VI. But what sort of a kingdom has Christ? Just such as you would expect such a King to preside over.

1. It is divinely ordered and ordained. Hear his own words: "I appoint unto you a kingdom, as my Father hath appointed unto me." (*Luke 22:29*). His regal power is no usurpation: "The Father of glory ... raised him from the dead, and set him at his own right hand in the heavenly places, far above all principality, and power, and might, and dominion, and every name that is named, not only in

this world, but also in that which is to come: and hath put all things under his feet, and gave him to be the head over all things to the church." (*Ephesians 1:17, 20-22*).

2. Christ's kingdom is not of this world. He says so expressly, (*John 18:36*). It is not based on worldly wisdom; it is not ruled by worldly maxims; it is not managed by crafty statesmanship. Scott says: "It has nothing to do with men's temporal interests or privileges; it leaves rulers and subjects in the same situation as it found them. It is therefore no fit object of jealousy to any government. Jesus never armed his followers. His disciples were inoffensive in their habits, and were forbidden to fight for him, even when he was apprehended. So that his kingdom is clearly not of a secular nature, but relates wholly to spiritual and heavenly things, and is supported entirely by spiritual sanctions and authority."

3. Christ's kingdom is not his without a cause. He has deserved all his honours and all his authority. He is not on the throne by an act of grace to him, but by his own amazing merits: He was "in the form of God," and "thought it not robbery to be equal with God: but made himself of no reputation, and took upon him the form of a servant, and was made in the likeness of men: and being found in fashion as a man, he humbled himself, and became obedient unto death, even the death of the cross. Wherefore God also hath highly exalted him, and given him a name which is above every name: that at the name of Jesus every knee should bow, of things in heaven, and things in earth, and things under the earth; and that every tongue should confess that Jesus Christ is Lord, to the glory of God the Father." (*Philippians 2:6-11*). All heaven publicly and adoringly ascribes his kingly exaltation to his own merits. (*Revelation 5:12*). Their cry ever is, "Worthy is the Lamb."

4. His kingdom is universal. It includes all worlds, all creatures, all causes. Nothing in heaven, nothing in earth, nothing under the earth is outside of it. His saints praise him. The angels adore him. The devils are subject to him. The king's heart is in his hands, and he turneth it whithersoever he will. His kingdom ruleth over all.

5. Christ's kingdom is supreme. He is over all God blessed for ever. There is no principality over him. His kingdom is not a wheel within another wheel, an *imperium in imperio;* but it is so exalted that there is nothing above it.

6. It is stable. Nothing can shake it. Many a bold conspiracy has been formed against it, but all in vain. Worms cannot spit their venom so as to reach the stars in their course. Nor can puny mortals reach the person or the power of our Immanuel.

7. Christ's kingdom is full of energy. By his own divine efficiency he carries on his government. He upholds all things by his powerful Word. He does his will in heaven and in earth. He is expecting till his enemies become his footstool. Not an empire rises or sinks but by his will. Not a sparrow falls to the ground without his notice. Every change on earth is by his providence. He is subverting wicked counsels and defeating wicked plots, till he shall have done his whole pleasure upon Mount Zion.

His work on his people is mighty. He subdues them to himself. By love, by power, by truth, by chastisement, by terrible things in righteousness, in mercy, in judgment, in faithfulness, in loving-kindness, he reigns their Lord and Master. He chains their great adversary; he subdues their iniquities under them; he strips the world of its fatal fascinations; he makes them willing in the day of his power; he leads them into all necessary truth. A joyful allegiance to Christ is a great element of true piety.

8. His kingdom is and perhaps ever will be above human comprehension. "God manifest in the flesh" is the mystery of mysteries. When Christ is about to do his greatest wonders, both of judgment and of mercy, he often gives no such notice as arrests attention. The kingdom of God cometh not with observation. The Lord comes suddenly to his temple. He doeth mighty things which we look not for. When we are shut up and cannot come forth, then he brings us out into a large place. When he turns our captivity, we are like them that dream. The resurrection of Christ, his ascension to heaven, the miracles of Pentecost, the release of Peter, the conversion of Paul surprised both good and bad men. It shall be so to the end of time. The judgment day itself will abound with wonders, beyond all the days of earth. One great mystery is that both we and the Captain of our salvation are "made perfect through suffering." Strange that he should scourge every son whom he receiveth; but so runs his counsel, and so we become partakers of the Divine nature.

Sometimes to us his delays are unaccountable, and we cry out, "O Lord, how long? Why tarry thy chariot wheels? Why do the wicked prosper? Why are waters of a full cup wrung out to thy chosen ones?" But we forget that with the Lord one day is as a thousand years, and a thousand years as one day. He inhabiteth eternity. His prospects are bounded by no horizon. His delays to punish are stupendous mercies. Without them no flesh would be spared.

*   *   *

1. Let us put our hand into our Saviour's hand to lead us as he will. A child of God was very sick. She had suffered long and severely. She was asked whether she would not prefer death to life. "Just as the Lord pleases," was her reply. "But," said one, "if God should refer it to you, which would you choose?" She replied: "Then I would refer it back again to God." She was right. She was wise. Should we settle such a question, it would almost certainly be decided wrong. If the Master determines it there will be no mistake. Besides, when we wholly submit our will to his will, his will becomes ours, and so we have our way because God has his way. When that which pleases the Lord pleases us, nothing can take away our rejoicing. Much of the bliss of heaven consists in this happy temper. No doubt things are constantly occurring in the realms above which would provoke resistance and rebellion in hearts not taught perfect submission to the will of God. The demand for hearty acquiescence is most reasonable, because the Lord is unerring. If he were ever unkind, if he were unwise, if he were feeble, we might hesitate. But he is too good, too perfect to be doubted.

2. The church is safe. The gates of hell shall not prevail against her. She enjoys her Monarch's love and her Monarch's care. Jesus lives and reigns for ever! To all believers we may boldly say, "Who shall harm you, if ye be followers of that which is good?" (*1 Peter 3:13*). The solution of a good man's perplexities, and the quelling of his fears, can often be had by remembering that our Saviour's throne is the throne of God, and that his ways are the ways of God. He giveth account of none of his matters. The Lord our God in the midst of us is mighty, – mighty to save all who take refuge in him, mighty to destroy all who dare rise up against Zion. Christ's kingly office is made illustrious in bringing good out of evil, light out of darkness, and joy out of sorrow. When the unhappy Dr Dodd was on his way to execution, a brutish man came and taunted him as a

culprit, though a minister of the gospel. He had indeed committed a great crime, but there is some reason to hope that he was a true penitent. In his anguish, heightened by the gaze of the multitude and the reproaches of this base accuser, he quoted those memorable words which the prophet Micah put into the mouth of the church: "Rejoice not against me, O mine enemy: when I fall, I shall arise; when I sit in darkness, the Lord shall be a light unto me. I will bear the indignation of the Lord, because I have sinned against him, until he plead my cause, and execute judgment for me: he will bring me forth to the light, and I shall behold his righteousness." (*Micah 7:8, 9*). The gloomy procession moved on, the crowd becoming more dense, until at last the man who had used the reproach was crushed to the earth and perished, though no one intended him evil. Thus were fulfilled the words of the very next verse, which Dodd had not quoted: "He that is mine enemy … shall be trodden down as the mire of the streets." Christ is the Prince of the kings of the earth.

3. We greatly misrepresent the church, and Christ also, when we teach that his kingdom is of this world, that the weapons of her warfare are carnal, that the linen white and clean of her members can be trailed in the mire of this world's maxims, usages, and policy, without being defiled. There is no risk in asserting that the cause of Christ has been more injured by being represented so as to sanction the vices and crimes and follies of men, than by all the fires that persecution ever kindled. The great error of the Jews respecting Messiah's kingdom was that it was of this world. His own followers laboured under this error for a long time. They said, "Lord wilt thou at this time restore the kingdom to Israel?"

4. Let all who are yet out of Christ be reconciled to him now while it is called today. He has a right to your highest homage. He is your rightful sovereign. Out of him you are undone. He has come and is calling for you. Will you accept his grace? He has done more for you than all your earthly friends united. He offers you the life that now is and that which is to come. Oh that you would be wise; wise for yourself, wise unto salvation, wise for eternity. "Kiss the Son, lest he be angry, and ye perish from the way, when his wrath is kindled but a little." (*Psalm 2:12*).

Now unto the king eternal, immortal, invisible, the only wise God our Saviour, be honour and glory for ever and ever. Amen.

10
Christ's Humiliation

SOME distinguish between Christ's *condescension* in assuming our nature, and his *humiliation* in suffering. But the distinction is useless. God "humbleth himself to behold the things that are in heaven, and in the earth!" (*Psalm 113:6*). Surely then he humbled himself when he became incarnate. This has already been considered.

Respecting the humiliation of the Saviour, the language of Scripture is strong: "He made himself of no reputation, [literally, he emptied himself] and took upon him the form of a servant, and was made in the likeness of men: and being found in fashion [form or figure] as a man, he humbled himself, and became obedient unto death, even the death of the cross." (*Philippians 2:7, 8*). This is an outline of our Lord's humiliation, which has long been and will for ever be the wonder and the song of angels and redeemed men. The whole of our Lord's history on earth was one series of acts of self-emptying and humiliation.

Let us begin with the humble circumstances in which he came into the world. The husband of his mother was an artisan, commonly supposed to be a carpenter. (*Matthew 13:55*). Both he and the mother of our Lord were descended from David. (*Luke 2:4*). But this family was fallen so low that when Joseph and Mary arrived in Bethlehem their descent from David secured them no attentions or civilities, but they were lodged in a house built for cattle. There the mother of our Lord brought forth her child, and wrapped him in swaddling clothes, and laid him in a manger, because there was no room in the inn. (*Luke 2:7*). And when she brought him to present him to the Lord, her offering was that of the poorest, "a pair of turtledoves or two young pigeons." The law of Moses admitted that offering for those who were "not able to bring a lamb." (*Leviticus 12:8*). Thus the most highly favoured among women was found in the depths of poverty and in great neglect. Her first-born shared her lot. I have heard of but one child born in a stable. That was the holy child Jesus.

At his birth our Lord had all the weakness of infancy. He was helpless and dependent like other children. The inspired history tells us that he "increased in wisdom and stature, and in favour with God and man." (*Luke 2:52*). He had the trials of childhood.

No sooner was his birth known than Herod the Great, a cruel and bloody man, became intent on his death. He killed all the young children in one district of the land in the hope that he would thereby surely destroy Jesus. By timely warning from God that infant Saviour was rescued from the threatened evil; but only by flight into Egypt – Egypt, the "Rahab" and "Leviathan" of Scripture. The cruel, idolatrous, and degraded people of that land had a hereditary and inveterate hatred against the Jews; but now their country was a safer asylum to this blessed family than any city or village of Judea.

On their return from Egypt, they settled in Nazareth. By some means this place had been rendered odious. Even the guileless Nathanael shared in the common aversion, and cried, "Can there any good thing come out of Nazareth?" (*John 1:46*). Here Jesus spent the most of his life till he was thirty years old. Nazareth is not once mentioned in the Old Testament, nor by Josephus. Prophecy said that Christ should be "despised and rejected of men." This was the same as saying he should be called "a Nazarene." (Compare *Isaiah 53:3* and *Matthew 2:23*). Nazareth was probably infamous for the fierceness and brutality of its people. (*Luke 4:16-30*). It was not the seat of any famous school. As a place of residence it had the advantage of privacy; and its geographical position was truly beautiful. Here our Lord lived and wrought at the same craft as Joseph, for his own countrymen said, "Is not this the carpenter, the son of Mary?" (*Mark 6:3*). If there was any school at Nazareth, Jesus does not seem to have attended it; for the Jews said, "How knoweth this man letters, having never learned?" (*John 7:15*).

Another part of Christ's humiliation consisted in his being tempted. (*Hebrews 2:18; 4:15*). True, the prince of this world found nothing in him. (*John 14:30*). In his holy soul was no fuel to be kindled by the fiery darts; but it must have filled him with anguish to have so foul suggestions made to him. So far as we know, his first great conflict with the adversary was in the wilderness. It lasted forty days. (*Luke 4:2*). Christ was about to enter on his public ministry, and retired to the wilderness under the best desires to commune with God. But Satan annoyed him continually. The temptation grew worse and worse to the close. The adversary then tempted him to use his miraculous power to prove his divinity to Satan, and to satisfy his own hunger, as he had eaten nothing for forty days. The wicked one also tempted him to an act of presumption by throwing himself from the pinnacle of the temple. Finally, he offered him immense possessions and great honours, the kingdoms of the world and the glory of them, if he would commit one act of idolatry. It added not a little to the power of these besetments that they were urged on Christ in his solitude. Although each assault was an utter failure, yet the devil departed from him but for a season. (*Luke 4:13*). The Saviour was tempted in all points like as we are, yet without sin.

As Jesus was born, so he lived and died poor. He said, "The foxes have holes, and the birds of the air have nests; but the Son of man hath not where to lay his head." (*Matthew 8:20*). During his ministry he seems to have chiefly subsisted upon the charity of some poor, pious women. Well did he know what it was to suffer hunger and want. When a capitation tax was demanded of him, though it was but half a crown for himself and Peter, he could not pay it without a miracle.

Another element of Christ's humiliation was his liability to affliction. Above all that ever lived he was the "man of sorrows." He was subject to disappointment, grief, vexation, a sense of wrong, a sense of the ingratitude of men, and the pangs arising from a disregard of all the principles of friendship. His holy soul was filled with anguish by his cruel rejection. "He was in the world, and the world was made by him, and the world knew him not. He came unto his own, and his own received him not." (*John 1:10, 11*). None of the princes of this world knew him. (*1 Corinthians 2:8*). "We hid as it were our faces from him ... we esteemed him not." (*Isaiah 53:3*). Those countless annoyances, called slights, must have pierced him deeply. The people of the city where he had been brought up were so offended at his first sermon in their synagogue, that they attempted to destroy his life by casting him down from a high rock. (*Luke 4:16-30*). And when he claimed existence prior to Abraham, the Jews took up stones to cast at him. (*John 8:59*). For saving two men from the most frightful torments, followed by the loss of some swine, the whole city of the Gergesenes "besought him that he would depart out of their coasts." They preferred their swine, madmen, and devils, to the Prince of Peace. (*Matthew 8:34*). Afterwards, on his trial, the Jews cried, "Away with him; away with him." (*John 19:15*). They preferred to have a murderer turned loose on their community, rather than that the Son of God should longer teach his heavenly doctrines. Their cry was, "Not this man, but Barabbas." During his whole ministry the leaders among his foes denied that God had sent him. (*John 10:24-26*). Never was a mission so well attested. Never were attestations so malignantly set aside.

And never were hard names and opprobrious epithets so heaped upon anyone. His enemies said he was a deceiver, (*John 7:12*); gluttonous and a winebibber, a friend of publicans and sinners, (*Matthew 11:19*). They said he was in league with the prince of the devils, and that by satanic power he wrought miracles. Surely above all others he endured the contradiction of sinners against himself. (*Hebrews 12:3*). Nor were these things without their dreadful effects on his refined and tender nature. "His visage was so marred more than any man, and his form more than the sons of men." (*Isaiah 52:14*). Speaking in his name the prophet said, "Reproach hath broken my heart; and I am full of heaviness: and I looked for some to take pity, but there was none; and for comforters, but I found none." (*Psalm 69:20*). The same prophet had elsewhere said in his name, "I am a worm, and no man; a reproach of men, and despised of the people. All they that see me laugh me to scorn: they shoot out the lip, they shake the head." (*Psalm 22:6, 7*).

The annals of our race furnish no parallel to his history in the want of sympathy under amazing sufferings. No terms of derision, no taunts in the midst of his agonies were by his enemies deemed indecent. (*Matthew 27:40-43*). In his greatest trial, when he most needed the offices of friendship, his "disciples forsook him and fled." (*Matthew 26:56*). The very boldest of all his followers denied him thrice, and even with oaths and curses. (*Mark 14:71*). Never by countenance did friend express such surprise, regret, and reproof, as when

Christ looked on Peter after the cock crew. He was not only denied by one disciple; he was betrayed by another in a manner full of base hypocrisy, even *with a kiss.* The general motive for his betrayal was the depravity of Judas. The special motive was covetousness. Yet the son of perdition sold him for the paltry sum of thirty pieces of silver, the amount fixed by the law of Moses as the price of a slave, to be paid to his owner if his death had been brought about by the goring of a neighbour's ox. (*Exodus 21:32*). In prophetically speaking of this sum, Zechariah ironically calls it a *goodly price.* He cast the amount in scorn to the potter in the house of the Lord. (*Zechariah 11:13*). Another element in our Lord's humiliation was the character of the testimony on his trial. The witnesses were all suborned. The Jews "sought false witness against Jesus, to put him to death, but found none: yea, though many false witnesses came, yet found they none." (*Matthew 26:59, 60*). That is, the law required two concurring witnesses, and they found not two who agreed. "At the last came two false witnesses, and said, This fellow said, I am able to destroy the temple of God, and to build it in three days." (*Matthew 26:60, 61*). These witnesses lied, for *they* had not heard him say anything about destroying the temple, and what he did say was quite unlike what they alleged. "Destroy this temple," (that is, kill this body) "and in three days I will raise it up." (*John 2:19*). The thing charged was absurd and frivolous as well as false. No wonder Jesus *held his peace and answered nothing.* The Jews evidently felt that they had made good no serious charge; for they tried to get from him a confession that he was *the Christ, the Son of the Blessed.* Our Lord felt it was the right time to speak, whereupon he made that "good confession," so precious in the church ever since. He said he was the Christ.

The course of the judge who sat on his trial, while it was a disgrace to himself, was a deep humiliation to Jesus. If history can be trusted, Pilate was a monster of perfidy, avarice, cruelty, and obstinacy. Previously he had fallen on some poor Galileans and butchered them while they were making their prescribed offerings, thus mingling their blood with their sacrifices. (*Luke 13:1*). No decency of life, no solemnity of religion could restrain him. Over and over again did he confess that Jesus had violated no law, had committed no offence. His wife warned him to do nothing against that just person. He knew that the chief priests had delivered him up for envy. He was afraid that he would lose his place if he did not give sentence against Jesus. Instead of abiding by his own clear convictions, he turned to the malignant enemies of the innocent sufferer before him and asked them what the sentence should be. (Compare *Matthew 27:18, 19, 24*, and *John 19:12-16*). Before yielding to the violence of the mob around the judgment-seat, this mercenary and vacillating creature made a feeble effort to convince the Jews that the prisoner before him ought not to die, saying, "Why, what evil hath he done?" (*Matthew 27:23*). This failing, he thought to save his popularity and the life of Jesus by working on their sympathies. So he delivered Christ over to be *scourged.* This was a dreadful infliction. The back was made bare, the arms were drawn up, the scourge was applied first with the right hand and then with the left. At the shocking sight men often grew faint. All this had been predicted by the evangelical prophet: "I gave my back to the smiters, and my cheeks to them that plucked off the hair: I hid not my face from shame and spitting." (*Isaiah 50:6*). But all this had no effect in appeasing the rage of the malignant throng. Nor did it strengthen any just purpose in the bosom of the judge. So he delivered his guiltless victim to be crucified. (*Matthew 27:26*). It is often asked, What became of Pilate? His murder of the Galileans and like acts of violence would probably have caused his dismissal, had not Tiberius died. He however fell under the displeasure of the successor of that emperor, was degraded from office, became a wretched outcast, and ended his days by committing suicide.

As the form of trial granted to Jesus was a mockery of all justice and decency, so mockery was kept up to the last. They spat in his face and buffeted him. Others smote him with the palms of their hands, and asked him, Who is he that smote thee? They stripped him, and put on him a scarlet robe, as though he were a royal personage. But all was in derision. And when they had plaited a crown of thorns, they put it upon his head, and a reed in his right hand: and they bowed the knee before him, and mocked him, saying, Hail, King of the Jews! And they spat upon him, and took the reed and smote him on the head. And after they had mocked him, they took the robe off from him, and put his own raiment on him, and led him away to crucify him. (*Matthew 26:67; 27:28, 29*).

It would be surprising indeed if so long and sleepless sorrow, such scourging and smiting, had not much exhausted his strength. And so we find it. At first by their bidding he bore his own cross, (*John 19:17*); but, as is supposed, growing faint under it, he could bear it no further. They met a man of Cyrene, Simon by name. Matthew says they compelled him to bear the cross. Luke says they laid the cross on him that he might bear it *after Jesus*. (Compare *Matthew 27:32* and *Luke 23:26*). Who this Simon was, friend or foe, or how he felt on the sad occasion, is not certain; but he was probably suspected of leaning to the cause of Christ. It is not certain whether he bore the whole cross or only the hinder part of it.

As the procession advanced, there followed him a great company of people, and of women which also bewailed and lamented him. But Jesus, knowing he should soon be through his troubles, and seeing the glory that should follow, turning to them, said, Weep not for me, but weep for yourselves and your children. He then foretold the awful doom of the holy city. (*Luke 23:27-31*).

Reaching the dreadful spot, Jesus was again stripped, and nailed to the cross. Truly this was the hour of darkness. A few days before the Son of God was in tears. The night before he had been in bloody sweat. Now he is on the cross, receiving at the hands of men a punishment reserved for the worst criminals, and those slaves. Some think hanging on the cross produced dislocation. So they understand that phrase, "All my bones are out of joint," (*Psalm 22:14*). Others think it is figurative language, descriptive of dreadful agony, as if all the bones were dislocated. Perhaps this is the more probable view. The theory of death by crucifixion was the extinction of life, not by strangulation, nor by loss of blood, but by nervous distress. The extremities, the seat of very tender sensation, were wounded and lacerated. The distortions of the frame were dreadful. The sufferer was confined to one position, itself great torture if long continued. One may read the history of crucifixion until his feelings are petrified. The details are indeed lacerating. No doubt a graphic description of them in a large assembly would make many swoon away. But the object of this chapter is not to harrow up sensibilities, but to show how Jesus humbled himself, and became obedient unto death, even the death of the cross.

Wondrous cross! Wondrous tree! The human mind, ever prone to superstition, has sought, and claims to have found, more wood belonging to our Saviour's cross than is found in one of our large edifices. But the efficacy of the cross is not in the wood, but in the blood shed by him who hung upon it. Pious minds must have experienced tangible relief when the first Christian emperor, considering the horrible nature of the torture, and wishing to put honour on the death of Christ, abolished punishment by crucifixion.

Every death by the cross was shameful. That of our Lord was peculiarly so. He was crucified between two thieves, and with every mark of ignominy.

Such was the agony of death by the cross that, as a matter of humanity, it seems to have been customary to administer some powerful narcotic to produce insensibility. "Wine mingled with myrrh" was offered to our Saviour, but he "received it not." (*Mark 15:23*). He drew his solace from another source. As he had despised their reproaches and cruelties, so he contemned their proffered stupefying cup. Christ would end his days with an unclouded intellect. He would not leave the world in voluntary stupor. Yet even the offer of wine mingled with myrrh was soon followed by renewed derision. (*Matthew 27:42, 43*).

The death of the cross is often called accursed. It was so indeed. Paul says: "It is written, Cursed is every one that hangeth on a tree." (*Galatians 3:13*). He refers to *Deuteronomy 21:22, 23:* "If a man have committed a sin worthy of death, and he be to be put to death, and thou hang him on a tree: his body shall not remain all night upon the tree, but thou shalt in any wise bury him that day (for he that is hanged is accursed of God;) that thy land be not defiled, which the Lord thy God giveth thee for an inheritance." These texts do not teach that eternal misery always followed this kind of death. We know this is not so. The penitent thief went from the cross to paradise.

A few remarks may aid us in understanding these verses.

1. Hanging in any way has always been esteemed odious, gibbeting the dead very much so, and crucifixion most of all. 2. The Jews contend that they never crucified the living, though they admit that, after the death of a vile criminal, they sometimes hung his lifeless body on a tree. Some contend that they crucified the living. Perhaps they did. (See *Joshua 8:29; 2 Samuel 21:9*). Josephus tells[1] of the crucifixion of eight hundred men by Alexander, king of the Jews.

---

1. lib. 13, cap. 22.

However this may be, the Jews and all ancient nations regarded hanging on the cross as the most execrable death. 3. In the passage cited from *Deuteronomy*, God himself teaches that whoever is righteously and according to the divine law delivered over to hanging, does therein receive the curse of God. 4. So terrible was this death, that God said it should be all the punishment and disgrace man should inflict on any criminal. It was "the curse of God;" that is, the extreme penalty provided for evil-doers in the Jewish commonwealth. Accordingly, at sunset the body was to be taken down, that the land might not be defiled by scenes which could but harden men's hearts. 5. Though the sentence given by Pilate was wholly unjust, and though it was with wicked hands that Jesus was crucified and slain, (*Acts 2:23*), yet, as he voluntarily and by God's approval stood in our place, he bore "the curse of the law," not for his own, but for our sins. No doubt the Mosaic law pointed to the death of Christ, for above all that ever lived, he was "made a curse," though not for himself, yet "for us." He was not only forsaken of men, but of God. The bitterest cry ever heard came from the cross: "Eloi, Eloi, lama sabachthani?"

Not long after, our Saviour cried with a loud voice, and gave up the ghost. That he was dead the executioners admitted, and neither friend nor foe doubted. The water that came from his side proved that he was dead and cold. But the Lord of heaven and earth had no sepulchre of his own. The love of one of his followers secured him burial. Joseph of Arimathea, an honourable counsellor and a rich man, who had hitherto shown much timidity, went in boldly to Pilate and craved the body of Jesus. He bought fine linen, and took him down, and wrapped him in the linen, and laid him in a sepulchre which was hewn out of a rock, and rolled a stone unto the door of the sepulchre. (*Mark 15:43, 46*). Here the Lord lay surrounded by a strong guard of Roman soldiers.

This was the end of his humiliation; for that clause in the Apostles' Creed which says, "He descended into hell," means no more than that his body was under the power of death, and that his soul was in the invisible world. That our Lord's soul was not in torment after his death is certain, for he said to the penitent thief, "This day shalt thou be *with me in paradise;*" and paradise is a place of bliss.

*   *   *

1. Why should we be in love with this world? It reviled, maligned, and crucified the Lord of life and glory. It deserves not our confidence or our love.

2. Let us not make much ado about our sufferings. Our Master fared far worse. If personal innocence and unswerving benevolence could screen anyone, our Lord had never met a rebuff.

3. Let us not be afraid of humiliation. In the end it will do us no harm. It is the highway to glory. If we would be very high, let us know the fellowship of Christ's sufferings, and be made conformable unto his death. (*Philippians 3:10*). If we would reign with him, let us suffer with him.

4. It is as safe as it is necessary to trust in the divine mercy granted to sinners through the blood-shedding of Christ. To believe in Christ is a duty, is wisdom, is eternal life.

11

General Views of Christ's Work

IT is common to many languages to put a part for the whole. The sacred writings abound in this figure. The whole nation of Israel is called Jacob. The law often signifies the whole Mosaic dispensation. The death of Christ, or the cross of Christ, is a term to denote the whole system of gospel truth. The fear of God and the love of God are used to express the whole of religion. So when the apostle says, "We preach Christ crucified," he intends to say that he and his co-workers set forth the whole of the gospel, giving a just prominence to the great fact of the sacrificial death of our Lord.

As preliminary to this discussion it may be observed:

1. Unless man is a sinner, he needs no other good news than that God is just. The whole need not a physician. The innocent require no pardon. The holy need no change of heart. In the righteous there is no room for remission. It is the lost who need a Saviour. Whoever denies his guilt rejects Christ. Let the Governor tender pardons where guilt has been proven; let him not insult the virtuous by an offer to remit the penalty for crime of which even the suspicion of guilt is a great wrong.

2. A full and thorough conviction that we are sinners is both right and useful. A vague and general suspicion of guilt will hardly lead anyone to embrace the gospel. Whenever one feels that he is wrongfully accused, and is fully conscious of innocence, he asks no relaxation of legal rigor. All he desires is sheer justice.

3. The gospel is rendered null and void as to any saving efficacy in regard to all men who refuse to say, in the spirit of the publican, "God be merciful to me a sinner." Its morality may secure to them

respectability; its civilising influences may soften the asperities of their character; its enlightening power may rescue them from barbarism, but its *saving* influences they will never feel while entertaining self-complacent views of themselves. Whoever would be cleansed in the fountain opened for sin and uncleanness must confess his guilt. Whoever would be made rich, must own his poverty. Whoever would be clothed upon with the righteousness of Christ, must bewail his own nakedness. To him who sees that floods of tears can never cover the mountains of his sins, it will be good news that, through Christ, God will cast them into the depths of the sea. God giveth grace to the humble, but he knoweth the proud afar off.

4. As many as are under the teachings of God's Spirit will always welcome even a plain and familiar explanation of the plan of mercy revealed in the gospel. Wisdom is justified of her children. All others will wonder and perish.

5. In preaching the gospel, nothing is to be concealed. It is at our peril if we withhold a truth because it is offensive to the carnal mind. We may not even disguise it or obscure it by the arts of rhetoric. Thus Paul says, "We preach Christ crucified, unto the Jews a stumbling-block, and unto the Greeks foolishness." (*1 Corinthians 1:23*). Nothing could have more offended the prejudices of Jews or assailed the wisdom of Greeks than preaching Christ crucified. To call upon them to believe in one that had been hanged on a tree seemed to them monstrous. Yet Paul preached this very doctrine. He knew its power. He says: "Unto them which are called, both Jews and Greeks, Christ" is "the power of God, and the wisdom of God." (*1 Corinthians 1:24*). Nor did he publish this vital truth in words which man's wisdom teacheth, but in words which the Holy Ghost teacheth. Let us follow his excellent example. Let us not try to render the gospel pleasing to men by denying or disguising its unwelcome truths. If we could persuade all men that Christ was never crucified, the work of salvation would be at an end, the humble would be cast into despair, the ignorant be rendered more brutish, and the world return by not very slow marches to idolatry and atheism.

6. While the death of Christ was the crowning event in his humiliation and an essential part of it, it is not to be separated from his incarnation, his perfect obedience, and his previous sufferings. His

whole life upon earth, followed by his death on the cross, and that by his exaltation at God's right hand, must be taken together.

7. The salvation of a sinner in no sense depends upon his fitness, but only on the fulness of Christ Jesus. If the gospel makes anything plain, it surely teaches that we are saved by grace through faith, that is in Christ the Lord.

With these explanations, let us notice several methods by which we often point to the effect of the death of Christ in saving lost men. The human mind is weak and full of darkness by reason of sin. It is a mercy, therefore, that in several well-chosen ways God makes this doctrine plain to our understandings.

I. Sometimes we represent Christ as taking our place; and so *substitution* is the name by which we designate the glorious plan of gospel mercy. This mode of expression is appropriate and striking. Among men substitution is common and well understood. One is drafted into the army; his brother or friend, seeing the importance of his presence at home, or a stranger moved by pecuniary reward, becomes his substitute. When once, with his own consent, he is thus enrolled, he is bound to obey all orders as if the lot had originally fallen on himself. In his case, as in any other, desertion is severely punished. Substitution, once admitted, binds in all its rigor. There can be no abatement in favour of him who voluntarily consents to stand in the place of another. When he has done all that the other was bound to do, and not before, is he released. So Jesus Christ voluntarily became our substitute. He took our place in the eye of the law, and "became obedient unto death." He perfectly fulfilled all his engagements. He never said, "It is finished," until he had showed us on the cross what temper he would have us exercise in the severest trials, and until he had drunk the dregs of "the cup of astonishment" put into his hands by the offended majesty of heaven. He entirely finished the work which God had given him to do. His release from the tomb was God's public declaration that the Substitute was bound to no more obedience or suffering for us. He who takes Christ as his substitute does therefore publicly approve of this method of salvation. By the act of faith in the Redeemer, he is released from the penalty of damnation, and from the law itself as a covenant of works, by the keeping of which unfallen creatures stand justified before God.

II. Near akin to substitution is *surety-ship*, in which one person undertakes to make good the engagements or liabilities of another. Christ is expressly called our *Surety*. In the Lord's Prayer, our sins are called *debts*. They are indeed dreadful debts. We could never pay them. We are said to owe ten thousand talents, a sum equal to twelve tons of gold. Who can meet such liabilities? Besides, we all owed a perfect obedience to the precept of the law, a sinless keeping of every commandment. Not one of Adam's race could meet such demands. Seeing our indebtedness and helplessness and poverty, Jesus mercifully became our Surety. He did not indeed endorse our worthless names, but he gave his own most worthy name to God. He bound himself to pay all our debts, that is, to suffer the penalty due to us for sin, and to obey the precept of the law for righteousness to us. He did it; he did it all. The law, either as to its curse on the rebellious or as a means of justification before God, claims nothing of believers. Their tears and groans pay no part of their debt incurred by transgression. Their works of love and faith prove their sincerity and adorn their profession, but form no part of their justifying righteousness. So wonderful was this surety-ship, and so perfect was the confidence of God in the engagements of the Surety, that "the souls of the elect were saved upon trust for four thousand years. The Father gave credit to Christ and glorified his saints on the footing of a sacrifice not then offered up, and of a righteousness not then wrought. Christ also, in the days of his flesh, went on credit with his Father every time previous to his death he said to a sinner, 'Thy sins are forgiven thee.'" (Ryland). Thus, though Jesus was not actually crucified till the days of Pontius Pilate, he was in the esteem of God "the Lamb slain from the foundation of the world." So that "if you have been looking at works, duties, and qualifications, instead of looking at Christ, it will cost you dear. No wonder you go to complaining. Graces are no more than evidences: the merits of Christ alone, without your graces, must be the foundation for your hope to rest upon." (Wilcox). Blessed be God, "Christ is not more rich himself than he is liberal to contribute of his treasures. He makes his people sharers to the uttermost of all that he has." (Crisp).

III. Sometimes we speak of Christ as meeting the demands of God's law against us, and then we call his undertaking a *satisfaction*, a satisfaction to the law of God, a satisfaction to divine justice. This mode of speaking goes on the supposition that God's law is holy, just, and good; that its demands, both in precept and penalty, ought to be met, and that God's justice is an amiable attribute, calling for no more than is right. The word satisfaction is often used in a general sense, not different from atonement, compensation, amends. But the primary meaning of satisfaction is, *doing enough.* To *satisfy* is to do all that is properly demanded. The judgment of all right-minded men the world over is, that God's precepts concerning all things are right, and that his judgments are equity and truth. To satisfy God's law is to meet its demands in all respects. This Jesus Christ did for us. He said: "I delight to do thy will, O my God: yea, thy law is within my heart," (*Psalm 40:8*); "Mine ears hast thou opened," (*Psalm 40:6*); that is, thou hast made me thy servant. As God's law is a transcript of his character, in full accordance with his justice and holiness, to do and suffer all the law demands is of course to satisfy justice – to do and suffer what justice requires. Christ's satisfaction goes upon this supposition, that mere absolute remission of undeniable guilt cannot take place without loosening the bands of good government. Guilt cannot be removed without what some theologians call "compensation," – without what most call satisfaction. If laws had no penalties, they would be mere advice. If their just penalties were not enforced, they would be idle appendages to the best laws, and so government would be at an end. But God's government is perfect; he never demands more than is right; he never unjustly condemns; he cannot pardon capriciously; he must show mercy, if at all, in some way consistent with the demands of law, justice, and good government. Hence the necessity for satisfaction. The satisfaction which Christ rendered is taken sometimes in an extended sense. It then includes all he did and suffered for us. Sometimes it is used in a more limited sense, and then it denotes his meeting all the demands of the law against us as sinners by enduring the penalty in our stead. Those who thus use the term speak both of the *satisfaction* and *merit* of Christ. By the latter they signify his obedience to the precepts of the law; by the former, his amazing sufferings, by which we are set free from the curse of the law. His satisfaction delivers us from death; his merit procures for us the inheritance of sons. By the one the chains of condemnation are taken off; by the other, the best robe is put upon us. One brings us out of Egypt; the other brings us into Canaan. This difference in terms, however, makes no difference in doctrine. Blessed is he who has accepted this full and glorious satisfaction made by God's dear Son. On him the second death shall have no power. God has declared the law met and justice satisfied by Jesus Christ. Is not that enough? Jesus gave himself for us that, "the justice of God being satisfied and the law fulfilled, sinners might be freed from the wrath to come."

How necessary this undertaking of Christ was is well stated by Owen: "To pardon sin without satisfaction in him who is absolutely holy, righteous, true, and faithful, the absolute, necessary, supreme Governor of all sinners, the Author of the law, and sanction of it, wherein punishment is threatened and declared, is to deny himself, and to do what one infinitely perfect cannot do." Another writer says: "The atonement may be defined as that satisfaction for sin which was rendered to God as the moral governor of the world, by the perfect obedience unto death of our Lord Jesus Christ – a satisfaction which has removed every obstacle, resulting from the divine perfections and government, to the bestowment of mercy upon the guilty." (Rev George Payne).

It is an objection of no force that the word satisfaction is never used in the Scriptures in regard to the work of Christ. We are not contending for words. The doctrine is taught, and that is enough for us. It is, however, a good word, and is used in Scripture on a like subject: "Ye shall take no satisfaction for the life of a murderer." (*Numbers 35:31*).

IV. Sometimes we represent the work of Christ for us by speaking of him as a *sacrifice*. It is expressly said in Scripture that Christ "hath given himself for us an offering and a sacrifice to God for a sweet-smelling savour;" "he hath appeared to put away sin by the sacrifice of himself;" "he offered up himself." (*Ephesians 5:2; Hebrews 7:27; 9:26*). He "bare our sins in his own body on the tree." (*1 Peter 2:24*). His soul was made an offering for sin. (*Isaiah 53:10*). Although the word sacrifice is sometimes used to denote every kind of offering, yet, a sacrifice, strictly speaking, differs from a mere oblation in this, that in a sacrifice there is a real destruction or change of the thing offered; while an oblation is a simple gift without any such change. Thus tithes, first-fruits, and every kind of property devoted to religious uses were oblations. But sacrifices, in strictness of speech, were either wholly or in part consumed by fire. They were of three kinds: first, *eucharistical*, to express gratitude for mercies received; secondly, *impetratory*, to obtain some favour; or, thirdly, *expiatory*, to atone for some sin. This last was specially and peculiarly the sacrifice of Christ. "He was made sin [a sin-offering] for us." (*2 Corinthians 5:21*). He died as a victim in our room and place. He put away sin by the sacrifice of himself. He offered one sacrifice for sins. The Jew, who had incurred ceremonial guilt, brought his lamb and confessed his sins over it; and it became his victim, and died for him, and for him alone. But when John the Baptist saw Christ he said, "Behold the Lamb of God which taketh away the sin [not of one man, or of one nation, but] of the world." (*John 1:29*). So that Paul well argues that there is no need of daily, yearly, or any more sacrifices, for by once offering himself to God, Christ hath for ever perfected them that believe, hath made an end of transgression, hath put away sin, and become the end of the law for righteousness to every one that believeth. Thus is Christ the propitiation for our sins. That is, his sacrifice averts from us the wrath of God, and renders God propitious to us. The word propitiation is borrowed from the propitiatory, or mercy-seat, which covered the tables of the law. So the propitiation of Christ covers up the handwriting that was against us, and opens the way for God's mercy to flow forth to us lost men. It should be for our perpetual joy that "the redeeming power of the blood of Christ is greater than the condemning power of sin." (Mather). The vilest sinners the world has ever seen, the murderers of Christ and the murderers of his saints, when they have been able to see the completeness of this one offering, have said, "It is enough: my conscience demands no more sacrifice: God requires no further offering."

V. Sometimes Christ's work for us is called his *obedience* – his obedience unto death. This mode of speaking is found in Scripture, and is often adopted by good writers. Paul says that "by the obedience of one shall many be made righteous;" that "though he were a Son, yet learned he obedience by the things which he suffered;" and that he "became obedient unto death, even the death of the cross." (*Romans 5:19; Hebrews 5:8; Philippians 2:8*). Christ's obedience was both active and passive. He kept the precept and he bore the penalty of the law. He obeyed in suffering. He suffered in obeying. In *Romans 5:19*, *obedience* in Christ is put in contrast with *disobedience* in Adam. This is *active* obedience. In *Philippians 2:8* we read of *obedience unto death*. This is *passive* obedience. Though we thus distinguish, we never separate these two kinds of obedience. They are inseparable. Had our Lord lived a blameless life, the example would have been good for us, and his life pleasing to God; but how could his life have saved us from wrath? On the other hand, if our Lord had not been holy, his death could in no way have availed for us. The whole obedience of Christ has these excellent qualities. It was obedience unto God. So he said, "I have finished the work which thou gavest me to do." "The cup which my Father hath given me, shall I not drink it?" It was perfect. There was no defect in it. He did all that God required. He suffered all God inflicted. His obedience was unfailing. He shrank from nothing. He came short in nothing. He was full of zeal for the honour of God. In his greatest darkness he prayed, "Father, glorify thy name." He was full of compassion to men. Having loved his own, he loved them to the end. It was because he loved us that he gave himself for us. (*Galatians 2:20*).

* * *

1. There is a rich and harmonious variety of modes of expressing and explaining the great doctrine of salvation by Christ. Every suitable method of teaching this truth is either used or suggested by the sacred writers. While we find this pleasing variety, there is no diversity in the scope of their teachings. They wonderfully agree.

2. It is of paramount importance that we believe and maintain the true doctrine respecting Christ's undertaking for us. At no time and at no hazard let us yield to the clamours or insidiousness of error. In the religion of a sinner all depends on the work and sufferings of the Saviour. Here alone can the guilty have peace with God, or the despairing have hope beyond the grave.

3. There is no danger in making Christ all and in all. "It is Christ that brings us everything we get … If you would have any good you must get it by Christ." (Crisp). "If you ever saw Christ, you saw him as a rock, higher than self-righteousness, Satan, and sin. And this rock follows you; and there will be a continual dropping of honey

and grace out of this rock to satisfy you." (Wilcox). Make much, make much of Christ. "Whoever hath Christ cannot be poor; and whoever is without him cannot be rich." (Dyer).

4. The salvation of Christ is no more rich than it is free. It gives milk and wine in abundance. And it gives without money and without price. If you would be saved, you must simply believe, simply accept the grace that is offered. An experienced Christian said: "I never had a more lively sense of my acceptance with God through Christ than when I was sensible of the greatest recumbency on him: when I laid most stress upon him, I always found most strength in him." (Thomas Coles).

5. As our persons, so also our services have acceptance through Christ. The love of God refuses nothing which the obedient love of his people offers through Christ Jesus. Imperfect indeed are all our doings. But perfect is the righteousness of Christ, through whom believing sinners and works of faith are graciously owned and accepted.

12
Redemption By Christ

IT has long been customary to speak of the recovery of lost men as the work of Redemption. Job, David, Isaiah, and Jeremiah, all speak of the Redeemer. Though the word redeemer is not in the New Testament, yet *redemption* and corresponding terms are there of frequent occurrence. In the Old Testament the same word is rendered Redeemer and Avenger. The avenging of blood and redeeming from bondage both devolved on the nearest male relative; so that a redeemer was a kinsman. Our Redeemer is our brother, bone of our bone, flesh of our flesh. In the New Testament are three verbs rendered *redeem*. One is from a noun which signifies a *market* and means simply *to buy*. It is found more than thirty times. It is the word used by our Lord when he speaks of *buying* a field, *buying* oxen, *buying* victuals. It is the word used by Paul, when he twice says, "Ye *are bought* with a price." (*1 Corinthians 6:20; 7:23*). It is used by John: "Thou hast redeemed us to God by thy blood." (*Revelation 5:9*. See also *Revelation 14:3, 4*). God's people are redeemed from the earth, from among men, from their sins by the blood of Jesus – a great price paid for such poor creatures – such sinful worms.

Sometimes we have another verb, a compound of the foregoing. It occurs four times. This is the word used by Paul when he says: "Christ hath *redeemed* us from the curse of the law;" "God sent forth his Son … to *redeem* them that were under the law." (*Galatians 3:13; 4:4, 5*). This word signifies to buy again, to buy out of the hands of another.

There is still another verb thrice used in the New Testament, and always rendered *redeem*. "We trusted that it had been he which should have *redeemed* Israel;" He "gave himself for us, that he might *redeem* us from all iniquity;" "Ye know that ye were not *redeemed* with corruptible things, as silver and gold, from your vain conversation received by tradition from your fathers; but with the precious blood of Christ, as of a lamb without blemish and without spot." (*Luke 24:21; Titus 2:14; 1 Peter 1:18, 19*). This word has a noun corresponding to it [lutron]. This is the word used by our Lord when he says: "The Son of man came not to be ministered unto, but to minister, and to give his life a ransom for many." (*Matthew 20:28; Mark 10:45*).

We have yet another word, a compound of the foregoing [antil-utron]. It is used by Paul when he says that Christ "gave himself a *ransom* for all." (*1 Timothy 2:6*). Each of these nouns points to the *price* paid for redemption.

In the Jewish Commonwealth redemption was well understood. If a man became poor, so that he could not pay his debts, he was sold into servitude until the year of Jubilee. But it was the privilege and the duty of his near and wealthy kinsmen to pay his debt, and let him go free. Among other nations also, before the coming of Christ, redemption was not unknown. In the early history of the world, prisoners-of-war were often put to death. At length, humanity forbade so cruel a practice, and they were sold as slaves. On the return of peace, their kin or their country sometimes sent and paid a ransom for them, thus redeeming them from their masters.

The moving cause of the redemption of sinners is not anything good in them, but only the sovereign, eternal, and unchangeable love of God. The procuring or availing cause of redemption is the humiliation and death of Christ. The end of redemption was the promotion of the divine glory, as it marvellously illustrated the divine perfections. The effect of redemption on man is full, complete, gratuitous, eternal salvation.

The subject of this chapter is *the wisdom of God in redemption*. In this matter it may aid us to keep clearly in view these truths:

1. God is a holy God. By the unchangeable rectitude of his nature, he hates sin. To him it is abominable.

2. God is the Creator of all things, and therefore he has a perfect right to treat all his creatures as he pleases. His awful challenge is, Shall I not do "what I will with mine own?" Who dares take it up?

3. God is every way fit to govern the world and all its inhabitants. He has all and infinite perfections. He justly claims and exercises the right of universal empire and control.

4. Man is a creature. He is therefore not independent. He is bound by his Maker's will. Nothing can release him from these everlasting bonds.

5. Man is a rational and voluntary agent. He is therefore a fit subject for moral government. He is rightly and justly accountable.

6. Man is a sinner. He has violated the law of his being. He is thus guilty, depraved, and miserable. He is under a curse, in a state of pollution, and a child of sorrow. He is not so unfortunate as he is criminal.

7. Sin is an evil of such magnitude as not to be manageable by finite beings. "It seems to be a law of mind that, once perverted, it should never be able to recover itself." It is easier to make breaches than to repair them, to pull down than to build up, to kill than to make alive. "He who cannot build a hut, may destroy a palace." One man may kill another, but all men united cannot give life. This is the law of our nature. Let it never be forgotten.

8. The whole problem of redemption was therefore beyond the solution of a finite mind. The limits of man's understanding and faculties are narrow. Our wisdom consists not a little in confessing our ignorance, in seeking instruction, in shunning dizzy heights. For human weakness to meddle with the great affairs of God can never be harmless.

9. Let us all, therefore, learn what we can, and pretend to no more than we have. Let us refresh ourselves in the river of truth, but let us not venture beyond our depth. Creation is beyond the reach of fair criticism. So also is redemption. Let us be lowly. There is a consanguinity between humility and solid advancement in knowledge. Paul confessed his insufficiency to fathom the deep things of God: "O the depth of the riches both of the wisdom and knowledge of God." (*Romans 11:33*). Such ignorance is wiser than all boasting.

10. All men do at times feel the necessity of some redemption-price being paid to God for them – some satisfaction being made to divine justice. Adam Smith, the author of the "*The Wealth of Nations*," whom none will suspect of too strong an inclination to Christian doctrines, says, "Man, when about to appear before a being

of infinite perfections, can feel but little confidence in his own merit, or in the imperfect propriety of his own conduct. To such a being he can scarce imagine that his littleness and weakness should ever seem to be the proper object either of esteem or regard. But he can easily conceive how the numberless violations of duty of which he has been guilty should render him the object of aversion and punishment; nor can he see any reason why the divine indignation should not be let loose, without any restraint, upon so vile an insect as he is sensible that he himself must appear to be. If he would still hope for happiness, he is conscious that he cannot *demand* it from *justice,* but that he must *entreat* it from the *mercy* of God. Repentance, sorrow, humiliation, contrition at the thought of his past conduct, are, upon this account, the sentiments which become him, and seem to be the only means which he has left of appeasing that wrath which he has justly provoked. He even distrusts the efficacy of all these, and naturally fears lest the wisdom of God should not, like the weakness of man, be prevailed upon to spare the crime, by the most importunate lamentations of the criminal. Some other intercession, some other sacrifice, some other atonement, he imagines, must be made for him, beyond what he himself is capable of making, before the purity of the divine justice can be reconciled to his manifold offences." Thousands feel as much as is expressed by this author; as he says, it is very natural that they should. A sense of guilt renders the existence of many almost intolerable; nor can it ever be effectually removed but by some great sacrifice like the blood-shedding of Jesus Christ.

11. Wisdom marks all the divine conduct. In actual operation wisdom selects good ends and right means to accomplish those ends. "The wisdom of God is formed of his omniscience and benevolence, united in planning and accomplishing all real good in the progress of his immense and eternal kingdom." (Dwight).

We are now prepared to look at the truth that there are unfathomable depths of wisdom in the dealings of God with our race in the great work of redemption.

It is evident that the illustration of any attribute of God or man, furnished by any work, is in proportion to the difficulties to be overcome. Some things are simple and have few relations. Others are vast and complicated, and have bearings remote and immediate. Their course is through a long duration. They involve the happiness of many. Such is the work of redemption. It is God's chief work. He has expended more on it than on all his other works; more than in creation and providence. It would seem as if it was known that God would redeem men, before it was known how he would do it. The wit of angels seems to have attempted no solution. The case was too wonderful for them. Of Jehovah it is said: "He saw that there was no man, and wondered that there was no intercessor: therefore his arm brought salvation unto him; and his righteousness, it sustained him." (*Isaiah 59:16*). Jehovah was the sole author of redemption. He alone devised it. He alone executed it. He alone applies it. "Salvation is of the Lord." Let us notice some particulars.

I. God's wisdom shines out in redemption, as his plan reconciles all the divine attributes. Redemption must not weaken the divine government, must not impair the divine honour. God could consent to nothing which should suggest the possibility of his denying himself. When human governments pass by offences, it is a confession of weakness. God could ignore no offence. Yet the eternal ruin of all men would have left the human and angelic races without a single case of mercy shown to the guilty.

"Mercy pleads, if man be ruined, the creation is in vain: justice pleads, if man be not sentenced, the law is in vain; truth supports justice, and grace abets mercy. What shall be done in this seeming contradiction? Mercy is not manifested if man be not pardoned: justice will complain if man be not punished; therefore an expedient is found out by the wisdom of God to answer these demands, and adjust the differences between them. The wisdom of God answers, I will satisfy your pleas. Punishment shall be inflicted, yet pardon shall be bestowed. Justice shall not complain for want of an infliction of wrath; nor mercy for want of an exercise of compassion. I will have an infinite sacrifice to meet the demands of justice; and the virtue and fruit of that sacrifice shall be the delight of mercy. The rights of both those attributes shall be preserved, and the demands amicably accorded in punishment and pardon, by transferring the punishment of our crimes upon our Surety, exacting a recompense from his blood by justice, and conferring life and salvation upon us by mercy without one drop of our own blood being required. Thus is justice satisfied in its holy severities, and mercy in its gracious indulgences. The riches of grace are entwined with the terrors of wrath. The glories of divine mercy are wound about the flaming sword of justice; and the sword of justice protects and secures the glories of mercy. Thus is God righteous without being cruel, and merciful without being unjust. His righteousness remains inviolable, and the sinner becomes recoverable. Thus is resplendent mercy brought forth in the midst of all the wrath threatened to the offender." (Charnock).

This scheme has no parallel in heaven or earth. Such a surety-ship as that of Christ was never before heard of. It stands by itself in the history of all worlds. Around the cross of Christ were assembled Jews and Gentiles, men and devils; but in the cross of Christ justice and mercy, righteousness and peace, severity and compassion embrace and kiss each other. So that now forgiveness to the believing sinner is no less consistent with justice than is the destruction of the unbelieving reprobate. "God is just to forgive us our sins, and to cleanse us from all iniquity." (*1 John 1:9*). All penitent souls may say: "We are justified freely by his grace through the redemption that is in Christ Jesus: whom God hath set forth to be a propitiation through faith in his blood, to declare his righteousness for the remission of sins that are past, through the forbearance of God." (*Romans 3:24, 25*). God's rational creatures had never before seen it on this wise. So far from being able to devise or execute such a scheme, man is not able to comprehend it. All he can do, at least the best he can do, is to embrace it, obey its calls, wonder, and adore.

II. The wisdom of God is displayed in the choice of his incarnate Son, as the Redeemer. Neither an infinite God, nor an enlightened sinner would be satisfied with the doings or sufferings of a mere creature. What our case demanded was something far above the power of worms. Any redemption wrought out by men or angels must have been wholly inefficacious; but if it could have saved anyone, it must have resulted in idolatry. No sinner saved from hell could have failed to give his heart to his deliverer. But the Lord Jesus Christ was in every way fit to be our Redeemer.

1. He was divine, and so able to lay his hand upon God. He counted it not robbery to be equal with God. He was the eternal Son. To worship him was no idolatry. Before all worlds he was the Well-beloved of the Father. If any redemption could avail, his would not be

powerless. He had no superior in nature. He was chosen, appointed, ordained of God to this very work. If any ask, Why was the second, and not the first or the third person of the Trinity chosen to be the Redeemer, we may not be able to tell what we shall know hereafter, and we ought both to think and speak reverently; but we may safely say that the Father could not fitly become incarnate and our surety, for then he must have stood in the relation of one answering for our guilt before the Judge of all the earth. This would have subverted the order of the Trinity. The Father is the first person in order. As such, there is a peculiar fitness in his demanding satisfaction for sins and receiving applications for mercy. He is the fountain of the Godhead. Besides, he could not properly be sent into the world, as it is of the Father to send the Son, and of the Father and Son to send the Holy Spirit. The order of subsistence in the divine persons is properly the order of their operations. The Father is of none. He was neither begotten, nor does he proceed from any. The Son is of and from the Father – eternally begotten. Whatsoever the Son doeth, he doeth of the Father: "The Son can do nothing of himself, but what he seeth the Father do." (*John 5:19*). When the Son came, it was as he was sent of the Father, and to "do the will" of the Father. Thus it appears that the Father was not the proper person to do the work of redemption.

Nor was the Spirit the proper person to undertake that work. True, he proceeds from the Father and the Son, and is sent by them, yet it was fit that the Third Person should glorify the Second in calling men to believe on him, rather than that the Second should call men to bow before the Third; for this would invert the order of divine operation. The Redeemer is the object of saving faith. The agent of saving faith is the Holy Ghost. In order, the object precedes the exercise of faith, and of course it precedes the author and existence of faith. It is meet that the Spirit should apply the redemption that is in Christ Jesus. Thus we see wisdom in sending the Second, and no other person of the divine nature, to be our Redeemer. His eternal Sonship in heaven well consists with his supernatural Sonship on earth. This double Sonship well fitted him to be our elder Brother, by whom we become sons and heirs of God.

2. This leads to the remark that God's wisdom is gloriously displayed in the incarnation of his Son. The glory of redemption much depends on its being effected in the very nature whose fall made

redemption necessary: "By man came death; by man came also the resurrection of the dead;" "As by the offence of one judgment came upon all men to condemnation; even so by the righteousness of one the free gift came upon all men unto justification of life. For as by one man's disobedience many were made sinners, so by the obedience of one shall many be made righteous." (*Revelation 5:18, 19*). The first Adam was earthy, and sank us in ruin; the second Adam was heavenly, and saves us from wrath. By the sin of one imputed we fell; by the righteousness of the other imputed we rise to sonship with God.

Thus by his two natures Christ is equal with God in glory and authority, and equal with man in lowliness and suffering. None is higher – none is humbler. The Father greets him with gladness: "This is my beloved Son, in whom I am well pleased." The sinner hails him with joy: "My Lord and my God!" Thus we see the wisdom of God in the choice of the Redeemer – one who can be safely trusted with the honours of God's throne and with the sins and sorrows and salvation of men; one who can be worshipped without idolatry and approached without terror.

III. The wisdom of God is also manifested in the works and sufferings of the Redeemer:

1. In his *works*. They were all faultless, perfect. Even Pilate found no fault in him. His works were without a blot or stain. They were many. They exemplified every perfection of God and every virtue of the creature. They set a pattern for every duty; they gave a measure for every attainment; they magnified every precept of the law. His obedience to law wrought out a spotless robe of righteousness for every believer. This is the linen white and clean, called the righteousness of saints. No robe of personal innocence is so glorious. Angels in heaven are not so beautifully adorned. And it is all by the merit of Christ. Thus is boasting excluded, God honoured, the dignity of the heavenly state unimpaired, and the sinner abundantly saved. Thus is God's wisdom displayed in Christ's works.

2. So also in Christ's *sufferings* do we see God's wisdom. He was subject to the penalty of the law. He suffered as one held guilty in law, not for himself, but for us, whose law-place he took. His sufferings began with his birth and lasted till he expired on Calvary.

They were not solely from man, but chiefly from God; not merely corporeal, but mainly mental; not confined to his last hours, but running through his whole life; not only present, but anticipated for long years. (*Luke 12:50*). "The radical error of the Unitarian system is, that men are saved solely by influence or power. But the truth is, we are not saved so much by any action as by a passion; not so much by exertion as by endurance; not chiefly by vital energy, but by dying blood. It was not finished till Christ died. We are made nigh by the blood of Jesus. We are *healed,* not at all by his words or deeds, but *by his stripes.*" (Nevius). Law is stern and uncompliant. It "ought to be severe and awful too, or it will excite nothing but contempt." By the suffering of death, Christ satisfied the demands of the law, and gave to the troubled conscience ground of hope. Now no justification is more perfect than that of sinners who believe in Jesus. Though without the shedding of blood there is no remission, yet by the shedding of Christ's blood there is no lack of forgiveness. He who poured out his soul unto death is exalted a Prince and Saviour, to grant both repentance and remission of sins. Thus is God's wisdom displayed in Christ's sufferings. The law is magnified, the sinner is saved.

IV. The wisdom of God is manifested in the effects of redemption on the universe:

1. We have seen how it harmonises the divine perfections; let us see how it illustrates them. In the cross we have the strongest possible expression of benevolence. The infinite dignity of the sufferer, the unparalleled humiliation he underwent, the debasement of those he would save, and the utter impossibility of ever adequately requiting his love, all show the amazing extent of the Divine compassion. If any ever doubted God's hatred of sin, all such uncertainty comes to a full end at Calvary. If God would not spare his own Son, when he suffered the Just for the unjust, surely he is the awful and determined enemy of all unrighteousness. The scheme of saving mercy demonstrates at once the greatest love to the sinner and the strongest abhorrence of his sins. "Christ was no partisan with the sinner against the law." In like manner it would be easy to show how God's truth, and faithfulness, and power, and all his perfections, are displayed in redemption.

2. The influence of redemption on holy angels is both great and benign. It affords them the most wonderful theme of inquiry. They

desire to look into it. It gives them new and delightful employment. They *minister to the heirs of salvation*. It gives them a new Head. Though Christ is not their Saviour, he is their Lord. It brings them and men into relations of amity and brotherhood, so that they make *one family, in heaven and earth*. It gives them great and new sources of joy. They are glad with exceeding joy when a sinner repents. (*Luke 15:10*). Nor have they any theme for songs so sublime as those concerning salvation.

3. To man the effects of redemption are glorious and elevating. He who is saved from death should be most of all struck with his deliverance – most of all drawn towards his Deliverer. None are so changed by redemption as the redeemed themselves. They pass from the lowest depths to the greatest heights; from just, perfect, and awful condemnation, to full, free, and irrepealable justification; from a state of the lowest depravity to a state of purity and holiness fitting them for fellowship with God; from a state of misery that cannot be conceived by sinless creatures, to a state of comfort and joy unspeakable; from a state of fearful estrangement from a holy God and holy angels, to a state of lasting friendship with their Maker and all right-minded creatures. The bond which binds them to God and to angels binds them also to one another, and that for ever.

*   *   *

1. How futile are all schemes of man's devising for securing the favour of God and his own happiness. None of them reach the real evils in his case. They do not dispose of sin, either in its power, or guilt, or pollution.

2. How vain are all objections to the gospel drawn from the feeble, erring, sinful soul of man. Never is man more a fool or a transgressor than when he sits in judgment on this greatest plan and work of God. Did any wise man ever undertake to show how God could have more fitly formed the dove, the eagle, or the horse? Yet many a prating simpleton undertakes to tell the world how he would like the plan of salvation, God's greatest work, to be arranged.

3. How attractive is the character of Jesus Christ. He is the perfection of a Saviour. Some have made the suggestion that he might have rescued many from sin and wrath without so full, and frequent, and amazing acts of condescension. But whoever taught that he ought to

have given higher evidences of compassion and tenderness? All the redeemed join in praising him, unite in crowning him, contend in the strife of extolling him. Each of them sings:

> "I was a stricken deer that left the herd
> Long since. With many an arrow deep infixed
> My panting side was charged, when I withdrew
> To seek a tranquil death in distant shades.
> There I was found by One who had himself
> Been hurt by the archers. In his side he bore,
> And in his hands and feet, the cruel scars.
> With gentle force soliciting the darts,
> He drew them forth, and healed, and bade me live."

Matchless Redeemer! None among all the sons of the mighty, none among the holy angels, can compare with thee.

4. If any desire a rich, pure, exalted, inexhaustible theme of study and inquiry, he has it in the redemption wrought out by Christ. He need go no further. Here the holy angels all stop, and bow, and worship.

5. Unconverted men ought to feel a lively and profound interest in the undertaking of Christ. It mightily concerns them to know something of its wonders. If they ever find life or peace, it must be here. In Christ are hid all the treasures of wisdom and knowledge. (*Colossians 2:3*). In him is life, and the life is the light of men.

6. Children of God, rejoice and obey. "Ye are bought with a price: therefore glorify God in your body and in your spirit, which are God's." (*1 Corinthians 6:20*). Give him all. Keep back nothing that can honour him. Hear the voice of mercy whispering good counsels to your souls. Present your whole selves a living sacrifice to him; and let the love of God, like holy fire, come down and consume you. Be not straitened in your charity. Be not slothful in your labours of love. Be not cold in your zeal for the Master. Be ye enlarged.

13
The Atonement

THE word *Atonement* is found but once in the English New Testament: "We also joy in God through our Lord Jesus Christ, by whom we have now received the atonement." (*Romans 5:11*). Yet the Greek word here rendered *atonement* frequently occurs elsewhere. Our word atonement is compounded of *at* and *one*. At-one-ment is therefore the same thing as a reconciliation. It brings together those who have been at variance. The words *reconcile, reconciled, reconciling,* and *reconciliation,* in application to the work of Christ, are found in the New Testament nine or ten times. "The ministry of reconciliation" is the ministry that makes known the atonement of Christ. "The word of reconciliation" is the doctrine of atonement. Here are four striking passages from the New Testament in which the word occurs: "In all things it behoved him to be made like unto his brethren, that he might be a merciful and faithful High Priest in things pertaining to God, to make reconciliation for the sins of the people." (*Hebrews 2:17*). "All things are of God, who hath reconciled us to himself by Jesus Christ." (*2 Corinthians 5:18*). "God was in Christ, reconciling the world unto himself, not imputing their trespasses unto them." (*2 Corinthians 5:19*). "It pleased the Father that in him should all fulness dwell; and having made peace through the blood of his cross, by him to reconcile all things unto himself." (*Colossians 1:19, 20*). In like manner *Daniel 9:24*, says: "Seventy weeks are determined upon thy people and upon thy holy city, to finish the transgression, and to make an end of sins, and to make reconciliation for iniquity, and to bring in everlasting righteousness." Each of these phrases used by Daniel is explanatory of the others. Each of them points to an atonement; and an atonement is a reconciliation, a bringing together of those who have been alienated. We have forsaken, insulted, and rebelled against God. He has followed us with mercies, reproofs, and expostulations, and yet we persist in iniquity. As a moral Governor, he must put down sin in his dominions. He is holy, and hates iniquity. His nature and his office both require that transgression be punished. He saw men ruined and lost, yet he pitied them. He provided a mode of reconciliation by the life and death of his Son. Jesus Christ is the Reconciler. He is fit for this work. He has the nature of God, and so can appear with honour before the heavenly Majesty. He has the nature of man, and is by experience acquainted with all our natural infirmities. He knows what temptation and sorrow and death are.

In the passage cited from *Colossians*, God is said "to reconcile all things to himself" by Jesus Christ. This mode of speaking is not unusual in the sacred writings. The reason of this seems to be, that God is the *offended* party and we are the offenders. As such, we have need to be reconciled to him. The price of reconciliation was, therefore, paid to him, not to us. The learned Grotius has very justly remarked that in heathen authors *men's being reconciled to their gods* is always understood to signify appeasing the anger of their gods. When our Saviour commanded the offending to go and be reconciled to his brother, the plain meaning is, that he should go and try to appease his brother's anger, obtain his pardon, and regain his favour by humility, entreaty, and, if required, by reparation or restitution. This is also the use of the word reconciled, in *1 Samuel 29:4*, where the Philistines say of David and his difficulty with Saul, "Wherewith should he reconcile himself unto his master? Should it not be with the heads of these men?" They thought David would try to assuage Saul's anger and regain his favour by destroying his enemies. Indeed, this is the ordinary sense of the term in Scripture. To make reconciliation, therefore, is to offer an atonement.

The doctrine of atonement is vital in the Christian system. It claims our candid and careful study. When we speak of atonement, we mean that "Christ, by his obedience and death, did fully pay the debt of all his people, and did make a proper, real, and full satisfaction to his Father's justice in their behalf." It was a *proper* satisfaction; that is, it was not figurative or emblematical. It was *real*, not imaginary, not feigned, not fictitious, not theatrical. It was *full*, and not partial. It was complete, entire, wanting nothing. The only possible ideas respecting the work and death of Christ are these:

1. That Jesus Christ fully satisfied all the penal claims of the law for all men, and that all shall therefore infallibly be saved. This was formerly the doctrine of Universalists. They held that Christ had paid all the debts of all men, and that God would certainly save all men by the merits of his Son.

2. Another theory respecting the atonement is, that Christ did not by his death satisfy Divine justice for any of the sins of any man; that he died merely as a martyr to the truth; that no man required any real atonement, and that God required no satisfaction to his justice. This was the view held by old the Socinians of Europe, and embraced by their modern followers.

3. Another theory of the death of Christ is, that he made atonement for some of the sins of all men, and left them by their own works and sufferings to satisfy for their other sins as best they could. This view presents the work of Christ as partial and incomplete. It is practically the theory of all who by pains, prayers, penances, and acts of voluntary humility, propose to make themselves acceptable to God.

4. The last view is, that Jesus Christ made full and complete satisfaction for all his people; that in him they are complete; that in him they possess full redemption and perfect righteousness before God. This is the true, Scriptural doctrine of atonement. It is full of comfort to all who are so humble as to be willing to be saved by sovereign grace. It puts the conscience at rest, so that it demands no more atonement. Indeed, it kindles up untold delights. "We joy in God through our Lord Jesus Christ, by whom we have now received the atonement," says the Scripture. (*Romans 5:11*).

As the doctrine of atonement is not of human origin, but is a matter of pure revelation from God, it is evident we must be guided in the formation of our opinions by the Scriptures alone. If they settle not the points involved, all our logic and metaphysics will be useless. Our appeal is directly to God's Word.

No one will deny that in the sacred writings Christ is called a Saviour, a Redeemer, a Deliverer, a horn of salvation. He is said to be the Bread of life, the Tree of life, the Water of life. Indeed, he is said to be the Life itself.

The Scriptures as clearly ascribe our salvation to the death of Christ. They say he "died for the ungodly;" that "to this end Christ both died, and rose, and revived;" that Christ "died for our sins;" that saints should live to him who died for them; that he died for us that we should live with him. (*Romans 5:6; 14:9; 1 Corinthians 15:3; 2 Corinthians 5:15; 1 Thessalonians 4:14; 5:10*).

The Old and New Testaments wondrously harmonise in their teachings on this subject. Isaiah says, "Surely he hath borne our griefs and carried our sorrows ... He was wounded [margin, tormented] for our transgressions, he was bruised for our iniquities: the chastisement of our peace [or, that procured our peace] was upon him; and with his stripes we are healed ... Thou shalt make his soul an offering for sin ... For the transgression of my people was he stricken ... The Lord hath laid on him the iniquity of us all ... He bare the sin of many." In sin are two things: one its defilement or pollution; the other its desert of punishment. To say that God laid on Christ the pollution of our sins is blasphemous; but to say that Christ "bare our sins in his own body on the tree," is a heavenly doctrine. When the prophet says, "Thou shalt make his soul an offering for sin," we know he refers not to any iniquity in Christ, for he had no sin. Nor did our Lord bear the sin of fallen angels. He took not on him their nature. Between them and God there is no mediator. They are reserved in chains under darkness, to the judgment of the great day. And yet his soul was an offering for sin. What sin can be meant but ours? One says, "We may, in many cases, say that the innocent suffers for the guilty, when one is exposed to loss or pain by means of another's fault, or for his benefit; but can it be said, with propriety, that the Lord lays upon the innocent sufferer the iniquity of the offender, or that the former bears the sins of the latter, when no translation or imputation of guilt is intended and no real atonement made? If so, what words can convey the ideas of imputation or atonement? What determinate meaning can there be in language?" (Scott).

Peter declares that "Christ also hath once suffered for sins, the just for the unjust." (*1 Peter 3:18*). If he suffered for sins, whose sins were they? They were the sins of the unjust, even of those whom he would rescue from a righteous and eternal destruction. Indeed, almost every form of language is employed to show that Christ's sufferings were vicarious, not for himself but for others. Paul says, "God hath made him to be sin [or a sin-offering] for us." (*2 Corinthians 5:21*). In the very same verse it is declared that Christ knew no sin. Surely he bore the wrath of God that was due to us.

When Peter says that he, "his own self bare our sins in his own body on the tree," (*1 Peter 2:24*), what is the meaning of this solemn language? The expression *bearing sin,* or *bearing iniquity,* occurs more than thirty times in Scripture, and in every instance it means to bear the sufferings or penalty of sin. Thus in *Leviticus 5:1,* God ordains that if a man hear swearing and is a witness and does not utter it, he shall "*bear his iniquity.*" This means that guilt shall so rest upon him that he shall be liable to punishment. So also in *Leviticus 22:9,* God says "they shall therefore keep mine ordinance, lest they bear sin for it, and die." So in *Ezekiel 23:49,* God says, "Ye shall bear the sins of your idols." Clearly, the meaning is, ye shall be held liable to punishment for worshipping your idols. Again, in *Leviticus 24:15,* the Lord says, "Whosoever curseth his God, shall bear his sin." In *Hebrews 9:28,* Paul says, "Christ was once offered to bear the sins of many;" and in *Isaiah 53:11,* God says, "My righteous servant … shall bear their iniquities." Could words more plainly teach that Christ endured the wrath of God for us, and bore the penalty of the law in our room and stead?

In *Galatians 3:13,* Paul says, "Christ hath redeemed us from the curse of the law, being made a curse for us." This passage seems specially intended to meet all cavillings. In the language of an Israelite, the law consisted of a precept, a statute, a rule, or a direction, and of a curse, or penalty, and of a promise or blessing. The rule or command was for all. The promise or blessing was for the obedient; the curse or penalty was for the transgressor. Indeed, our Anglo-Saxon word *curse* has precisely the same meaning with the Latin word *penalty.* As we were all transgressors, we were all under the curse. But Christ has redeemed us by enduring the penalty or by being *made a curse* for us. The slight variations in the sense of the word *curse* in this passage need mislead no one. In the latter case, it means a victim, one devoted or accursed for us. In quite a number of passages is Christ spoken of as a lamb, a Lamb slain, a Lamb that takes away sin, as a Lamb that is worshipped in heaven, a Lamb slain from the foundation of the world. (*Isaiah 53:7; John 1:29; Acts 8:32; 1 Peter 1:19; Revelation 5:8, 12; 13:8*). It is admitted that Christ resembled a lamb in his uncomplaining gentleness. But in what sense did a lamb ever take away sin, but by dying in the place of the offerer, and how could Christ as a lamb take away sin, but by the sacrifice of himself? If he were slain, it was not for himself, but for us. All the lambs offered in sacrifice died the innocent for the guilty, the spotless for the criminal. Do not these things clearly teach that Christ endured the penalty of the law, that he died as a substitute for others?

The same doctrine is variously taught in the Scriptures in connection with the phrase, *the blood of Christ*. It is expressly said that he "made peace through the blood of his cross," (*Colossians 1:20*); that "by his own blood he entered in once into the holy place, having obtained eternal redemption for us," (*Hebrews 9:12*); that his blood shall purge our "conscience from dead works to serve the living God," (*Hebrews 9:14*); that "the blood of Jesus Christ … cleanseth us from all sin," (*1 John 1:7*); that he hath redeemed us to God by his blood, (*Revelation 5:9*); and that we "are made nigh by the blood of Christ." (*Ephesians 2:13*). Now the shedding of the blood of Christ by his enemies was the greatest crime ever committed in Jerusalem or on this earth. It is impossible that such wickedness could be pleasing to God. In what sense then does his blood cleanse us from sin? It cannot be otherwise than as he offered himself as a Lamb without spot unto God; poured out his soul unto death, that we might live for ever. Blood, innocent blood, calls for vengeance. The blood of Abel cried from the ground, and the cry went up to heaven. But the blood of Christ speaketh better things than that of Abel. It calls for salvation to all who believe.

The Scriptures no less clearly declare that Christ endured his sufferings for the iniquities of his people. Isaiah says, "For the transgression of my people was he stricken;" (*Isaiah 53:8*). Paul says that "he was delivered for our offences," (*Romans 4:25*); that he "died for our sins according to the Scriptures," (*1 Corinthians 15:3*); and that he "gave himself for our sins," (*Galatians 1:4*). There is no desirable sense in which Christ could have done and suffered these things for sin, unless it be as an atonement. And it is very clear from the New Testament that Christ's dying for sin is a matter of exultation to all the pious. Indeed the only feast instituted under the gospel is a feast expressly ordained to show forth his death until he come. The Scriptures no less frequently declare that Christ died for guilty men.

"This is my body which is given *for you.*" (*Luke 22:19*). "I lay down my life for the sheep." (*John 10:15*). "In due time Christ died for the ungodly." (*Romans 5:6*). "While we were yet sinners, Christ died for us." (*Romans 5:8*). There is danger of weakening the force of such clear and solemn passages by any explanation. Still it may be asked, In what conceivable sense could Christ die in our place if it be not as a vicarious, atoning sacrifice?

The Scriptures also declare that all hope of pardon for us lost men is centred in Christ. But why in him if he is not our atoning priest? Thus says Peter, "Him hath God exalted with his right hand to be a Prince and a Saviour, for to give repentance to Israel and forgiveness of sins." (*Acts 5:31*). Paul says as explicitly, "Be it known unto you therefore, men and brethren, that through this man is preached unto you the forgiveness of sins." (*Acts 13:38*). Again, "in whom we have redemption through his blood, the forgiveness of sins, according to the riches of his grace." (*Ephesians 1:7*). Where is the fitness of connecting the remission of sins in so remarkable a manner with the person and the blood of Jesus Christ unless he is indeed the substitute of his people and their Saviour in the highest sense ever claimed by the Christian world?

*　　*　　*

These clear, Scriptural proofs and statements receive confirmation and elucidation from the following considerations:

1. If we deny that Jesus Christ endured the penalty of the law, and that his sufferings were vicarious, then we must deny that he was the substitute of his people, and that their sins are imputed to him. If this be true, we are of all men most miserable; for we have given up this world in the hope of attaining a better through Christ's substitution for us. But all our sins still remain, unless we have remission through his blood. We are disappointed, and our guilt is still upon us. If we go thus far, we must in consistency maintain that justice is unsatisfied and must ever remain so, and that if there is any salvation for sinful men, it must be in derogation of the justice of God; it must be by trampling underfoot the penalty of God's law.

2. Some who deny that Christ's death and sufferings were vicarious and for us, yet admit that the Scriptures *seem* to teach that doctrine. But they warn us against being led astray by figurative language. To

this these answers may be given: *a.* If figurative language teaches nothing, then it is nonsense. *b.* In all languages, the very strongest things that are said are said in metaphor. *c.* A great variety of metaphors is employed by the sacred writers on this subject. *d.* Oftentimes the Scriptures speak in language perfectly plain. "He bare the sin of many;" "He was wounded for our transgressions;" "He died for our sins;" and "He suffered the Just for the unjust," are forms of expression as free from figure as language can well be.

3. If the Scriptures which are generally relied on as teaching the doctrine of a vicarious atonement may be so explained as not to teach it, then it is useless to attempt to prove anything by the Word of God.

4. Any scheme of doctrine which opposes the retributive justice of God will, if carried to its legitimate results, subvert also the doctrine of the Divine holiness. God punishes sin because his nature leads him to abhor it.

5. If God has set aside the penalty of his law without a full satisfaction, must it not have been at first too severe? And if the penalty was at first wrong, may not the precept for the same cause be too strict? Thus by our speculations we subvert the whole law.

6. In like manner we shall subvert the gospel. What the convinced sinner needs and seeks is, not merely that he may escape hell and reach heaven, but he wishes to do it in a manner that will secure the honour of God. He wishes to see how God can be just and yet justify the sinner. On the old Bible doctrine of a vicarious atonement, all is plain; but on any other scheme there is no way of satisfactorily accounting for the death of Christ or the offer of salvation. If Jesus Christ bore the penalty, all is clear; if he did not, why did God smite the man that was his fellow?

7. How well does the true doctrine, and how ill does the opposite doctrine, agree with the types of the Old Testament. Without referring to the many great offerings in detail, let anyone carefully consider the offering of even the young pigeons or the rite of the scape-goat, and see what can be the meaning of such services, if Jesus Christ did not die for us. If Christ bears our sins, well may we be forgiven.

8. How well does the true doctrine, and how ill does the opposite doctrine, harmonise with the worship of heaven: "The songs of the

redeemed in heaven, even of those 'who had come out of great tribulation,' and had shed their blood in the cause of Christ, afford an unanswerable argument in favour of a real atonement and a vicarious sacrifice in the death of Christ. Without one discordant voice, they ascribe their salvation to 'the Lamb that was slain, and redeemed them unto God by his blood,' who washed them from their sins in his own blood. But in what sense could *the Lamb that was slain wash them from their sins in his own blood, unless he was literally an atoning sacrifice?*" (Scott). What is there to make exultant the worship of sinners saved if, after all, God merely connives at their transgressions?

9. It cannot be safely denied – indeed it is commonly admitted – that the early Christian writers, the reformers, and the Christian world generally, until after the middle of the eighteenth century, held and taught that Christ bore the curse and endured the wrath of God in the room and stead of sinners. Is not this fact a strong presumptive proof that the doctrine is true? Is it possible that God's hidden ones have so generally mistaken the prophets and apostles, and been left to embrace delusion?

10. It is a great fact confirmatory of the true doctrine, that it has a mighty power over all right hearts. "O what a melting consideration is this, that out of Christ's agony comes our victory; out of his condemnation our justification; out of his pain our ease; out of his stripes our healing; out of his gall and vinegar our honey; out of his curse our blessing; out of his crown of thorns our crown of glory; out of his death our life: if he could not be released, it was that we might be; if Pilate gave sentence against him, it was that the great God might never give sentence against us; if he yielded, that it should be with Christ as they required, it was that it might be with our souls as well as we can desire." (Hopkins). Hearts must be harder than the rocks, if the love and death of Christ do not move them, When he died, the rocks were rent.

14
The Folly of Objecting to the Atonement

THE minds of inspired men were warm with saving truth. The more fully the way of salvation was understood, the more did they glory in the cross and in its power to save. With them philosophy was as nothing. Learned men without revelation had wasted centuries in idle debates, in refuting one another, and in deceiving mankind; but they had effected nothing truly useful. Not a sinner was reformed, not an aching heart found ease, not an idol was abolished. But when the gospel was fully and faithfully preached, it wrought wonders. It saved men's souls. It was full of power. The early preachers of righteousness gave to mankind the triumphant challenge, "Hath not God made foolish the wisdom of this world?" (*1 Corinthians 1:20*). Yet the wise, the scribe, and the disputer, had many objections. They mocked; they cavilled; they scorned; they counted the gospel foolishness. Then they pretended to reason. Their utmost powers were directed against the cross and the person of Jesus Christ. They hated the doctrine of atonement. It is even so still. Time, which mends many things and wears out many things, has not improved the temper of the carnal heart, nor exhausted its fondness for debate.

Let us look at some of the objections made against the atonement. These are sometimes stated, with apparent modesty, in the form of questions, and sometimes categorically and polemically.

1. It has been urged against the doctrine of vicarious atonement, that it involves a transfer of moral character. To meet this, it is

sufficient to ask, Is there not a difference between the penalty of sin and its pollution? between the penalty of the law incurred and the vileness of the heart indulged? between legal responsibility and moral character? If an innocent man pays the forfeiture for the non-appearance of a bad man to stand his trial, does that make the surety a partaker of the moral character of the criminal? Surely one may voluntarily assume pains and penalties for even a bad man without approving of his wrong, or without being like him in moral character. The truth is, a transfer of moral character is simply impossible; but nothing is more common than a transfer of legal responsibilities. The correct doctrine on this subject is well expressed by Owen in his work on justification: "Nothing is more absolutely true, nothing more sacredly and assuredly believed by us, than that nothing which Christ did or suffered, nothing that he undertook or underwent, did or could constitute him, subjectively, inherently, and therefore personally, a sinner, or guilty of any sin of his own. To bear the guilt or blame of other men's faults – to be *alienae culpae reus* – makes no man a sinner, unless he did unwisely or irregularly undertake it."

2. Again, it is urged that if Christ bore the curse due to us, and fully satisfied Divine justice, then it is no mercy in God to forgive and accept us. But was there no mercy in God's providing that justice should be satisfied, so that salvation might flow forth to sinners? Was it not mercy in God so to love the world as to give his only-begotten Son, that whosoever believeth in him might not perish, but have everlasting life? Is it not mercy in the blessed Spirit of God to purify our hearts? To Christ, indeed, who has bought us with his blood, justice and the covenant of God require that he have a seed to serve him. But to the seed who do serve him, considered in themselves, salvation from first to last is the fruit of infinite grace. To believers, considered as in Christ and confessing their transgressions, God is faithful and just to forgive their sins. He is faithful and just to himself, faithful and just to his Son. But to those forgiven it is never of debt, but all of mercy, pity, and love. The whole objection goes on the supposition that justice and mercy, in the gospel scheme, even after all that Christ has done, are antagonistical to each other. Whereas Christ's first and great work was to satisfy the claims of justice; and now justice and mercy gloriously harmonise

in man's salvation. Mercy abounds and grace is free, because justice is fully satisfied. "The transcendent graciousness of the gospel covenant consists not in requiring less righteousness to give title to life than was done at first; not in requiring a perfect righteousness of us personally to that end; but in providing and accepting that of the Surety, according to the apostle, (*Romans 8:3, 4*). The law could not give us life, because, being weakened by sin, we could not perform the perfect righteousness which it required; but what the law could not do, Christ has done, giving us a title to life, fulfilling the righteousness of the law on our behalf." (Clarkson).

3. It is sometimes said that if Christ bore the curse due to us for sin, there is no increase of happiness in the universe by means of his mediation. Such an objection goes on the supposition that Christ's sufferings were in exact proportion to the number of those who shall finally be saved, and that they were in amount equal to what would have been the everlasting sufferings of all his people if they had not been rescued from wrath. But this is not the doctrine of the Scriptures. It is wholly unsupported by the Word of God. It is shocking to the feelings of pious men. It is not maintained by one enlightened friend of the doctrine of a vicarious atonement. It utterly overlooks the infinite dignity of the eternal Son of God, from which his sufferings derive their chief value, and which puts them far beyond all comparison with the sufferings of mere creatures. So that there is no ground whatever for the objection. His sufferings, though great, were short. They were soon followed by unparalleled glory, in which all his redeemed partake. The happiness of the universe is already infinitely increased by the death of Christ; and yet his kingdom is far from being completed, and all its subjects have an eternity of bliss before them.

4. Sometimes it is asked, How could Christ make an atonement for us? How could he bear our sins, endure the penalty of the law for us, and for us work out a perfect righteousness?

So far as there is a real difficulty in this matter, and so far as it has not its seat in our depravity, let the following things be carefully considered:

(1.) God was under no obligation to provide any Saviour for us. He might justly have left us to perish as he did the fallen angels. But if in his mercy he has provided a Redeemer, who has satisfied divine justice, why should we find fault? If the demands of the law and Lawgiver are fully met, it is perverseness in us to cavil or object.

(2.) God could not relax his demands and accept a righteousness less perfect than the law requires. "Christ's righteousness is called the righteousness of the law. For, though righteousness does not come by our obedience to the law, yet it does come by Christ's obedience to it. Though by the deeds of the law as performed by man no flesh living can be justified; yet, by the deeds of the law as performed by Christ, all the elect are justified." (Gill – *Romans 8:4*). So the penalty of the law is death, and without the shedding of blood there is no remission, even though Christ undertake for us.

(3.) The whole work of Christ from first to last was voluntary. He was not forced to obey the law or bear the curse for us. No man took his life from him. He laid it down of himself.

(4.) Mere suffering even of such a one as Christ would not of itself avail for us without the consent of the sufferer and of God the Lawgiver. Jesus Christ died in fulfilment of a covenant between himself and his Father. Hence the efficacy of his blood-shedding.

(5.) When we say that Jesus Christ bore the penalty of the law in the stead of sinners, we do not deny that his sufferings were different from those of sinners on whom the curse falls. He felt neither despair nor remorse. His holy soul could feel neither, because he had done no sin, and because he knew his sufferings would soon be followed by great glory. But despair and remorse are nowhere said to be the penalty of the law. They are indeed incidents to the wicked, who suffer the curse, but they are not the curse itself. Christ also suffered but for a short time, whereas sinners who bear their own iniquity must suffer eternally. The reasons of this difference in the duration of sufferings are, first, Christ's infinite dignity and glory, which made his humiliation in time, to avail more than the anguish of man to all eternity; and secondly, when Christ bore our sins, he bore them all, and made provision that his people should cease from sin; but the wicked, who fall under the wrath of God, sin always, and provoke the Most High by new transgressions for ever. But an eternity of suffering is nowhere in Scripture said to be an inherent element of the penalty of the law. It accompanies it only when borne by finite creatures, themselves sinners. The death of the body and that endurance of the wrath of

God in the mind, which is properly called the death of the soul, constitute the penalty of the law. Jesus Christ bore these, for all admit that his body died and was buried; and that his soul was exceeding sorrowful even unto death. This is the sense and the only sense in which any sound writer maintains that Christ bore the penalty of the law.

Admitting these views, how plain is it that God could be just and yet justify the ungodly. But if we reject these views and maintain that in saving his people it was the deliberate purpose of God to set aside the penalty of the law, who can conceive of the object of Christ's death? All admit that he died not for his own sins, for he had none. If divine justice requires the punishment of sin, how is God just in not punishing his people, unless the wrath due to them was borne by their Substitute? We cannot prove that God is righteous in permitting anyone personally innocent, not standing in the place of the guilty, to suffer much or little. Good angels have sometimes visited our world in the form of men; and some have sought to harm them. But God never permitted one of them to endure the least pain. There can be no greater injustice than to visit with stripes one who is under no penalty. The sufferings of Christ can never be reconciled with justice, unless he bore the wrath of God due to us. To inflict pain on one who has done no wrong or who has not assumed legal responsibilities for others, is absurd.

Some hold that Christ's sufferings were not penal, yet that his death was an exhibition of God's justice, and hatred of sin. But how can it illustrate these excellent attributes of the Most High to inflict unparalleled sufferings on one who had never displeased him, and who had not undertaken to bear the penalty of the law in the place of others? The only legal obstacle to the salvation of any sinner is the penalty of the law. If that is not borne, it remains in full force, and forever demands satisfaction. To admit men to heaven with the penalty of the law still unsatisfied, would be trampling the law underfoot. No government can maintain its authority when the penalty of its laws is not enforced. The penalty not executed, the precept falls into contempt. If sinners were thus saved, the heavens would be filled with thieves and robbers, as Christ speaks, that is, with men who would be there in spite of law and right, and in contempt of God's retributive justice.

Where, then, is the difficulty in the case? God, the Judge of all, objects not to our salvation by the death of his Son. The Son died and lives for this great purpose. The Holy Spirit calls men to repentance. Why should we waste our lives in crying, "How can these things be?" A little simple faith in Jesus Christ will scatter the difficulties men make about this doctrine.

5. Others say that if Jesus Christ made a vicarious atonement for those who believe on him, and laid down his life for his sheep, how can we offer the salvation of the gospel to all men, as we are commanded to do?

Let us look at this matter candidly and fairly. In reply it may be stated that the Scriptures clearly teach that Christ died to save his people, and with the covenant engagement on the part of his Father that he should effect that great end. He himself says, "I lay down my life for the sheep;" and prophecy said, "He shall prolong his days; he shall see his seed." Yet we have the example of God, of the prophets, of the Lord Jesus Christ, and of the apostles, in favour of making an indiscriminate and urgent offer of salvation to our fellow-men. But it is no part of the true doctrine of the atonement that the merit of our Saviour is exhausted in the salvation of those who believe on him. No respectable writer teaches that Christ's humiliation and sufferings would have been less if the number of his chosen people had been smaller; nor that his humiliation and sufferings would have been greater, if the number to be saved had been greater. The old standard writers all held that the offer of salvation was to be made to men indiscriminately, earnestly, and tenderly; that it was entirely consistent to make such an offer, that there is an infinite fulness in Christ, a sufficiency of merit to save the souls of all who should come. Mark the testimony of eminent divines.

Calvin: "We know the promises to be effectual to us only when we receive them by faith: on the contrary, the annihilation of faith is the abolition of the promises. If this is their nature, we may perceive that there is no discordance between these two things: God's having appointed from eternity on whom he will bestow his favour and exercise his wrath, and his proclaiming salvation to all. Indeed, I maintain that there is a most perfect harmony between them."

Owen: "It was, then, the intention and purpose of God that his Son should offer a sacrifice of infinite worth, value, and dignity, sufficient in itself for the redeeming of all and every man, if it had pleased the Lord to employ it for that purpose; yea, and of other worlds also, if the Lord should freely make them and would redeem them. Sufficient, we say then, was the sacrifice of Christ for the redemption of the whole world, and for the expiation of all the sins of all and every man in the world. This sufficiency of his sacrifice hath a two-fold rise. First, the dignity of the person that did offer and was offered. Secondly, the greatness of the pain he endured, by which he was able to bear and did undergo the whole curse of the law of God due to sin: *and this sets out the innate, real, true worth of the blood-shedding of Jesus Christ.*"

Thomas Boston: "There was virtue and efficacy enough in Christ's oblation to satisfy offended justice for the sins of the whole world, yea, and of millions of worlds more; for his blood hath infinite value because of the excellency and dignity of his person."

John Brown of Haddington: "Such is the infinite dignity of Christ's person that his fulfilment of the broken law is sufficient to balance all the debts of all the elect, nay, of millions of guilty worlds … In respect of its intrinsic worth as the obedience and sufferings of a divine person, Christ's satisfaction is sufficient for the ransom of all mankind: and being fulfilled in human nature, is equally suited to all their necessities."

What broader, surer foundation for a sincere and consistent offer of mercy, than is found in such views as these, can anyone demand?

Hervey: "The obedience and atonement are as sufficient to secure perfectly all sinners that fly by faith under the covert of his wings, as the immeasurable circuit of the sky is roomy enough for a lark to fly in, or as the immense brightness of the Sun is lightsome enough for a labourer to work by. When the thunders roar, and the lightnings flash; when the clouds pour down water, and a horrid storm comes on; all that are in the open air retire under the branches of a thick tree, or fly to some other commodious shelter. So the blood and righteousness of Christ are a covert. Hither we may fly and be screened; hither we may fly and be safe."

Witherspoon: "I shall lay down three propositions which I think can hardly be called in question, and which are a sufficient foundation for our faith and practice.

"1. The obedience and death of Christ is of value sufficient to expiate the guilt of all the sins of every individual that ever lived or shall live on earth. This cannot be denied, since the subjects to be redeemed are finite, the price paid for their redemption is infinite. Christ suffered in the human nature, but that nature was intimately and personally united to the divine; so that Christ the Mediator, the gift of God for the redemption of sinners, is often called his own and his eternal Son. 'He that spared not his own Son, but delivered him up for us all, how shall he not with him also freely give us all things.' (*Romans 8:32*). Such was the union of the divine and human nature in Christ, that the blood which was the purchase of our redemption, is expressly called the blood of God. (*Acts 20:28*). This is the great mystery of godliness, God was manifest in the flesh, in which all our thoughts are lost and swallowed up.

"2. Notwithstanding this, every individual of the human race is not in fact partaker of the blessing of the purchase, but many die in their sins, and perish for ever. This will as little admit of a doubt. Multitudes have died who never heard of the name of Christ, or salvation through him; many have lived and died blaspheming his person and despising his undertaking; many have died in unbelief and impenitence, serving divers lusts and passions, and if the Scripture is true, he will at last render to them according to their works.

But "3. There is in the death of Christ a sufficient foundation laid for preaching the gospel indefinitely to all without exception. It is the command of God that this should be done: 'And he said unto them, Go ye into all the world, and preach the gospel to every creature.' (*Mark 16:15*). The effect of this is, that the misery of the unbelieving and impenitent shall be entirely at their own door: and they shall not only die in their own sins, but shall suffer to eternity for the most heinous of all sins – despising the remedy and refusing to hear the Son of God.

"Let us neither refuse our assent to any part of the revealed will of God, nor foolishly imagine an opposition between one part of it and another. All the obscurity arises from, and may be resolved into, the weakness of our understandings; but let God be true, and every man a liar. That there is a sense in which Christ died for all men, and even for those who perish, is plain from the very words of Scripture."

In like manner Symington: "We hold that the sacrifice of the Lord Jesus possessed an *intrinsic value sufficient for the salvation of the whole world.* In this sense it was adequate to the redemption of every human being ... The worth of Christ's atonement we hold to be, in the strictest sense of the term, *infinite, absolute, all-sufficient ... This all-sufficiency is what lays the foundation for the unrestricted universality of the gospel call* ... Such is my impression of the sufficiency of the atonement, that were all the guilt of all mankind concentrated in my own person, I should see no reason, relying on that blood which cleanseth from all sin, to indulge despair."

So also Dr Candlish has written at length to show that there is a fitness in the "universality of the gospel offer," and that it is sincere and in "good faith on the part of God."

"We maintain that the death of Christ lays the foundation for the offer of the gospel to all men universally, and lays the foundation for that offer being honest and free on the part of God."

Precious as is the doctrine of a vicarious atonement, and glad as must be the heart of him who hopes that he personally is interested in the sacrifice of Calvary, yet it abates nothing from the riches of divine grace, but on the contrary, enhances its glories, that the blood of Christ will never lose its power; and when all the redeemed shall have obtained a full supply, the treasure of gospel grace will be as ample as ever. Let sinners everywhere know that, if they perish, it is not because there is not merit in Christ sufficient to meet all the demands of law and justice against them. Let them all turn and embrace the kind, the sincere, the urgent call to life and salvation by mere gratuity on the part of God: "Whosoever will, let him take the water of life freely." (*Revelation 22:17*). As God is not mocked, so neither does he mock any of his creatures.

Other objections have been urged against the doctrine of a vicarious atonement, but it is not necessary here to dwell upon them.

*   *   *

1. Let the Christian glory in the fulness and sufficiency of the work of Christ. His crown and his inheritance are sure. In this world's possessions you may be poor; but "a ragged saint is dearer to God than a godless millionaire." "God is a portion of which his people can never be robbed. Impoverished you may be, but not undone; discouraged,

but not disinherited." (Arrowsmith). I recommend Christ to you more and more. Hold fast to him. Never let him go. Especially,

2. Let all sinners everywhere accept the salvation that is so fully provided and so freely offered. Why will men stand and cavil, and wonder, and perish, when they are called to return to God and seek salvation? "There is mercy enough in God, and merit enough in Christ, and power enough in the Spirit, and scope enough in the promises, and room enough in heaven." O why will men refuse salvation?

15
Christ's Resurrection

THE humiliation of Christ being completed in his death and burial, his exaltation began in his resurrection from the dead. This is a great cardinal truth in the Christian system. It has often been shown to be so. It is so by the confession of all Christians, and of the apostles themselves. Paul says, "If Christ be not risen, then is our preaching vain, and your faith is also vain ... If Christ be not raised, your faith is vain; ye are yet in your sins. Then they also which are fallen asleep in Christ are perished. If in this life only we have hope in Christ, we are of all men most miserable." (*1 Corinthians 15:14, 17-19*). Clearly this doctrine is fundamental. It should be often preached and never yielded. "It is the cardinal fact of Christianity, without which all her other facts lose their importance." (Mason).

It is agreed by Jews, Christians, and Infidels, that Christ was dead and buried. For a time his body was lifeless. Any decent regard to truth must admit this. Of his death there is no doubt. Himself admitted it more than fifty years afterwards: "I am He that liveth, and was dead; and, behold, I am alive for evermore." (*Revelation 1:18*).

It is also clear that prophecy required that Christ should rise from the dead. "My flesh also shall rest in hope. For thou wilt not leave my soul in hell; neither wilt thou suffer thine Holy One to see corruption." (*Psalm 16:9, 10*). That this does not apply to angels is certain, for angels are pure spirits and have no "flesh." They never die. That it does not refer to any mere man is certain, for the person here spoken of is called God's *Holy One,* and all mere men are sinful. That it does not apply to David, who wrote the Psalm where it is found, Peter proved on the day of Pentecost: "Men and brethren, let me freely speak unto you of the patriarch David, that he is both dead and buried, and his sepulchre is with us unto this day;" we know that he has seen corruption, for he has been lying in the grave for centuries. But, continues Peter, David "being a prophet, and knowing that God had sworn with an oath to him, that of the fruit of his loins, according to the flesh, he would raise up Christ to sit on his throne; he seeing this before spake of the resurrection of Christ, that his soul was not left in hell, neither his flesh did see corruption." (*Acts 2:29-31*). Jesus foretold his own resurrection: "Destroy this temple, and in three days I will raise it up." (*John 2:19*). "He spake of the temple of his body."

In the resurrection of Christ there was a concurrence of all the divine persons. Peter says, "God raised him up." (*Acts 10:40*). Paul also says, "God the Father raised him from the dead." (*Galatians 1:1*). But this work is not ascribed to the Father alone. The divine nature of Christ was employed in quickening his own dead body. Himself said of his own body, "I will raise it up." "I have power to lay down my life, and I have power to take it again." (*John 10:18*). The Son of God participated in the resurrection of his own body. And in *Romans 8:11* the same work is said to have been effected by the Spirit of God. As in creation and providence, so in the raising of Christ's body, each person of the Godhead concurred.

Peter says that Christ was raised up the *third day.* (*Acts 10:40*). In reckoning time, both Hebrews and Greeks frequently counted the part of a day on which a thing began as one day, and the part of a day on which it ceased as another day, and, putting these to the intermediate day or days; gave the total. Thus, among the Hebrews, the day on which a child was born was set down as one day, and the day on which it was brought to be circumcised was put down as another day, and only six entire days intervened between its birth and circumcision, and so it frequently happened that a child was not seven times twenty-four hours old when it was circumcised, and yet the law required that sign and seal to be put on the child on the eighth day. Greek antiquities show that the same mode of reckoning was often used in Eastern Europe. At other times the Hebrews counted only the entire days. (Compare *Luke 9:28* and *Mark 9:2*). So that either mode might be used. The gospels state that Christ was buried the afternoon of the day before the Jewish Sabbath, and that he rose very early on the day after the Jewish Sabbath. So that he continued under the power of death one whole day and a part of two others. This method of computing time explains the phrases *three days* and the third day. Jesus arose the third day; this was the time fixed by his own prophecies; had he risen sooner, some might have doubted the reality of his death; had he remained longer in the grave, the season of terrible fear and darkness to his people would have been needlessly prolonged; had he remained much longer under the power of death, his body must have "seen corruption," which prophecy had said should not be.

Christ's raised body was a real body, and not merely the appearance of a body. In the minds of his followers there were doubts on this point. Once when he stood in the midst of them they were "affrighted, and supposed that they had seen a spirit." To settle this point he said, "Handle me, and see; for a spirit hath not flesh and bones, as ye see me have." (*Luke 24:36-39*). Their sight and their touch alike informed them that there was no illusion.

Jesus Christ had the same body after his resurrection that he had before. The sepulchre was opened and the sacred body it contained arose. After his resurrection our Lord said to his disciples, "Behold my hands and my feet, that it is I myself." To unbelieving Thomas he said, "Reach hither thy finger and behold my hands; and reach hither thy hand and thrust it into my side; and be not faithless, but believing." Christ's risen body was the same as his dead and buried body.

Do any ask, Why did not Christ's followers recognise him immediately? In at least one instance "their eyes were holden" that they should not know him, until by reasoning with them out of the Scriptures, he had satisfied them that he "ought" to have suffered these things, and then enter into his glory. And although Christ had plainly foretold his own death, burial, and resurrection, yet through the strange power of unbelief, his disciples did not understand or receive those truths. This error was not wholly removed from their minds till near the time of his ascension. When he was dead, the best thing they could bring their feelings to say was, "We trusted that it had been he which should have redeemed Israel." Moreover, in a mind greatly afflicted, there is a strange unwillingness, amounting almost to incapacity, to believe good tidings. It looks upon any very good news as too good to be credited. Luke tells us that this was the state of mind in the followers of Christ: "They believed not for joy, and wondered." (*Luke 24:41*). Such a state of mind is not unusual, as might easily be shown.

Let us now examine the evidence by which the fact of Christ's resurrection is established. Peter says: "God ... showed him openly; not to all the people, but unto witnesses chosen before of God, even to us, who did eat and drink with him after he rose from the dead." (*Acts 10:40, 41*). It is worthy of notice that to the disciples there were two heavenly witnesses of Christ's resurrection. Luke indeed speaks of them as "two men ... in shining garments;" but John expressly says they were "two angels in white." (*Luke 24:4-6; John 20:12, 13*). These elder sons of God were the first, and they were fit witnesses of the wonderful event.

Respecting the witnesses of Christ's resurrection, several things may be stated:

1. Their number was large, between five and six hundred. From the days of Moses to this time, the most enlightened nations have admitted the testimony of two or three men. Here we have two or three hundred times the number of witnesses required to prove even that a mother killed her own child. Five or six hundred witnesses are as good as five or six thousand. The number is sufficient.

2. The witnesses were competent. They had the use of all their senses, and they had the best opportunities of obtaining correct information. Peter says the witnesses "did eat and drink with him after he rose from the dead." (*Acts 10:41*). In *Acts 1:3,* Luke says that "he showed himself alive after his passion by many infallible proofs, being seen of them [the apostles] forty days, and speaking of the things pertaining to the kingdom of God." So that the witnesses fearlessly say, "That which we have heard, which we have seen with our eyes, which we have looked upon, and our hands have handled, of the Word of life ... declare we unto you." (*1 John 1:1, 3*). In Scripture are mentioned eleven particular instances in which our Lord was seen by some or all of these witnesses.

His first appearance was to Mary Magdalene, who at first mistook him for the gardener, and to whom he announced his early ascension into heaven, (*Mark 16:9; John 20:14-17*). Christ's second appearance was to Mary Magdalene, and Joanna, and Mary the mother of James, and other women, who had prepared spices to embalm his sacred body. (*Matthew 28:1-10; Luke 24:1-12*). His third appearance was to the two disciples, as they went into the country on their way to Emmaus. (*Mark 16:12, 13; Luke 24:13-35*). He was afterwards seen by Peter, (*1 Corinthians 15:5*). He was afterwards seen by James, (*1 Corinthians 15:7*). He was then seen by the ten apostles, Thomas being absent, (*John 20:19-24*). Eight days afterwards he was seen by all the eleven apostles, (*John 20:26-29*). He was next seen by his disciples at the sea of Tiberias. There were seven apostles present on that occasion, (*John 21:1-14*). He was also seen at one time by more than five hundred brethren, (*1 Corinthians 15:6*). Perhaps it was on this occasion that he ascended to heaven in the sight of the men of Galilee. Paul also, on his way to Damascus, perhaps about two years later, saw him in his resurrection body, and conversed with him. In these interviews with his disciples, they had every opportunity to be certified of his being truly the risen Saviour. There is no reason to believe that the evangelists have told us all the instances in which Christ was with his friends. Both John and Luke would lead us to this conclusion, (*John 20:30; Acts 1:3*). Christ conversed with them. The pious women held his feet and worshipped him. These witnesses saw him walk; they heard his arguments and his reproofs; they saw his wounds; they received both his command to spread his gospel, and his blessing. Infidelity itself has never impugned the competency of the witnesses. Their testimony was not built on rumour, on the report of others, but on what was submitted to their own senses and observation.

3. The testimony of these witnesses agrees. Some mention things that others did not see or hear; but all agree that he rose from the dead, and that they saw him in his resurrection body. There is no contradiction between the witnesses. They agree in all things of which they speak. The early infidels laboured to find out some contrariety in their testimony, but their labours were a singular compound of ignorance and malice.

4. The witnesses, by lives of humility, benevolence, uprightness, and self-denial, proved that they were good men, and their word could be relied on. There is an almost universal belief that the apostles were pious men, and afraid of offending God, which they would have done by fabricating falsehood. It is not even pretended that any of them ever amassed fortunes by maintaining that Jesus had

risen. They lived and died poor men. The sublimest of the apostles was willingly a tent-maker. Jesus forewarned all his followers that adherence to him was the highway to poverty. These witnesses too were banished, stoned, slain with the sword, and crucified. They were hated of all men; ignominy was heaped upon them. They foresaw it would be so, and they were not disappointed. They were not in quest of fame, or ease, or pleasure. They counted it joy to suffer reproach for Christ. They hailed with composure the fire and sword of persecution. "There were no motives to corrupt them … It is evident that nothing desirable in this world had the least influence on the apostles. Nay, on the contrary, whatever was terrible to nature discouraged them. They suffered all temporal evils, even death itself, for this testimony." The enemies of the Christian religion do commonly admit all this. The way of weakening this testimony is by such insinuations as these:

1. The witnesses were unlettered and unphilosophical men. Suppose this were true, it would not prove that they were not good witnesses. Science and literature do not qualify men to tell the truth respecting a matter of fact occurring before their faces. But men who could speak all the languages of their times ought not to be held up to the world as liable to contempt for their ignorance. And men who have revolutionised the moral sentiments of mankind must have had something better than mere science. Such men were capable of being witnesses.

2. Some have said the apostles were credulous, and so are not worthy of confidence. But the whole history shows that they were not credulous. Mark says they "believed not." (*Mark 16:11*). Again, on the next declaration of the fact, he says: "Neither believed they them." (*Mark 16:13*). Again: "He appeared unto the eleven as they sat at meat, and upbraided them with their unbelief and hardness of heart, because they believed not them which had seen him after he was risen." (*Mark 16:14*). Indeed, Christ often reproved their slowness to believe on this point. The whole history shows that they were not credulous. Notice here the unfairness of these infidels. When we state how slow Christ's followers were to believe his resurrection, some say, Why did they doubt, if the evidence was good and sufficient? Then when we give the reasons of their hesitancy, and show that finally the evidence was complete and to everyone satisfactory,

we are told that they believed only because they were easy of belief. One of these statements destroys the other. Neither is true.

3. But some have said that the witnesses in this case, and especially the apostles, were fanatics, and therefore not to be believed. It is freely admitted that a well-established charge of fanaticism must impair confidence in any testimony; but who has adduced the slightest evidence of the truth of such a charge in this case? It is no evidence of wild enthusiasm to believe an extraordinary yet possible thing when it is proven to us. It is no evidence of fanaticism to say that we are witnesses of what we thus believe. Fanaticism relies on impulses and unaccountable impressions. It pays no just regard to evidence. But the apostles appealed to well-known facts. They said, "Ye know" so and so. "These things were not done in a corner." "We testify that which we have seen." This is not the language of madmen. Fanatics are proud, and boastful, and arrogant. All history shows that the apostles were humble, meek, and modest men. They avoid all needless allusion to themselves. They record their own imperfections. They praise not themselves. The chiefest of them says he was "not worthy to be called an apostle;" that he was "the least of all saints;" yea, that he was "the chief of sinners." Fanatics could never have sent forth a system claiming to be divine, and accompanied with such evidences as to deceive such men as Milton, Locke, Boyle, Bacon, and Newton, and a large portion of the most enlightened nations of the earth, for the last eighteen hundred years.

But it is worthy of notice that the Jews at first generally denied Christ's resurrection. They said that while the soldiers were asleep, his disciples stole away his body. This story cannot be believed for the following reasons:

1. The guard at the sepulchre was unusually large – as large as Christ's enemies desired it should be. (*Matthew 27:65, 66*).

2. It is wholly incredible that a guard, a large guard of Roman soldiers, should be asleep on their posts. The season of the year, at least during the night, was cool. The penalty for falling asleep on guard was death.

3. The dead body of our Saviour could have done nothing in producing the belief that he was alive.

4. During the hours that Christ lay in the sepulchre, his disciples spent their time very much in mourning and weeping. (*Mark 16:10*).

It is incredible that this company of unarmed, dispirited, heart-broken followers of Jesus Christ should have laid and executed a plan to rescue the precious body of their Lord from a trained and armed soldiery.

5. The testimony of these soldiers, as eventually given, was wholly incompetent; for it related to a fact which they said occurred when they were asleep.

6. Their testimony, as first given, was full and satisfactory in favour of our Lord's resurrection. Of the two stories they gave out we are at full liberty, yea, we are bound, to believe the one that they told without "large money."

If Jesus Christ was not the Son of God, and did not rise from the dead, then he was a gross deceiver. Nevertheless, his followers, in that case so cruelly misled, were willing to lay down their lives for him. Is not that very strange?

If Jesus Christ did not rise, then a few men, who never had nor claimed any political power, any fortune, any favour with civil rulers, were able to convince hundreds of thousands of Greeks, Romans, and Hebrews, that one who suffered as a malefactor, was the Saviour of men, and yet all in the teeth of evidence to the contrary.

If Jesus Christ did not rise, then we must believe that millions have "madly suffered imprisonments, tortures, and crucifixions, to spread an illusion."

If Jesus Christ did not rise, then it is true that "ten thousand miracles were wrought in favour of falsehood."

All admit that Christ died. Yet "his death is incomparably a greater wonder than his resurrection." Surely it is less to be expected that "the Son of God, who originally possessed immortality, should die, than that the human body united to him should be raised to a glorious life." "It was not possible" that he should have been holden of death. (*Acts 2:24*). His eternal power and godhead forbade it. Divine justice required his resurrection that his innocence might be vindicated.

*   *   *

Many important truths, essential to the comfort of a Christian life, are suggested and confirmed by this discussion:

1. The resurrection of Jesus Christ incontestably proves that in nothing was Jesus an impostor.

2. Christ's resurrection clearly manifests his divinity and his Sonship with God. If he raised himself from the dead, he must have been divine. If he claimed to be equal with God, and the Father and the Spirit co-operated in his resurrection, then he was equal with God, for God would not work a miracle to establish a lie. Paul says expressly that he was "declared to be the Son of God with power," that is, in a powerful manner, "by the resurrection from the dead." (*Romans 1:4*).

3. Christ's resurrection gave ample proof of the completeness of his satisfaction to the law and justice of God. So Paul argues: "Who was delivered for our offences, and was raised again for our justification." (*Romans 4:25*). "Who is he that condemneth? It is Christ that died, yea rather, that is risen again, who is even at the right hand of God, who also maketh intercession for us." (*Romans 8:34*). Paul says "the God of peace … brought again from the dead our Lord Jesus." (*Hebrews 13:20*). He was the God of peace because his justice had been fully satisfied. "His death appeased God, his resurrection assures men … Justice incensed, exposed him to death; and justice appeased, freed him from the dead."

4. If Christ rose from the dead, so shall his people. "Now is Christ risen from the dead, and become the first-fruits of them that slept." (*1 Corinthians 15:20*). He is "the first-born from the dead." "If we believe that Jesus died and rose again, even so them also which sleep in Jesus will God bring with him." (*1 Thessalonians 4:14*). "Our Saviour's victory over death was obtained by dying, his triumph by rising again. He foiled our common enemy in his own territories, the grave." We shall be raised "in the likeness of his resurrection." (*Romans 6:5*). Our vile bodies shall be fashioned like unto his glorious body. (*Philippians 3:21*).

5. If we would know the fulness of the blessings of eternal life hereafter, we must know the power of Christ's resurrection here. (*Philippians 3:10*). One of Whitefield's best sermons is on this subject.

6. On the fact and doctrine of Christ's resurrection depend all our hopes for eternity. So the apostles taught, (*1 Peter 1:3, 4*). There is no room for doubt here. We cannot yield this point without surrendering all that is worth contending for.

7. How wonderful is that providence of God, which permitted death to come by man, and which arranged that by man also should come the resurrection of the dead. (*1 Corinthians 15:21*).

8. The Bible is true. Christianity is divine. Its author was the Son of God. Obedience to him is required, and is most reasonable. Will you believe and obey the Son of God?

16

Christ's Ascension and Session at God's Right Hand

THE first step in Christ's exaltation was his resurrection; the second, his ascension to heaven; the third, his sitting at the right hand of God. Having considered the first, let us now meditate on the other two.

I. His Ascension

1. Our Lord, having risen, did not at once ascend to heaven, but remained on earth forty days. (*Acts 1:3*). By this delay:

(1.) He would give his followers all reasonable proof of his humanity: "Behold my hands and my feet, that it is I myself: handle me, and see; for a spirit hath not flesh and bones, as ye see me have. And when he had thus spoken, he showed them his hands and his feet." (*Luke 24:39, 40*). Long after his ascension to heaven, the last surviving apostle testifies: "That which was from the beginning, which we have heard, which we have seen with our eyes, which we have looked upon, and our hands have handled, of the Word of life … declare we unto you." (*1 John 1:1, 3*).

(2.) Christ would give all reasonable satisfaction concerning the reality of his resurrection. This he did in many ways, calling one poor doubter to reach forth his finger and behold his hands, and to reach forth his hand, and thrust it into his side. (*John 20:27*). Indeed he showed himself alive after his passion by many infallible signs. (*Acts 1:3*).

(3.) Christ remained on earth for a season that he might aid his disciples in recovering from the terrible shock which their faith had received at the crucifixion, and that he might further confirm and instruct them in the nature and things of his kingdom. "These are the words which I spake unto you, while I was yet with you, that all things must be fulfilled, which were written in the law of Moses, and in the prophets, and in the psalms, concerning me. Then opened he their understanding, that they might understand the Scriptures." (*Luke 24:44, 45*).

2. Prophecy required the ascension of our Lord, and the Scripture cannot be broken. So we read, "God is gone up with a shout, the Lord with the sound of a trumpet." (*Psalm 47:5*). "Thou hast ascended on high, thou hast led captivity captive: thou hast received gifts for men; yea, for the rebellious also, that the Lord God might dwell among them." (*Psalm 68:18*). Of this prediction we have an inspired and so an infallible interpretation given by Paul in *Ephesians 4:8-13*. Daniel foretold the same thing: "I saw in the night visions, and, behold, one like the Son of man came with the clouds of heaven, and came to the Ancient of days, and they brought him near before him. And there was given him dominion, and glory, and a kingdom, that all people, nations, and languages, should serve him," etc. (*Daniel 7:13, 14*).

Our Lord himself often foretold his own ascension: "I go unto the Father." (*John 14:28*). "I go my way to him that sent me." (*John 16:5*. See also *John 1:51*). Much more did he say to the same effect. So that beyond all doubt several predictions, running over the space of at least a thousand years, required that Christ should ascend to God.

3. With the prophecy, the historic record well and fully agrees. Neither Matthew nor John in the gospels bearing their names record Christ's ascension. Yet it is declared in four books of the New Testament. The testimony of Mark on the subject is, "So then after the Lord had spoken unto them, he was received up into heaven, and sat on the right hand of God." (*Mark 16:19*). In his gospel Luke says, "And he led them out as far as to Bethany, and he lifted up his hands, and blessed them. And it came to pass, while he blessed them, he was parted from them, and carried up into heaven. And they worshipped him, and returned to Jerusalem with great joy: and were continually in the temple, praising and blessing God." (*Luke 24:50-53*). In *Acts 1:9-11*, we read: "And when he had spoken these things, while they beheld, he was taken up; and a cloud received him out of their

sight. And while they looked steadfastly towards heaven as he went up, behold, two men stood by them in white apparel; which also said, Ye men of Galilee, why stand ye gazing up into heaven? this same Jesus, which is taken up from you into heaven, shall so come in like manner as ye have seen him go into heaven." In *1 Timothy 3:16*, Paul says he was "received up into glory." Thus the record agrees with the prediction and explains it.

4. On the south-east side of Jerusalem, and separated from it by the valley of the brook Kidron, is a mountain-ridge running north and south. Its summit is about half a mile from the wall of the holy city. For many thousand years it has been famous for its olive-trees, and from the days of Samuel to the present time it has been called Olivet, or the Mount of Olives. (*2 Samuel 15:30*). Over this David fled weeping, as he retired from his palace in the rebellion of Absalom. The road to Jericho and the Jordan crosses this ridge. At its base on the west lay the ever-famous garden of Gethsemane. On its eastern slope was the retired village of Bethany, so often favoured with the presence of the Saviour. Often did he cross Olivet. This mount, which rises about two hundred feet above Jerusalem, is chosen by Zechariah either as the place or the emblem of great and terrible judgments. It witnessed many of the wonders and mercies and sufferings of our Lord. From it he ascended. Tradition attempts to mark the spot whence he arose; but all this is uncertain. On this mount he had beheld the holy city and wept over it. At its base he had been sorrowful and very heavy; yea, "his sweat was as it were great drops of blood falling down to the ground." It had witnessed his human weakness and his dreadful sufferings. At his ascension, it witnessed his triumph and amazing glory. Here he had fought with the powers of darkness. Here he now "made a show of them openly."

5. From Olivet Christ ascended to heaven. His going to heaven is expressly said to have been necessary: "Whom the heaven must receive until the times of restitution of all things." (*Acts 3:21*). God's purpose, the truth of prophecy, and the fitness of things, required Christ's ascension into heaven. Mark says: "He was received up into heaven." Luke says: "He … was carried up into heaven." Christ himself says: "No man hath ascended up to heaven, but he that came down from heaven, even the Son of man, which is in heaven." (*John 3:13*).

In *Acts 1:11* we have the words of the angels: "This same Jesus, which is taken up from you into heaven, shall so come in like manner as ye have seen him go into heaven." Stephen saw "the heavens opened, and the Son of man standing on the right hand of God." Paul warns masters to be kind and gentle, and gives this as a reason, "knowing that your Master also is in heaven." (*Ephesians 6:9*). Again: "Our conversation is in heaven; from whence also we look for the Saviour, the Lord Jesus Christ." (*Philippians 3:20*). Again: "Christ is not entered into the holy places made with hands, which are the figures of the true; but into heaven itself, now to appear in the presence of God for us." (*Hebrews 9:24*). Peter also says, "He is gone into heaven." But Paul says he is "made higher than the heavens." (*Hebrews 7:26*). This mode of speech may have reference to the Jewish idea of three heavens – first the aerial heavens, and then the starry heavens. Christ is made higher than these heavens, and has entered the third heaven, often called the heaven of heavens.

6. When we speak of Christ ascending, we speak of his human body and human soul. His divine nature fills, and has always filled, heaven and earth. Essentially it fills all space, is confined to no place, but pervades immensity. When Christ was walking here on earth, he spoke of the Son of man as being then in heaven. (*John 3:13*). At all times this was true of his divine nature, and of it only. The effect of this exaltation on the human nature of Christ was not to annihilate it, not to sublimate it so that it ceased to be human nature, but to glorify it, to crown it with glory and honour. When Saul of Tarsus saw him, soon after his ascension, he shone with a lustre above the brightness of the sun. The vision produced blindness, which was miraculously healed. About sixty years later John saw him, and he fell at his feet as dead. The ordinary mode of explaining this wonderful change in the appearance of Christ is that, while he was here on earth, his glory was veiled. At his transfiguration the veil was taken away, and his raiment became white and glistering. In heaven there is no veil, no covering. The glory shines out brightly, and nothing obscures it.

7. The manner of Christ's ascension is worthy of our attention. Christ ascended not figuratively, but literally; not spiritually, but corporeally; not insensibly, but visibly. His disciples saw him ascend to heaven as clearly as they saw him on the cross, or on the

ship, or at the seaside. He ascended in a cloud. No one has told us how bright that cloud was, or what was its appearance; but it was like the cloud in which he will come to judgment. (*Acts 1:11*). Nor was he taken away suddenly. He was seen to leave the earth, and seen for some time after he left it. They gazed upon him as he went up. His ascension was triumphant. Forty-three days before he had ridden into Jerusalem on the colt of an ass. He now ascends triumphantly into the heavenly Jerusalem. He left the world speaking words of encouragement and benediction to the humble. The first nine sentences of his Sermon on the Mount began with the word *blessed*. The last thing he ever did on earth was, to pronounce a blessing on his people. His ascension to heaven was in every way glorious. His appearance was doubtless such. And his retinue was first the heavenly host of angels. In *Acts* mention is made of but two angels having been seen. But the prophecy which expressly foretells his ascension begins by saying, "The chariots of God are twenty thousand, even thousands of angels: the Lord is among them as in Sinai, in the holy place." (*Psalm 68:17*. Compare verse *18* and *Ephesians 4:8-12*). The law on Sinai was given by angels. The Saviour shall come to judgment with his angels *in like manner* as he left the world. Our Lord's ascension was in every way a joyous event, and was so regarded by his disciples, as Luke expressly informs us. It was the blessed fruit of his sufferings and obedience. And it was witnessed by a sufficient number of competent and credible witnesses, not less than five hundred. (*1 Corinthians 15:6*). No man has ever suggested a plausible pretext for anyone saying that he had seen him ascend, unless it was true.

II. His Sitting at the Right Hand of God

This is the third measure of our Lord's reward; the third step in his exaltation.

This was required by prophecy. David had said: "The Lord said unto my Lord, Sit thou at my right hand, until I make thine enemies thy footstool." (*Psalm 110:1*. Compare *Luke 20:42, 43; Hebrews 1:13*). Both Peter and Paul prove that this applies to Christ. Christ himself foretold the same thing when he was in the hands of his murderers: "Hereafter shall the Son of man *sit on the right hand* of the power of God." (*Luke 22:69*).

This session at the right hand of God is much spoken of in Scripture. Mark says, he "sat on the right hand of God." (*Mark 16:19*). Paul says, God "set him at his own right hand in the heavenly places." (*Ephesians 1:20*). Peter says, he "is on the right hand of God." (*1 Peter 3:22*).

1. The question then arises, What is the import of the phrase, "sitting at the right hand"? The word *sitting* does not teach that our Lord's body is always in a sitting posture. Indeed, mere posture is not referred to at all. Peter and Paul, each once, simply say, he "is *at* the right hand of God." And Stephen, dying, saw "the Son of man *standing* on the right hand of God." (*Acts 7:56*). Standing is a posture in which one is ready to receive another, or give him assistance. This was just what Stephen needed.

(1.) The first thing taught by Christ's "*sitting* at the right hand of God" is that he now has quiet repose. He is entered into his rest. He hath ceased from his own works. Thus says Micah: "They shall *sit* every man under his vine and under his fig-tree; and none shall make them afraid." (*Micah 4:4*). So in *Revelation*: "To him that overcometh will I grant to sit with me in my throne, even as I also overcame, and *am set down* with my Father in his throne." (*Revelation 3:21*). It is right that after toil should come rest; after war, peace. After the conflict, both Christ and his people rest from their labours and sorrows.

(2.) The term *sitting* also denotes permanency of abode and possession. Thus it is said, "Asher continued [literally, *sat*] on the sea-shore," (*Judges 5:17*); that is, he had permanent possession of that country. Christ has rest and a permanent abode and a rightful possession in heaven.

(3.) Sitting also expresses authority and dominion. "Sit thou at my right hand, until I make thine enemies thy footstool," (*Psalm 110:1*), is parallel to "He must reign till he hath put all enemies under his feet." (*1 Corinthians 15:25*). It is not meet that the king should stand in the presence of his subjects, even of those admitted nearest to his throne.

(4.) Sitting is also a fit posture for a judge. Solomon speaks of "a king that *sitteth* in the throne of judgment." (*Proverbs 20:8*). Speaking of Christ, Isaiah says: "In mercy shall the throne be established: and he shall sit upon it in truth in the tabernacle of

David, judging, and seeking judgment, and hasting righteousness." (*Isaiah16:5*). And he shall not fail nor be discouraged till he have set judgment in the earth; yea, "he shall judge the poor of the people, he shall save the children of the needy, and shall break in pieces the oppressor." (*Psalm 72:4*).

2. Sitting, being, or standing *at the right hand* is figurative. God has no bodily parts. He uses such language in condescension to human weakness. The figure is one of frequent use in the Scriptures. Jacob put his right hand on the head of Joseph's younger son wittingly, to give him the greater blessing. In *Psalm 80:17* are these words: "Let thy hand be upon the man of thy right hand, upon the son of man whom thou madest strong for thyself." What is the import of the figure?

(1.) The hands are the chief instruments of human bodily power, and by reason of use the *right hand* is commonly the stronger of the two. It is a fit emblem of strength, and is often used to denote the almighty power of God. Thus in Moses' song: "Thy right hand, O Lord, is become glorious in power: thy right hand, O Lord, hath dashed in pieces the enemy." (*Exodus 15:5*). So Jesus Christ, at the right hand of God, has all power. He is able to do all his will.

(2.) With the right hand gifts were commonly bestowed and received. So when Christ ascended up on high he received gifts for men, and for himself glory and dominion. (*Ephesians 4:8*).

(3.) The right hand of regal power is by men esteemed a place of enjoyment. As such it is much sought after. So in *Psalm 16:11*, which much relates to Christ, we read: "In thy presence is fulness of joy; at thy right hand there are pleasures for evermore." Our Saviour is no longer "a man of sorrows." Grief reaches him no more.

(4.) The right hand, according to Hebrew ideas, is the post of honour. When Solomon would confer peculiar honour on his mother he caused her to sit on the right hand of his throne. (*1 Kings 2:19*). To say that Christ is on the right hand of God is to declare that he is exalted by his Father to great dignity and glory. This corresponds with the declaration of Paul in *Philippians 2:9*. Our translation is, "God hath highly exalted him." The Syriac is, "God hath multiplied his sublimity." The Arabic is, "God hath heightened him with a height." Justin renders it, "God hath famously exalted him." God has heard his prayer and glorified him with himself, with the glory which he had with the Father before the world was. Yes, "we see Jesus crowned with glory and honour." (*John 17:5; Hebrews 2:9*). To a higher degree of rest, and rule, and bliss, and favour, and power, and majesty, Christ could not be raised.

In this glorious state Jesus Christ executes all the mediatorial offices. He is the great Prophet of the church. With him is the residue of the Spirit. By his Spirit he convinces the world of sin, of righteousness, and of judgment. We may not say, as some do, that the Spirit was purchased by Christ, much less that he is the minister of Christ. The Holy Ghost is "free." (*Psalm 51:12*). He has no guide or counsellor. He is equal with the Father and the Son. He is sovereign in all his acts. (*1 Corinthians 12:11*). He cannot be purchased either with money, or tears, or blood. But there is a glorious harmony in the counsels of the Trinity. The Holy Ghost proceeds from the Father and the Son. There is no diversity of counsel or of will in the Godhead. On the day of Pentecost Peter said, "Jesus, being by the right hand of God exalted, and having received of the Father the promise of the Holy Ghost, he hath shed forth this, which ye now see and hear." (*Acts 2:33*). So the Holy Ghost is the Spirit of Christ. He enlightens our minds, works faith in us, and saves us. Christ also raises up, qualifies, and sends forth every real, genuine gospel minister. He is head over all things to the church.

In his exalted state Christ continues to be our Priest. He makes, indeed, no more offerings; but he gloriously intercedes for us. The glory of his intercession may be learned from these facts: 1. The person of the intercessor is ineffably gracious; 2. He is the delight of his Father; 3. His intercession is full of authority; 4. It always prevails; 5. It is alone; 6. It continues for ever.

In his exaltation Christ is also a King. In this his great glory is: 1. His kingdom is spiritual, and so has its seat in the hearts of his people. 2. It is wholly ordered in truth, and equity, and righteousness. 3. It is as stable as the throne of God. 4. It is for ever and ever.

*   *   *

1. We have a right to expect the conversion of all God's chosen. Native depravity and long-continued habits of sinning may seem to render a change of heart hopeless; but because Christ is *sitting at*

God's right hand, his *people shall be willing in the day of his power.* (*Psalm 110:1, 3*).

2. There will be no failure in the completion of all God's plans and schemes: "The Lord at thy right hand shall strike through kings in the day of his wrath. He shall judge among the heathen … He shall drink of the brook in the way: therefore shall he lift up the head." (*Psalm 110:5-7*).

3. The church is safe. Her Head is exalted, and he loves her, and bought her with his blood. He has graven her on the palms of his hands. Her success depends on an arm full of power, on grace that is infinite, on intercession never unavailing. Humble and exclusive confidence in the Captain of our salvation can never be disappointed.

4. To what a glorious state believers in Christ are rapidly tending. Heaven, the heaven of heavens, the third heaven, paradise, the new Jerusalem, the city of God, are some of the names by which the glory of the spirits of just men made perfect is shadowed forth. The glory of that blessed world is, that the Lamb is the light thereof. We shall be like him, for we shall see him as he is. Our vile bodies shall be fashioned like unto his glorious body. We shall be for ever with the Lord.

5. Hearty and universal submission and obedience to Christ are both reasonable and obligatory. Submit we must, either joyfully unto salvation, or reluctantly unto destruction. Now men may affect, and even feel, contempt for religion and its Author: but those are shallow thinkers who do not know that inconsiderate courage soon gives way to appalling dismay, while sober apprehension prepares the mind for the worst. No cries for mercy will be more loud, no shrieks of anguish will be more piercing, no moanings of despair will be more heart-rending, than those uttered at the last by men who all their lives made light of eternal things. If you are yet in your sins, one of two things is true – either your conscience is at perpetual and fear-ful war with your practice, or you have embraced some error which strips life of dignity and death of hope.

17
Christ in Heaven

PIOUS souls feel a profound interest in the person, life, and glory of Christ. Let us consider him in his exaltation; and the benefits received from him by his people.

I. Christ in his exaltation.

1. His exaltation is deserved. He has merited all the honour and glory he has. He is the only one who has in the highest sense earned all that he has received of God. Originally possessed of infinite perfection, and freely consenting to great humiliation, his merit consists in his perfect obedience to the law, and in his bearing its curse for us. Holy angels have never sinned against God; but they owed all the obedience they have ever rendered. None but Christ has ever supererogated. All Christ merited for us was as our Mediator, was by a blessed covenant with his Father, and was through the gift by grace, which has abounded unto many. (*Romans 5:15*). He is worthy to live and reign for ever.

2. Christ's life is immortal. He was dead, but he dieth no more. (*Romans 6:5*). He says, "I am he that liveth, and was dead; and, behold, I am alive for evermore." (*Revelation 1:18*). It is greatly to the joy of the child of God that his Saviour can be spat upon no more, can be wounded no more, can be crucified no more, can be laid in the sepulchre no more. He hath immortality.

3. Christ's exaltation is very glorious. His very scars are resplendent with light and radiance. Soon after his ascension Saul of Tarsus saw him, and his light was above the brightness of the sun, and such was the glory that it covered the persecutor's eyes with scales. John says,

"I saw ... in the midst of the seven candlesticks one like unto the Son of man, clothed with a garment down to the foot, and girt about the paps with a golden girdle. His head and his hairs were white like wool, as white as snow; and his eyes were as a flame of fire; and his feet like unto fine brass, as if they burned in a furnace; and his voice as the sound of many waters. And he had in his right hand seven stars; and out of his mouth went a sharp two-edged sword: and his countenance was as the sun shineth in his strength, And when I saw him, I fell at his feet as dead." (*Revelation 1:12-17*). Among all the bright objects in glory, far the brightest is the Son of man, the Son of God, our great deliverer. There is no mistaking him for another, or another for him, in that bright world above.

4. Christ's exaltation is full of authority. He has the keys of hell and of death. (*Revelation 1:18*). On his vesture and on his thigh is a name written – King of Kings, and Lord of Lords. (*Revelation 19:16*). He is far above all principality, and power, and might, and dominion, and every name that is named, not only in this world, but also in that which is to come. (*Ephesians 1:21*). He is the head of all principality and power. (*Colossians 2:10*). Indeed, before his ascension he said, "All power is given unto me in heaven and in earth." (*Matthew 28:18*). Blessed be God, our Saviour sways the sceptre of universal empire. There is none above him. He is Lord of all. He has no rivals. He shall never be superseded.

5. And yet his love is unchanged. Great is the change in his state; but he is as meek, as lowly, as gentle, as tender-hearted as when he gave his face to spitting and his back to the smiter; as when he cried, "Learn of me;" as when he set a little child as the model he would have us copy; as when he wept at the grave of Lazarus; as when he prayed for his own murderers. Change of state has not changed his heart, his love to his people, or his pity for sinners.

6. Christ's exaltation is full of holy action. He is not sunk down into the repose so much celebrated in Hindu theology. His rest, like that of the spirits of just men made perfect, is consistent with eternal activity. His toils, and sorrows, and weariness are over. But his energy and operations remain.

He is still executing the offices of Prophet, Priest, and King. No man knows the Father but as the Son reveals him. He ever liveth to make intercession for us. "He must reign till he hath put all enemies under his feet." He feeds, and guides, and protects all his people. He is the Angel that leads Israel in all the wilderness, and in the heavenly mansions.

Wherever and whenever a sinner is made penitent and is pardoned, it is by and through him. For he is on the hill of Zion to grant repentance and remission of sins. He leads his chosen like a flock. He gathers the lambs in his arm and carries them in his bosom. He is present at every closet of secret devotion. He hears all our weeping and supplications. He says: "I will not leave you comfortless: I will come to you." "He that loveth me shall be loved of my Father, and I will love him, and will manifest myself to him."

He is present at every social meeting of his people, however small it may be. Two or three are enough to claim the fulfilment of his promise. (*Matthew 18:20*). To all such gatherings he says, "Whatsoever ye shall ask in my name, that will I do, that the Father may be glorified in the Son. If ye shall ask any thing in my name, I will do it." (*John 14:13, 14*).

He is no less present at all our solemn assemblies. When he sent forth his disciples to preach the gospel to every creature, he said, "Lo. I am with you alway, even unto the end of the world." (*Matthew 28:20*). Many a time his servants have failed to meet their appointments; but our Lord has always been true to his word.

He is always ready to help his people in their temptations. His promise is: "My grace is sufficient for thee." Never, in any case, does he fail to make good his engagement. A thousand times would their feet slip, and their profession be covered with reproach, but for his timely aid and succour. His *peace* is their solace when Satan roars. (*John 14:27*).

He is also with his chosen in sorrow. Into deep affliction he often brings them. There for a long time he often keeps them. But never does he leave them to bear their sorrows alone. For intrepid consistency in fearing God the three faithful Hebrews were cast into the burning fiery furnace. But though its intense heat consumed those who cast them in, yet the smell of fire was not on their garments. Not a hair of their heads was singed. Nor are we at a loss to account for their preservation. The tyrant of Chaldea, though a heathen, found out the cause of their preservation: "Then Nebuchadnezzar the king was astonished, and rose up in haste, and spake, and said unto his counsellors, Did not we cast three men bound into the midst of the fire? They answered and said unto the king, True, O king. He answered and said, Lo, I see four men loose, walking in the midst of the fire, and they have no hurt; and the form of the fourth is like the Son of God." (*Daniel 3:24, 25*). This explains the whole mystery, not only of this, but of all cases of Christian endurance. The presence of Christ shut the mouths of the lions, that they hurt not Daniel. It made Paul and Silas pray in the jail at Philippi, and sing praises, so that the prisoners heard them. Ten thousand times it has converted deserts into Bethels and dungeons into sanctuaries.

The Lord Jesus also receives all departing saints. He said he would, (*John 14:3*); and he keeps his word. Not a soul of a believer passes out of time but Jesus does for it what he did for Stephen in his dying hour, though he does not always before death give like full evidence of his being at the gate of heaven ready to put forth his hand and take in his dove.

Christ is also building the heavenly Jerusalem. In the Divine purpose, this blessed abode was prepared from the foundation of the world. So also has its location long since been determined. But ever since his ascension, the Redeemer has been enlarging and beautifying it, and bringing the glory of the nations into it. To his sorrowing disciples he said, "I go to prepare a place for you. And if I go and prepare a place for you, I will come again, and receive you unto myself; that where I am, there ye may be also." (*John 14:2, 3*). In a sense, the works of creation were finished from the foundation of the world. (*Hebrews 4:3*). Yet Providence has in a thousand ways made great changes here. Had sin never entered, there is no telling to what heights of advancement things would before this have been carried on our globe. As there is no sin in heaven, and as there is the abode of the Redeemer, and as there is the city of the living God, we know not what its glory is. Of this city we know some things, though the half is not told us. It is the city of the great King. It is his abode. He is its Builder and Maker. It is stable. It hath foundations. (*Hebrews 11:10*). It is the true "Zion, the city of our solemnities … Jerusalem, a quiet habitation, a tabernacle that shall not be taken down; not one of the stakes thereof shall ever be removed, neither shall any of the cords thereof be broken. But there the glorious Lord will be unto us a place of broad rivers and streams; wherein shall go no [enemy's] galley with oars, neither shall gallant ship pass thereby." (*Isaiah 33:20, 21*). It is the city of truth, (*Zechariah 8:3*); the perfection of beauty, (*Lamentations 2:15*); the city of praise and joy. (*Jeremiah 49:25*). "Great is the Lord, and greatly to be praised in the city of our God, in the mountain of his holiness." (*Psalm 48:1*). It is the city of righteousness. (*Isaiah 1:26*). All its inhabitants are righteous. The fearful, and unbelieving, and the abominable, and murderers, and whoremongers, and sorcerers, and idolaters, and all liars are shut out of its pure precincts. (*Revelation 21:8, 27*). Inside of its walls are no sickness, no poverty, no sorrow, no weeping, no tears, no crying, no pain, no death, no curse. (*Revelation 21:4; 22:3*). This too is the greatest of all cities. Babylon was fifteen miles square; but this city is represented as twelve thousand furlongs, or fifteen hundred miles square. (*Revelation 21:16*). This is the capital of Immanuel's dominions, that great city, the holy Jerusalem, having the glory of God. Her light is like unto a stone most precious, even like a jasper-stone, clear as crystal. (*Revelation 21:10, 11*). The walls of this city can never be scaled. "The length and the breadth and the height of it are equal." (*Revelation 21:16*). They are walls of salvation, impregnable, girt with omnipotence. (*Isaiah 26:1*). In it is no temple; for the Lord God Almighty and the Lamb are the temple of it. And it has no need of the sun, neither of the moon, to shine in it: for the glory of God did lighten it and the Lamb is the light thereof. Nor is it a desolate, uninhabited city; for it has in it the nations of them that are saved. Nor is it a poor, mean city; for the kings of the earth do bring their glory and honour into it. (*Revelation 21:22-24*).

II. The benefits received from Christ in his exaltation. These are expressed very forcibly in the last gospel: "Because I live, ye shall live also." (*John 14:19*).

1. Because he lives and reigns, all who believe shall be justified. Now if any rises up to condemn us, we cry, "It is Christ that died, yea rather, that is risen again, who is even at the right hand of God, who also maketh intercession for us." (*Romans 8:34*). As he rose from the dead, so are believers risen with him from the death of sin. (*Colossians 3:1*). He sat not down at the right hand of God, till he

had by himself purged our sins. (*Hebrews 1:3*). As the expiation of Christ was complete and perfect, so is the justification of all who have fled to him.

2. By the life of Christ his people are sanctified. We are dead – dead to the world, dead to sin – and our life is hid with Christ in God. When Christ, who is our life, shall appear, then shall we also appear with him in glory. (*Colossians 3:3, 4*). Christ is made of God unto us sanctification. (*1 Corinthians 1:30*). The Spirit of Christ, sent into our hearts by the Saviour, purifies them. In so doing, he puts great honour on the death and life of Christ by using them as means and motives of our purification. (*Colossians 3:1*).

3. Sometimes the word *live* seems to be nearly synonymous with *being happy;* as where Paul says, "Now we *live,* if ye stand fast, in the Lord." (*1 Thessalonians 3:8*). So we live and are happy because Christ lives and is happy. He is beyond the reach of malice or misery. For thousands of years it has been for a song in Israel: "If we be dead with him, we shall also live with him: if we suffer, we shall also reign with him: if we deny him, he also will deny us: if we believe not, yet he abideth faithful: he cannot deny himself." (*2 Timothy 2:11-13*). Though we see him not, yet believing that he lives and is blessed, we live and rejoice with joy unspeakable and full of glory.

4. By Christ's present glorious life, believers have every encouragement. They are fully authorised to expect that, as he has overcome and sat down with his Father on his throne, so they shall overcome, and sit down with Christ on his throne. (*Revelation 3:21*). It is a reasonable duty and a great help to *look unto Jesus,* and to *consider him* that endured such contradiction of sinners against himself, lest we be wearied and faint in our minds. All good hopes spring from the cross and centre in the person of Christ.

5. By Christ's living and reigning above, the natural life of believers is continued and made safe as long as is on the whole best. Each child of God is immortal till his work is done. The very hairs of his head are all numbered. Every believer may say to every persecutor as Christ said to Pilate: "Thou couldest have no power at all against me, except it were given thee from above." (*John 19:11*). Every lion is chained. Not a dog can move his tongue against God's people, unless God gives permission. (*Exodus 11:7*). Daniel never spent a night more safely than that he spent in the lions' den.

6. It is by the life of Christ that the bodies of all his people shall be raised to life and beauty. So teach all the Scriptures: "Thy dead men shall live, together with my dead body shall they arise. Awake and sing, ye that dwell in dust: for thy dew is as the dew of herbs, and the earth shall cast out the dead." (*Isaiah 26:19*). "Now is Christ risen from the dead, and become the first-fruits of them that slept." "As we have borne the image of the earthy, we shall also bear the image of the heavenly." (*1 Corinthians 15:20, 49*). Christ's resurrection put the resurrection of his people beyond all doubt. Each one may shout and sing: "I know that my Redeemer liveth, and that he shall stand at the latter day upon the earth: and though after my skin worms destroy this body, yet in my flesh shall I see God: whom I shall see for myself." (*Job 19:25-27*).

7. By the life of Christ his people are fully saved. So argues blessed Paul: "While we were yet sinners, Christ died for us. Much more then, being now justified by his blood, we shall be saved from wrath through him. For if, when we were enemies, we were reconciled to God by the death of his Son, much more, being reconciled, we shall be saved by his life." (*Romans 5:8-10*). No man can find in mathematics more conclusive and irrefragable argument than this.

8. Because Christ lives, all his people have and shall have everlasting life. They cannot be condemned, because they are accepted in the Beloved. They cannot be overcome, because he overcame. They cannot fail of eternal life, because they hold their title to it through the merits of him that sits on the throne. If they could fail of salvation, Jesus would fail of his reward; for they are the purchase of his agonies.

*   *   *

1. Humility well becomes the saints. They are less than the least of all God's mercies. In themselves they are poor creatures, yea, they are nothing. Christ is all. He is their life. It is easy for us to esteem Christ too little and ourselves too much; but it is not possible for us to think too much of him, and too little of ourselves. In a life of faith, the more we think of Christ, the lower do we put ourselves. We cannot be too low in self-esteem. The Lord giveth grace unto the humble. Wisdom is with the lowly.

2. The true, blood-bought, blood-washed church of God is safe. She is loved by her Redeemer, and he is strong. The high priest

carried the names of the twelve tribes inscribed on his breastplate. But his church is graven on the palms of the hands of her Redeemer. (*Isaiah 49:16*). If a dying Saviour could redeem, a living Saviour can give the victory.

3. The ministers of Christ have a peculiar interest in this subject. Let them hope in him for ever. Each of them may say as Cyprian: "While I oversee the church, Christ oversees me." Most of the promises personally made by Christ when on earth were first made to his ministers, and through them to all believers.

4. God's people are truly blessed. With them all is right. Nothing can harm them, nothing can destroy them, because they are in Christ, and he lives for ever. If they die, they sleep in Jesus. If they leave this world, they go to be with Jesus. He is everything to them. A pious, sorrowful widow used to say, "Jesus lives!" Once a wretched state of nerves and a sore surprise for the moment seemed to rob her of courage, and she burst into tears. Her little child, who knew her habits of cheerfulness and the ground of her courage, recalled her to her trust by saying, "Mamma, is Jesus dead?" The child supposed nothing could go wrong in life if Jesus lived. The mother was thus reproved, and regained her Christian heroism. So blessed are the people of God, that even in this world a company of believers could not in a day or a year count up their privileges.

Some time ago, a number of eminent servants of Christ were together, and each one was asked to repeat as sweet a text of Scripture as he could then think of. One said: "Unto you therefore which believe he is precious." This is, indeed, refreshing. Another said, "God so loved the world that he gave his only begotten Son, that whosoever believeth in him should not perish, but have everlasting life." What an eternal rock is this! Another, since gone to glory, said: "We know that all things work together for good to them that love God, to them who are the called according to his purpose." Another gave this as his text: "God is love." Another this: "As the Father hath loved me, even so have I loved you." Another said: "Jesus Christ, the same yesterday, and today, and for ever." Such a string of pearls might be made ten times as long, and yet it would be but the beginning of all that God has said and done for his people.

5. But how sad is the state of the wicked. Instead of promises and assurances, the Scriptures are full of woes and threatenings to such,

saying, "They shall not see life;" "God is angry with the wicked every day;" that Christ the judge of all will say, "Depart accursed;" that the Most High will laugh at their calamity, and mock when their fear cometh; and that they shall endure "the wrath of the Lamb." The Bible gives whole chapters to show the necessity and the dreadfulness of the doom of impenitent men. See (*Ezekiel 15; Isaiah 14; Matthew 25*). Surely the wicked must turn or burn; must repent now or mourn for ever; must embrace Christ or embrace death. The very truths and principles which secure the eternal life of the righteous, make certain the eternal death of the wicked.

18

Christ's Personal Absence from this World

THE family of Christ was the most interesting society that ever existed on earth. Most of its members were remarkable characters; and the head of this household was the most wonderful person that ever appeared in any world.

In such a brotherhood we should look for affecting scenes. Nor are we disappointed. It is not rash to say that the last interview, before the crucifixion, between Christ and his disciples, was as tender and overpowering as any of which the human mind can form a conception. While inspiration employs no epithets to characterise it, we yet have the substance of what was said and done. The chief source of affliction to the disciples in the upper chamber, where for the last time they celebrated the Passover, and for the first time partook of the Lord's Supper, was the prospect of their Master's leaving them. To prepare their minds for this event, he said many soothing things, yet did he not conceal the fact of his departure: "I go away;" "I go unto my Father;" "I tell you the truth; it is expedient for you that I go away." (*John 14:3, 12; 16:7*).

The subject of Christ's absence from the visible church is in many respects one of great interest, and has always been made to hold an important place in Christian doctrine, and in pious meditations. Their belief on this point greatly affects men's comfort and efficiency.

From the best views we can get, it is clear that it was in itself proper that our Lord should go to his Father when he did. In proof it may be said:

That it is fit and right that honour should succeed faithful and eminent service, and that the highest honours should follow so distinguished services as those rendered by Jesus Christ. This is the Scriptural method of speaking on this subject: "When thou shalt make his soul an offering for sin, he shall see his seed, he shall prolong his days, and the pleasure of the Lord shall prosper in his hand. He shall see the travail of his soul, and shall be satisfied." (*Isaiah 53:10, 11.* Compare *Philippians 2:7-9*).

It was right that Moses, after serving God and his generation, should enter upon his reward; but Moses was a mere servant, and an imperfect one too. He owed all the obedience he ever rendered. But Christ was a Son, and his whole work was in the highest sense voluntary. Yet in the form of a servant he rendered perfect and blameless obedience. He never once failed. Truly did he say to his Father, "I have glorified thee on the earth." He brought to God such a revenue of honour as none else in heaven or earth ever did or can do. Well, therefore, might he say, "Now, Father, glorify thou me:" in the presence of all thy creatures, let suitable honours succeed my humiliation. If angels, who owe all the obedience which they render, are crowned with heavenly glory, how much more proper that Christ should receive honour and glory from God. If he who so pre-eminently merited the richest gifts of God had failed to receive them, how could poor sinners, though they believe in him, hope for anything good?

Moreover, ever since Christ's incarnation, a large majority of his real people have been in heaven, and it seems proper that as their bliss and glory are in and through Christ, he should be personally with them, and by his presence make them glad. From the days of righteous Abel to the time of Christ, there was a long succession of pious men, who believed in the Redeemer, and walked with God. They endured much for his name. They loved him. They saw his day approaching and rejoiced in it. They were as dear to Christ as the people of God in any age could be. They were saved by his blood. And there were many of them. Even in one nation, and when there was a great apostasy, God says there were seven thousand who had not revolted to idol-worship. What number of souls before Christ's birth were saved, none can tell; but beyond a doubt far more of the redeemed have for long centuries been in heaven than have been living on the earth at any one time. Is it not proper that the great body of Christ's followers, who are in heaven, should enjoy his personal presence? Is he not their light and life and glory? Is he not the admiration of all his saints? Yes; the Lamb is the light of that bright world. His presence fills it with radiance and effulgence. His ascension brought to it a vast accession of gladness. It may then be asked, Would it be proper that we upon earth, a mere handful, should have his bodily presence, while all heaven should be left without it? Blinded as we are by ignorance and sin, even we may see a fitness in this arrangement. Surely it is right that the great cloud of witnesses, who have, in ages of darkness long gone by, stood in their lot and fought the good fight, should have with them the great Captain of salvation and rejoice in his fulness and glory, even though we, who for the trial of our faith remain on the earth, should be deprived of his blessed presence.

Besides, it seems proper that one having so vast dominions should dwell in the capital of his empire. Christ's authority and government are over all creatures and all worlds. This earth is a mere speck in creation. It probably constitutes not a millionth part of the intelligent universe. Since sin has entered, this world has become peculiarly unfit for the residence of anyone in a glorified state. Much less is it suited to be the great centre of influences in the kingdom of God. When Christ was in the world, it was in a way of voluntary exile from his proper home and country. One thing we know: he has chosen another part of the universe for the seat of his throne; having fixed the centre of his kingdom there, it is right that he should not seem to desert it.

It is also expedient for Christ's people on earth that he should not be in this world, but in heaven. Suppose that he were here; he must be here either in glory or in humiliation; either bearing the signs of majesty and divinity which now attend him in heaven, or in apparent weakness, his godhead covered with a thick veil, and himself appearing much like other men. If here in glory, who could abide his coming? His brightness is intolerable to the eyes of mortals. Even when Moses had been in the mount but forty days, conversing with God and beholding his glory, his countenance acquired such brightness that upon his coming among the people it was necessary that he should put a veil upon his face. They could not look upon him. Yet

Moses was a mere man, and a sinful man too. How then could we, with open face, behold the KING in his glory? Isaiah saw Him in a vision before His incarnation, and the sight so overpowered him as to make him cry out, "Woe is me! for I am undone; because I am a man of unclean lips, and I dwell in the midst of a people of unclean lips: for mine eyes have seen the King, the Lord of hosts." (*Isaiah 6:5; John 12:41*). When Christ was transfigured before his disciples, and his raiment became shining, even his most intimate friends who were present became "sore afraid," so much so that Mark says Peter "knew not what to say." If the transfiguration produced such terror even on bosom friends, how could the mass of men, even of good men, while in the body, endure his divine effulgence?

From these and like known facts, it is apparent that a full vision of Christ's unveiled glory would not be to us, in our present state, tolerable. In his *History of Redemption*, Edwards properly says: "It is not to be supposed that any man could subsist under a sight of the glory of Christ's human nature as it now appears." At such a vision we should, like Saul of Tarsus, become blind; or like John, as dead men. Should Christ, therefore, be personally present on earth for our good, it could not be in his glorified condition, but in a state of humiliation. And is it right that the Son of God should again humble himself and assume the form of a servant? If he should reappear in a lowly state on earth, where would be the assurance that his faithful followers shall ever be glorified? The servant may not expect more honour than the Master; the disciple will not rise higher than his Lord. How then could we believe that our glorification should ever come and never cease, if Christ should be brought back to earth in a lowly condition? Verily it is expedient for us that Christ, having overcome, should sit down on his Father's throne, and thus certify us that when we shall have overcome we shall sit down with him on his throne.

Nor is this all. If Christ were here in person, that is, in his human nature, in any state in which we could bear his presence, it is evident that he could not be everywhere on earth at once. Ubiquity belongs not to manhood in any state. Christ's human nature possesses not the attribute of omnipresence. If then he were here, he must at any one time be in some particular place in a sense in which he could not be in other places. Then, in order to enjoy his bodily presence, the whole church must be assembled in one spot or vicinity, and thus the perishing nations would be left without the light of holy examples and gospel preaching; or the Saviour would of necessity travel over the earth, visiting every portion of the world; and even then many of his devoted followers would never see him. The sick, and the poor, and the prisoner would be among the less favoured of his followers. Thus would be created continual dissatisfaction in the church, some thinking one place too highly favoured, and others neglected. Indeed it is very probable that, blind as we are, all the pious now feel the Saviour to be nearer to them than they would if he were anywhere upon earth. Is not this view of the matter just and important?

There is still another thought upon this subject. The absence of our Saviour is the means of furnishing an excellent test of character. In the parable of the talents, our Lord seems to teach this doctrine. He represents himself as one "travelling into a far country," and "after a long time coming and reckoning with his servants." In this way all motives except those arising from genuine love to him lost their force; and if his servants were not sound at heart, they would demonstrate their true character by disregarding his will; and if they really loved him, their devotion to his interests would not die out as he left them. Eye-servants are often very industrious when their master is looking on; but faithful servants are governed by higher principles. Their controlling purpose is to do right, whether they are applauded, or neglected, or blamed. Our Lord alludes to this matter when he says, "Blessed are those servants, whom the lord when he cometh shall find watching: verily I say unto you, that he shall gird himself, and make them to sit down to meat, and will come forth and serve them … But and if that servant say in his heart, My lord delayeth his coming; and shall begin to beat the men-servants and maidens, and to eat and drink, and to be drunken; the lord of that servant will come in a day when he looketh not for him, and at an hour when he is not aware, and will cut him in sunder, and will appoint him his portion with the unbelievers." (*Luke 12:37, 45, 46*). No man ever loved Christ who did not love him present or absent; and all must admit that cheerful and uniform obedience to him in his absence is to us and to our neighbours the best proof we can give of sincere attachment to his cause and his person.

Furthermore, if Christ were here upon earth in an humble state, would not the feelings of his people be continually mortified and deeply wounded by the direct insults and personal indignities offered him by his foes? The world is in no better humour with holiness than it ever was. Christ's presence on earth would be a continual and sharp rebuke to the abounding wickedness of every age and country; and those who are in love with sin, and determined not to forsake it, would bear reproof no better now than formerly. To a good man, what could be more trying than to have continual slanders uttered respecting the daily conduct of his Saviour, and to know that wicked conspiracies were constantly forming against his person? Even if all plots should be defeated by miracle or otherwise, it would still keep the church in deep distress to witness fearful exhibitions of deadly malice against the Beloved. Or if the Lord were here and invulnerable, his friends would be subjected to unusual and dreadful persecutions for cleaving to One whose light terribly condemned the world. Now the Christian rejoices that, however malevolence may vent itself against Christ, he is for ever beyond its reach. May not this explain what he means by that saying, "If ye loved me, ye would rejoice, because I said, I go unto the Father?" (*John 14:28*).

Again, in Christ's absence faith has full scope for exercise; whereas, were he present we should walk somewhat at least by sense, and not by faith only. Any arrangement friendly to the vigorous growth of faith is advantageous to the pious. It was, indeed, a great privilege to be able with the disciples to say: "We have seen with our eyes … and our hands have handled of the Word of life." Compared with ages preceding, the lifetime of our Saviour afforded great privileges to the godly. Nor is it asserted that faith and sight necessarily destroy each other; but we may say that faith has now fewer obstacles to overcome than if Christ were here. For then it would not be easy to separate, or even distinguish emotions awakened by sight from those which spring from a living faith. In the days of our Lord's flesh many, moved by what they saw, outwardly became his followers. Though they had no pious confidence in him, nor reliance on him, yet they mistook their strong feelings for true piety; but the root of the matter was not in them. Under one pungent discourse many such forsook him. (*John 6:66*). It is indeed true that the distance of the sun makes it appear to us very small; but by the aid of science, we learn his dimensions and know its vastness. Now faith is "divine reason," as Leighton calls it. It corrects the errors of sense. It teaches us firmly to believe, and on the best grounds – the Word of God – that the Sun of Righteousness is far more glorious than we can conceive; and of course more glorious than we could possibly apprehend by our senses. Foster well says that it is "evident that to see the Messiah in his personal manifestation was a mode of contemplating him very inferior, for the excitement of the sublimer kind of affection, to that which we have to exercise by faith. It is true that to those who regard him as nothing more than a man, all this will appear impertinent and fantastic. But those who solemnly believe that their salvation depends on his being infinitely more, will feel the importance of all that gives scope to their faculties for magnifying the idea of their Redeemer." Now that he is in heaven "we have no exact and invariable image, placing him before us as a person that we know; exhibiting him in the mere ordinary predicament of humanity." Now "we can with somewhat more facility give our thoughts an unlimited enlargement in contemplating his sublime character. Thus also we are left in greater freedom in the effort to form some grand though glimmering idea of him as possessing a glorious body, assumed after his victory over death. Our freedom of thought is more entire for arraying the exalted Mediator in every glory which speculation, imagination, devotion can combine to shadow forth the magnificence of such an adored object."

Our Saviour himself has pronounced a special blessing on those who believe without sight. To Thomas he said, "Because thou hast seen, thou hast believed: blessed are they that have not seen, and yet have believed." (*John 20:29*). This settles the point. We may fearlessly assert that the present arrangement is more advantageous to believers, however weak their faith, than if our Lord had continued on earth after his resurrection, or were now to return again to this world.

We should not forget that no carnal view of Christ is profitable to the soul. Thousands saw him, conversed with him, travelled with him, ate with him, heard his sermons, witnessed his miracles, and were as little profited as if he had been a common man. It is a remarkable fact that no picture of our Saviour was ever taken, fables to the contrary notwithstanding, and that we have no reliable description of his stature, of his figure, of his gait, of his complexion, or of anything respecting his personal appearance. The Bible says, "his visage was so marred more than any man, and his form more than the sons of men;" and there it leaves the matter, as if to warn us not to indulge in carnal thoughts of him.

If an artist should give to the church a perfect likeness of our Saviour, as he appeared in the days of his flesh, he might indeed lead many into idolatry; but he would render no real service to any true believer. It is as true of the Son as of the Father that he who worships him must worship him in *spirit*. Does anyone seriously believe that our spiritual conceptions of the glory and grace of Christ would be in the least aided by the knowledge of anything respecting his outward appearance as a man?

It is enough for us to know that the Son of man is glorified, and that he shines with a brightness above the brightness of the sun. His is a "glorious body."

Nor should we forget that our Saviour assigns yet other reasons for leaving his disciples: "I go to prepare a place for you;" "I tell you the truth; It is expedient for you that I go away: for if I go not away, the Comforter will not come unto you; but if I depart, I will send him unto you." (*John 14:2; 16:7*). The great promise of a copious descent of the Spirit is in importance second to none ever made. The Holy Ghost is God, has all divine perfections, has never been incarnate, works in the church unseen, yet mightily. He is essentially everywhere present, he is infinitely loving and tender, and in all respects suited to apply the work of redemption. He comes not to speak of himself, but he takes of the things of Christ, and shows them. He glorifies Christ. (*John 16:13-15*).

Should any inquire why Christ's abode on earth was inconsistent with the abundant gracious presence of the Holy Spirit, we might, perhaps, without irreverence, assign certain reasons of fitness in the case, drawn from the nature of things. We might dwell upon the fact that the word *Comforter* and the word *Advocate* are in the original the same word, that both the second and the third persons of the Trinity are called Advocates or Comforters, and both make intercession for us, though in different ways. (*John 16:7; 1 John 2:1; Hebrews 7:25; Romans 8:26*). It seems proper that so long as a part of the church is above and a part below, one of the Advocates or Comforters should be on earth, while the other is in heaven. We need not speculate, but rest the whole upon Christ's word – that if he went not away the Spirit would not be poured out. He lays this down as an ultimate, though certain truth. The church may not expect the personal presence of Christ, and the copious effusion of the Holy Ghost at the same time. There were days of Pentecost when our Lord was on earth, but none of them was marked by the descent of the Spirit, like a mighty rushing wind, converting thousands in a day. All the glorious revivals witnessed since Christ's ascension, have been in consequence of his absence from the church below. He said: "He that believeth on me, the works that I do shall he do also; and greater works than these shall he do; because I go unto my Father." (*John 14:12*). The blessed Spirit comforts ten thousands, yea, ten millions of hearts at once, filling with joy the souls of believers, at the same hour, in different parts of the world. This is better than Christ's personal presence on earth. The Spirit is in all, through all, over all. He is just such a Comforter, just such an Advocate, as the church militant needs. His presence may revive ten thousand churches at once, and each of them be as much blessed as if his visit was to it alone.

* * *

1. The present arrangement of all things concerning the church is the best. If there ever was a point respecting the expediency of which the pious might have doubted, it was Christ's leaving them on earth. Yet even his personal followers lived to see that this dark event was for the best. Man, with his ignorance and folly, will never be able to suggest any improvement in God's method of governing the world and saving the church. It is best that Christ should be on the other side of Jordan and beckon us over. Rays of heavenly brightness from the upper world light up our darkness even in our passage to eternity. The Sun of Righteousness gilds the path of dying saints. The departing believer now rejoices that he is going to his Saviour. Death is far less dismal than it would be if, in leaving earth, we were going away from the blessed Redeemer.

Besides, after the High Priest has shed his blood, what is so proper as that he should go into the holy of holies, sprinkle the mercy-seat, appear for us in the presence of God, and execute the full work of intercession for his chosen?

As things now are, Christ is the great attraction to heaven and heavenly-mindedness.

2. Let the people of God everywhere and always rejoice in a Saviour risen and made higher than the heavens. Let them do this in adversity as well as in prosperity. Bates says: "One of the sorest and most dangerous temptations of the afflicted is, that they are out of God's favour. The mourning veil darkens the eyes of their minds, that they cannot reconcile his gracious promises with his providential dispensations, the good things he hath prepared for hereafter with the evil he sends here. Gideon complained to the angel, 'If God be with us, how comes all this evil to us?' Augustine introduces God as thus addressing his afflicted and tempted child: 'Is this thy faith? Did I promise temporal prosperity to you? Were you made a Christian that you might flourish in this world?'" Blessed be God, who has said, "As many as I love, I rebuke and chasten." God had one Son in this world without sin, but never a son here without affliction. His promise is, I will bring them through the fire, and they shall be refined as gold and silver is tried; and they shall say, The Lord is my God. (*Zechariah 13:9*). If it were expedient for the Master to leave the disciples, surely it is no great stretch of faith to believe that it may be for our good that friends, and health, and prosperity, and reputation should leave us. He who overrules for good the heaviest losses will not permit lesser ones to do us harm.

3. All things are now ready for the conversion of sinners and for subduing the world to knowledge, to love, and to obedience. The atonement is finished. Christ has made an end of transgression. His work has been owned and accepted before heaven and earth. His ascension was a public triumph in the presence of angels and men. In it he led captivity captive, and received gifts for men. The chiefest of the mercies he sends down to accompany pardon of sin and acceptance is the sanctifying, enlightening, and comforting presence of the Holy Ghost. In God's government, all obstacles to the salvation of sinners who will believe have been removed. The propitiatory has been sprinkled with precious atoning blood. It is now indeed a mercy-seat, and it is accessible to all the guilty sons of men who are willing to bow before it; so that we may now proclaim aloud: "Let us come boldly unto the throne of grace, that we may obtain mercy, and find grace to help in time of need."

(*Hebrews 4:16*). If we need more grace, more liveliness in our affections, more success in our labours, we have access to God. The door is open to poor, perishing men, the guilty and the helpless. Let them only look and live, believe and be saved.

19
Christis on the Judgment-Seat

THE fourth and last step in Christ's exaltation is yet future. It consists in his coming to judge the world.

No man knows that he will ever see the sun rise or set again; but it is certain that everyone shall see the Son of man coming to judgment, and witness the solemn transactions of the last day.

Conscience forebodes a solemn reckoning. She says it will be right and fair to have a final settlement of all things. The resurrection of Christ from the dead gave assurance of a judgment-day. (*Acts 17:31*). It is in itself proper that God should show to the whole universe that in all things he has done right. This can fitly be done in the assizes of an assembled world. The doctrine of a Day of Judgment was not a secret to any of the prophets. Enoch foretold it as clearly as any apostle. The author of *Psalm 1* says: "The ungodly shall not stand in the judgment;" and the author of *Psalm 50* gives a full account of its awful grandeur, and of the principles on which its awards shall be made. Solomon says: "God shall bring every work into judgment, with every secret thing, whether it be good, or whether it be evil." (*Ecclesiastes 12:14*). Time would fail us to show how often and clearly Christ himself, and Paul, and James, and Peter, and John speak of such a day. This solemn subject now claims attention.

I. God hath appointed a day in the which he will judge the world. Respecting this day several things are noticeable.

1. *To God it is a day certain.* He has *appointed* it. (*Acts 17:31*). Nothing can hasten it: nothing can retard it. The purpose of God concerning it is fixed, unalterable.

2. *To all creatures it is a day uncertain:* "Of that day and hour knoweth no man, no, not the angels of heaven." It is clear from the teachings of Scripture, that God designed that no conjecture should be formed by any generation of men respecting the precise time of the judgment. Twice is it said, it will come as a thief in the night, (*1 Thessalonians 5:2; 2 Peter 3:10*. Compare *Matthew 24:36, 42, 44; Luke 21:35, 36*).

3. The Day of Judgment will be *the great day*. So inspired men often call it. It will be the greatest day in the annals of the universe. It is the day for which all other days were made. There will be more done that day than was done perhaps for thousands of days, or even years, of former times. This day is so well known to inspired men, that they call it *the day, that day,* as pre-eminent over all others.

4. It will be *the day of the Lord*. (*2 Peter 3:10*). Christ will then appear in his glory. On that day men will not question his divinity, or his humanity, or his authority. Then he will be crowned Lord of all. It will be exclusively his day.

5. It will be *the last day*. It is so called by Christ himself, (*John 6:39, 40*). After it, time will be no longer. Duration will no more be measured by seconds, minutes, days, months, years, centuries, cycles; but all will be boundless, shoreless, fathomless, unmeasured eternity.

6. It will probably be a *long day* – how long we are not informed, but long enough to answer all the purposes for which it was appointed, displaying God's justice, vindicating the right, condemning the wrong.

7. It will be a *very bright day*. Other days had their dawn, their twilight, and their clouds; but this day will begin, continue, and end in ineffable effulgence. They had their light from the sun; but this will have its light from the brightness of Immanuel.

8. It will be a *day of unusual noises:* "The Lord himself shall descend from heaven with a shout, with the voice of the archangel, and with the trump of God." The heavens shall pass away with a great noise. To these shall be added the shouts of the redeemed and the wailings of the impenitent.

9. It will be a *day of wonderful clearing up* of the character of the innocent. God will then bring forth their righteousness as the light and their judgment as the noonday. The slandered will that day have

the sting of calumny for ever removed; the persecuted will no longer clank their chains; those with whose lives and liberties witnesses, juries, judges and rulers treated so cruelly, will no more fear the minions and myrmidons of cruelty.

10. It will be a *day of astounding exposures.* Villainy will be covered up no more. Every disguise will be taken away. There is nothing covered that shall not be revealed; neither hid, that shall not be known. Indeed, there never was anything kept secret, but that it should come abroad. (*Luke 12:2; Mark 4:22*). "Some men's sins are open beforehand, going before to judgment; and some men they follow after." (*1 Timothy 5:24*).

11. It will be a *day of unwonted grandeur:* "Our God shall come, and shall not keep silence: a fire shall devour before him, and it shall be very tempestuous round about him. He shall call to the heavens from above, and to the earth, that he may judge his people." (*Psalm 50:3, 4*). For majesty and glory, for sublimity and grandeur, the pomp of all other days shall, in comparison with this, be as nothing. If Felix trembled when Paul merely reasoned of judgment, how will sinners tremble when Christ shall come to judgment?

12. From first to last it shall be a *day of miracles.* "All the wonders ever exhibited before will be nothing to the wonders of this day. Indeed, all that is natural will end on this day, and everything will be miraculous."

13. Of course it will be a *day of intense excitement.* There will be no listless spectators of those scenes. Every faculty of the intellect and of emotion will be aroused to the highest possible exercise. Men may sleep under sermons concerning the judgment, but they will not be dull when they go to judgment.

14. It will also be *a day of separation.* The precious and the vile, the wheat and the tares, the sheep and the goats, saints and sinners, shall no longer mingle together. The separations of this day will be final. The righteous and the wicked shall part that day to meet no more.

15. It will be *a day of decision.* The tribunal of Christ is the court of last resort. Causes and destinies will be inquired into no more. Saved that day, saved for ever. Lost that day, lost for ever. Holy that day, holy for ever. Filthy that day, filthy for ever.

16. It will be *a day of triumph.* Christ and his people will fill the heavens with their peals of exultation. At his ascension from Olivet

the Redeemer went up with a shout. (*Psalm 47:5*). He shall come to judgment with a shout. (*1 Thessalonians 4:16*). His return to heaven will be with vehement notes of triumph still louder. When the Israelites brought the ark of the covenant into their camp they shouted with a great shout, so that the earth rang again. But when all the elect shall receive their welcome plaudit, their shout shall fill the heavens with its thunder.

17. It shall be *a day of despair* to all sinful creatures. The last hope will be gone from fallen angels and incorrigible men. Everywhere sinners will be crying to the rocks and the mountains: "Fall on us, and hide us from the face of him that sitteth on the throne, and from the wrath of the Lamb." (*Revelation 6:16*). Was ever despair more dreadful than this?

18. This will be *a day full of surprise.* Not only will it come unexpectedly, but its awards will fill saints and sinners with astonishment. So Christ teaches at length in *Matthew 25.* The wicked will be amazed *that* they are lost, and *how* they are lost. They will be especially surprised that God sets no value on their self-righteousness. The sons of God will receive more honour than they ever asked or thought of. The sons of Belial will receive more wrath than they ever feared. Christians will marvel why they *are* saved. Sinners will wonder why they are *not* saved. Each class of persons will cry, "Lord, when saw we thee an hungred, or athirst, or a stranger, or naked, or sick, or in prison?" Many will be saved and more perhaps be lost contrary to the judgments formed of them by their neighbours. But more will be saved and more will be lost contrary to the opinions they had formed of themselves.

II. The Bible says on that day God will judge *the world.* In the Greek Testament are three words rendered *world.* One of these signifies duration past, present, or future, but often with a limit. It is the word used by our Saviour when he speaks of "this world," of "that world," of "the end of the world," and of "the world to come." In this way of using it, it is equivalent to age. In the plural it often signifies eternity. It is never used to teach whom God will judge.

A second word, rendered world, is of frequent occurrence. It is found in *Acts 17:24:* "God that made the *world* and all things therein." Here it evidently means the universe; so also in many other cases. Often it means the earth, and then its inhabitants. It is often used in connection with the judgment. In *Romans 3:6* it is said: "God shall judge *the world.*"

But in *Acts 17:31,* "He hath appointed a day in the which he will judge *the world,*" yet another word is used for *world.* In *Luke 21:26* it is rendered *the earth;* in all other cases, *the world.* In *Luke 2:1,* it is put for the Roman empire, because that embraced most of the known world. But commonly it means *the habitable earth.* It occurs fifteen times, and, with the exception already noticed, is uniformly rendered *the world,* as when Jesus says, "This gospel of the kingdom shall be preached in all the world for a witness unto all nations." (*Matthew 24:14*).

The Scriptures declare that all men shall be judged. The Lord "shall judge the earth," "shall judge the ends of the earth," "shall judge the people," shall judge "all nations," "shall judge them that are without," "shall judge his people," "shall judge the righteous and the wicked," "shall judge the quick and the dead."

Other Scriptures say that angels shall be then judged. Christ shall bring all his holy angels with him. (*Matthew 25:31; Mark 8:38; Luke 9:26*). They shall be the reapers on this great harvest-day. (See also *2 Peter 2:4*). It seems to be intimated that all angels, fallen and unfallen, all men, saints and sinners, great and small, quick and dead, shall be judged. All rational creatures shall make up the assembly. The servant and his master, the prisoner at the bar and the judge that sat on his trial, the assassin and the assassinated, the seducer and his victim, the invader and the invaded, the hireling and his oppressor, the king and his subjects, the fool and the wise man, the persecutor and the persecuted, the apostate, the hypocrite, the child of God and the child of the devil, the angels that stood and the angels that fell, shall all be there. No rational creature shall be so mighty, no mortal shall be so mean as to elude the eye or the sentence of him that shall sit upon the throne of judgment.

What a mighty concourse will this be, when prophets, apostles, martyrs, confessors, saints of all ages, when sinners, liars, infidels, blasphemers, moralists, and murderers, shall all be there; when the sea and the dry land shall give up their dead, when the third heaven shall pour forth its glorious legions, when death and hell shall deliver up the dead that are in them, when all that lived before the flood, all that have lived since the flood, and all that shall have lived to the end of time shall stand before God. This will be the first and the last assembly in which may be found every rational creature that God ever made.

III. This great assembly shall be judged in righteousness. No injustice shall be done. Even the condemned will have nothing to allege against the equity of their doom. Every mouth will be stopped. The evidence will be full, the record complete. For "the books shall be opened:"

1. The volume of nature. It shows forth the eternal power and godhead of the Most High. Its lessons are taught everywhere. "There is no speech nor language, where their voice is not heard." So that all men are "without excuse." (*Psalm 19:3; Romans 1:20*).

2. There is the book of providence. How many disregard all its lessons! They despise the riches of God's goodness, and forbearance, and long-suffering. They never think that his goodness should lead them to repentance; but after their hard and impenitent heart treasure up to themselves wrath against the day of wrath. (*Romans 2:4, 5*).

3. There, too, will be the book of conscience. On it is written the work of the law. Now this volume may be closed. There it will show its faithful records.

4. Then, too, will be opened the book of holy Scripture. Christ says that even infidels, who refused to believe God's Word, shall be judged by it. "He that rejecteth me, and receiveth not my words, hath one that judgeth him: the word that I have spoken, the same shall judge him in the last day." (*John 12:48*). Wilful ignorance is no excuse. Wilful rejection of the Bible enhances men's condemnation.

5. Then, too, will be opened the *book of remembrance*. Its record will be full, minute, infallible. When it is opened every sinner will say, "Innumerable evils have compassed me about: mine iniquities have taken hold upon me, so that I am not able to look up; they are more than the hairs of mine head: therefore my heart faileth me." (*Psalm 40:12*).

Thus will be revealed all forms and degrees of sin; open sin, which proclaims its guilt on earth; secret sin, which no man could prove, or without uncharitableness suspect, (*Romans 2:16*); sins of commission, which were acted out; and sins of omission, which in every case will make a formidable array. The fig-tree was cursed because it had no fruit. Indeed, in his solemn account of the judgment, in *Matthew 25,* Jesus Christ mentions no sins but those of omission. The life of man consists in thoughts, emotions, words, and deeds. For all these he shall give account.

(1.) Thoughts. "The thought of foolishness is sin." (*Proverbs 24:9*). God destroyed the old world because the imagination of the thoughts of man's heart was evil, and that continually. (*Genesis 6:5*). It is an alarming charge against the wicked that "God is not in all his thoughts." (*Psalm 10:4*). "The thoughts of the righteous are right." (*Proverbs 12:5*). "The thoughts of the wicked are an abomination to the Lord." (*Proverbs 15:26*). All good thoughts and all evil thoughts shall be judged.

(2.) Emotions. Malice, lust, covetousness, envy, sinful anger, hatred, inordinate affection on the one hand; and love, hope, joy, peace, gentleness, patience on the other; all good emotions and all sinful emotions shall be tried.

(3.) Words. "Every idle word that men shall speak, they shall give account thereof in the day of judgment. For by thy words thou shalt be justified, and by thy words thou shalt be condemned." (*Matthew 12:36, 37*). Not a word, good or bad, shall be passed over. "Whatsoever ye have spoken in darkness shall be heard in the light; and that which ye have spoken in the ear in closets shall be proclaimed upon the housetops." (*Luke 12:3*). All vain, false, unchaste, impudent, provoking, profane, blasphemous speeches, and all pure, pious, loving, wise, right words, shall alike and properly be noticed.

(4.) Deeds. All our good deeds shall be reported before the Judge. And he will not wipe out our good deeds that we have done. (*Nehemiah 13:14*). To the ungodly Jehovah will give "according to their deeds, and according to the wickedness of their endeavours: give them after the work of their hands; render to them their desert." (*Psalm 28:4*). "According to their deeds, accordingly he will repay." (*Isaiah 59:18*). He says: "I will recompense them according to their deeds, and according to the works of their own hands." (*Jeremiah 25:14*). The matter, the manner, the motive of every act, good and bad, will be tried.

(5.) As no man has a good thought, or feeling, or speaks a good word, or does a good deed, but by divine grace, and as in this life sin cleaves to all men so as to mar their best performances, and as all the wicked do nothing but sin, if there was no other book besides these to be opened, all must perish. But there is another. It is *the book of life of the Lamb slain from the foundation of the world.* (*Revelation 13:8*). In the other books was nothing found that could save any man. But this contains the names of all those who shall have washed their robes and made them white in the blood of the Lamb. According to this book all who believe in Christ shall be justified. They shall receive a rich, free, gratuitous salvation. But "whosoever was not found written in the book of life was cast into the lake of fire." (*Revelation 20:15*).

IV. The Judge will be the Lord Jesus Christ, called in Scripture, *the man whom God hath ordained* to that work: "For the Father judgeth no man, but hath committed all judgment unto the Son." (*John 5:22*). "We must all appear before the judgment-seat of Christ." (*2 Corinthians 5:10*). Christ shall come not only in the glory which he had with the Father before the world was, but in his glorified human nature; God has given him authority to judge, because he is the Son of man. (*John 5:27*). Christ the Lord will be the righteous Judge. Others shall approve the sentences he shall pronounce, and in this sense saints are said to judge angels. (*1 Corinthians 6:3*). But in the full sense shall Christ alone "judge the quick and the dead." (*2 Timothy 4:1*). How altered the state and appearance of the Saviour will be from what it was when he walked and wept on earth, and especially when he hung upon the cross, or lay in the sepulchre of Joseph. His coming shall be visible to all: "Every eye shall see him, and they also which pierced him." (*Revelation 1:7*). Even those born blind shall see him. Christ will come visibly, and be seen as a man. We shall behold him in human form. So he himself declared more than once: "Ye shall see the Son of man coming in the clouds of heaven." (*Matthew 24:30; 26:64; Mark 13:26; 14:62*). So testified the angels at his ascension: "This same Jesus, which is taken up from you into heaven, shall so come in like manner as ye have seen him go into heaven." (*Acts 1:11*). But Jesus ascended visibly; so will he descend visibly. He ascended in human nature entire; he shall descend in human nature entire. He shall come with great power and glory. (*Mark 13:26*).

At his presence nature shall dissolve. The elements shall melt with fervent heat. (*2 Peter 3:10*). Great signs and terror shall witness his coming: The heavens shall depart as a scroll when it is rolled together and every mountain and island shall be moved out of their places, and the kings of the earth, and the great men, and the rich men, and the chief captains, and the mighty men, and every bondman, and every freeman shall hide themselves in the dens, and in the rocks of the mountains. (*Revelation 6:14, 15*).

The sentence passed by the Judge will be solemn and irrevocable. That of the righteous will be: "Come, ye blessed of my Father, inherit the kingdom prepared for you from the foundation of the world." That of the wicked will be: "Depart from me, ye cursed, into everlasting fire, prepared for the devil and his angels." In both cases the sentence will be at once executed. (*Matthew 25:34, 41*).

*   *   *

1. Let us not be much troubled by the apparent confusion we now witness in human affairs. Here vanity often rides in splendour, while worth is clothed in rags; folly rolls in chariots, while wisdom lies in chains; brutality wields unlimited power over decency and piety; and oppression puts its iron heel on all that good men love; but the last day will set all things right. (*Ecclesiastes 2:14-17; 5:8*).

2. What a mighty argument is the Day of Judgment for a holy life. So Peter says: "Seeing then that all these things shall be dissolved, what manner of persons ought ye to be in all holy conversation and godliness, looking for and hasting unto the coming of the day of God." (*2 Peter 3:11, 12*).

3. Nothing but uprightness and consistency will stand the test of the last day, and be followed by glory and honour: "Thinkest thou this, O man, that judgest them which do such things, and doest the same, that thou shalt escape the judgment of God?" (*Romans 2:3*).

4. In his address to the people of Athens, Paul uses this subject as an argument to repentance: "God … commandeth all men everywhere to repent: because he hath appointed a day, in the which he will judge the world in righteousness by that Man whom he hath ordained." (*Acts 17:30, 31*). The call to repentance thus given is solemn and full of authority. It is a command from God. It is urgent. The judgment is coming. The Judge standeth before the door. The time is short. There is no work, nor device, nor knowledge, nor wisdom, nor repentance in the grave, whither thou goest. Some say,

God has not made us to punish us. But if they die in their sins, they will find that "He that made them will not have mercy on them, and he that formed them will show them no favour." (*Isaiah 27:11*). O drunkard, how wouldst thou look and feel if called to go raving and reeling into the presence of thy Maker and thy Judge? No drunkard shall inherit the kingdom of God. (*1 Corinthians 6:10*). And thou shameless profligate, unless thou dost speedily repent, thou wilt be for ever given over to appetites and passions which will sink thee to the lowest hell. I pray thee to repent. And thou profane man, who minglest thy Maker's name with thy ribaldry, thy passions, or thy lies, beware lest thou become one of those "that cannot cease from sin … to whom the mist of darkness is reserved for ever." Oh repent while thou mayest. Thou abuser of holy time, if thou sinnest a little longer, thou wilt be in a state where thou wouldst give ten thousand worlds for another Sabbath in a gospel church. Thou foul-mouthed man, with thy present love of sin thou canst never sing, Hosanna to the Son of David. When, on his trial, Latimer heard the pen of the notary running behind the curtain, he was careful what he said. Take heed what thou speakest. The recording angel is about. Thy words will meet thee at God's bar. Art thou an apostate? "If any man draw back," says God, "my soul shall have no pleasure in him." Tertullian says: "The apostate seems to put Christ and Satan both in the balance, and having weighed the service of each, prefers that of the devil, and proclaims him master." Surely thou must repent: "God will make his sword drunk in the blood of apostates." Finally, art thou an unbeliever, perhaps moral, serious, kind to the poor, well-behaved in the house of God, yet without living faith in Jesus? Repent, and believe the gospel, else it had been good for thee if thou hadst not been born. Let every sinner cry for mercy. Let him cry mightily, O thou Son of David, have mercy on me!

20

Christic the Good Shepherd

WITH the exception of the Egyptians, (*Genesis 46:34*), the ancients appear to have held in high esteem the occupation of shepherd. Much of the romance and poetry of antiquity related to pastoral life. It was therefore very natural for the sacred writers by a shepherd and his flock to represent the relations between rulers and their subjects, between ministers and their people, and between God and his church. There is peculiar propriety in thus setting forth the character and offices of the Saviour and the relations subsisting between him and believers. Quite a number of inspired writers employ such language. With his own blessed lips our Lord said, "*I am the Good Shepherd.*" We may here consider:

I. The *qualities* of a good shepherd, as they are found in Christ.

One of these is, *devotedness to his office.* He who would well fulfil the place of shepherd must not be idle. He holds no soft option. He must be very attentive. He has a great work on hand. This is the case when the shepherd has but a small flock, and they of little value. It is much more true when he has the care of souls. It is above all true of the Saviour of men. Who ever served God or his generation like the Redeemer? Even when on earth, he was often wearied and hungry and thirsty, yet nothing could divert him from the great business he had undertaken. In every age he has fully performed the engagement to each believer, "I will never leave thee nor forsake thee." At home and abroad, in sickness and health, in the height of prosperity and in the perfection of trouble does he attend his "little flock." He is not merely a

Saviour afar off, but also a Saviour at hand – a very present Help in time of trouble.

Another quality of a good shepherd is, *love for his office.* If his heart should be set more intently on something else, he cannot possibly succeed. If he prefers some other calling above that in which he is engaged, disaster must come on the flock. It is delightful to be able to assert, on the authority of single promises and of the tenor of Scripture, that no object in creation lies nearer the heart of the good Shepherd than the care and salvation of his flock. This was so in the countless ages of a past eternity, as he himself declares: "Then I was by him as one brought up with him: and I was daily his delight, rejoicing always before him; rejoicing in the habitable part of his earth; and my delights were with the sons of men." (*Proverbs 8:30, 31*). When he was here, "having loved his own … he loved them unto the end." (*John 13:1*). Never did he neglect one of his flock. Never did he slight his appropriate work. As one whom his mother comforteth, so does he comfort his saints. To Zion he says: "Behold, I have graven thee upon the palms of my hands; thy walls are continually before me." (*Isaiah 49:16*).

Another important quality of a good shepherd is, *watchfulness:* "Thy shepherds slumber, O king of Assyria," (*Nahum 3:18*), was among the saddest signs of Nineveh's ruin. To the church God saith: "He that keepeth thee will not slumber. Behold, he that keepeth Israel shall neither slumber nor sleep." (*Psalm 121:3, 4*).

> "Those wakeful eyes,
>   That never sleep,
>   Shall Israel keep
> When dangers rise."

"The eyes of the Lord run to and fro throughout the whole earth, to show himself strong in the behalf of them whose heart is perfect toward him." (*2 Chronicles 16:9*). It is a great mercy that God's people are so seldom allowed to fall under the temptation to believe that their way is hid from the Lord and their judgment passed over from their God. But even when Satan does gain a temporary advantage, in such a case they know that it is not for the want of loving care and tender watchfulness in their God and Saviour.

Another desirable quality in the shepherd is *wisdom*. Woe to the flock whose guide has only "the instruments of a foolish shepherd." (*Zechariah 11:15*). When the shepherd takes the whip rather than the crook, the scourge rather than the staff of Israel, when he would only drive, and not at all allure, it is sad indeed for the flock. Alas for the "shepherd that cannot understand." (*Isaiah 56:11*). But the good Shepherd employs no unwise instruments or measures. He knows what is best. He sees the end from the beginning. He understands all our case. He chargeth his angels with folly. He taketh the wise in their own craftiness. No plot is so deep, and no machination so cunning, that he cannot at once, and with infinite ease, pour confusion upon their authors.

Another necessary quality in a shepherd is *strength*. Without it the sheep are defenceless. With it they are safe. In *Amos 3:12,* we read of the shepherd taking out of the mouth of the lion the two legs of one of his sheep. With supernatural strength God endowed David, when he was but a shepherd boy, that he might deliver his flock from a lion and a bear. It may be in special reference to the power of Christ that he is called "that great Shepherd of the sheep." (*Hebrews 13:20*). He is also styled "the chief Shepherd." (*1 Peter 5:4*). In strength, as in all other good qualities, he excels all shepherds: "God hath spoken once; twice have I heard this; that power belongeth unto God." (*Psalm 62:11*). In Scripture our Shepherd is called "the mighty God." (*Isaiah 9:6*). He claims for himself the awful title, "The Almighty," (*Revelation 1:8*); and one Almighty is more than all mighties. Indeed, our Shepherd "appeared unto Abraham, unto Isaac, and unto Jacob, by the name of God Almighty." (*Exodus 6:3*).

It is a matter of no small weight that a shepherd be no intruder, but be *rightfully in his office*. This is the case with our Shepherd. Before he gave the commission under which the gospel is now preached, he assured his church, saying, "All power [authority] is given unto me in heaven and in earth." (*Matthew 28:18*). Indeed, early in his ministry he said to his disciples: "All things are delivered unto me of my Father." (*Matthew 11:27*). Even long before his advent, prophecy declared that there should be "given him dominion, and glory, and a kingdom, that all people, nations, and languages, should serve him." (*Daniel 7:14*).

No quality of a shepherd is of higher value than *love to the sheep*. This shows itself in gentleness, in constant care, in readiness to encounter danger for their defence. O how wondrously loving is our Shepherd. He is so gentle. He neither strives, nor cries, nor lifts up, nor causes his voice to be heard in the streets. When reviled, he reviled not again; when he suffered, he threatened not. How different was he from the shepherds of the flock of slaughter. They pitied not the distresses of those for whom they were bound to care. It was love; O, it was compassion like a God, that caused the Good Shepherd to lay down his life for the sheep. Some of the Roman emperors claimed to be shepherds to their people. Trajan was such a one. He sent his own raiment to bind up the wounds of his soldiers; and for that kindness many loved him. But Jesus, the Good Shepherd, had his flesh torn, and his blood shed, and his heart melted like wax, that he might heal our wounds. He has the only sovereign balm. This pity of Jesus shows itself in his readiness to receive and tenderly treat the weakest and most sickly of his flock. Continually does he fulfil the prophetic promise, "He shall feed his flock like a shepherd: he shall gather the lambs with his arm, and carry them in his bosom, and shall gently lead those that are with young." (*Isaiah 40:11*). One of the last charges of the chief Shepherd to Peter, and through him to all ministers, was, "Feed my lambs, feed my sheep, feed my sheep." Jesus never forgot the lambs. Jesus never forgot one of his sheep. When a bird, frightened by a hawk, flew into the bosom of a man, though he was a heathen he said, "I will not betray thee to thine enemy, seeing thou comest to me for sanctuary." So in time of danger the Good Shepherd loves to have his affrighted sheep come close to him and abide with him. In a sense, all times are times of danger; so we cannot cleave too closely to the Redeemer. This ardent love to the flock secures fidelity, as our Lord has said: "He that is an hireling, and not the shepherd, whose own the sheep are not, seeth the wolf coming, and leaveth the sheep and fleeth: and the wolf catcheth them, and scattereth the sheep. The hireling fleeth, because he is an hireling, and careth not for the sheep." (*John 10:12, 13*). But Jesus saw the wolf coming, and stood his ground, and laid down his life for his sheep, and saved them.

II. Let us consider the *offices* which the Good Shepherd actually performs for his people. It would do no good to a flock to have a shepherd ever so well qualified, if he exercised not himself on their behalf. Our Shepherd unceasingly seeks and promotes our good.

It is required of a shepherd that he know his flock. The words of Jesus, so full of comfort, are, "I … know my sheep, and am known of mine." (*John 10:14*). And in *verse 3* he says, "He calleth his own sheep by name." Sometimes in Scripture the word *know* has the same sense as *foreknow*. In this sense Jesus knew his people. "Whom he did foreknow, he also did predestinate." (*Romans 8:29*). He saw Nathanael under the fig-tree, and Zacchaeus in the sycamore-tree. He knew all about them. Sometimes the word *know* is equivalent to *distinguish*. In this sense, also, Christ knows his people: "The Lord knoweth them that are his," that is, he distinguishes the sheep from the goats. Sometimes to *know* denotes *familiarity*. So our Lord Jesus says: "I will come unto you;" "I will make my abode with you;" "Lo, I am with you alway, even unto the end of the world." Sometimes to *know* denotes *recognition* as of friends. So Jesus says, "Henceforth I call you not servants; for the servant knoweth not what his lord doeth: but I have called you friends; for all things that I have heard of my Father I have made known unto you. Ye have not chosen me, but I have chosen you." (*John 15:15, 16*). Besides, he himself has taught us how a good shepherd will seek a lost sheep, and rejoice over it when he has found it. Thus he illustrates the emotions awakened in heaven over a lost sinner recovered from the snare of the wicked one. And he explicitly tells us that he came to seek and to save that which was lost, and to do it by dying the death. Indeed, "All we like sheep have gone astray; we have turned every one to his own way; and the Lord hath laid on him the iniquity of us all." (*Isaiah 53:6*). With what joy each believer sings,

> "Jesus sought me when a stranger,
>   Wandering from the fold of God;
> He to rescue me from danger,
>   Interposed his precious blood."

By Ezekiel, (*Ezekiel 34:6*), God complains, "My sheep wandered through all the mountains, and upon every high hill: yea, my flock was scattered upon all the face of the earth." He then adds, *verses 12-14*, "As a shepherd seeketh out his flock in the day that he is among his sheep that are scattered; so will I seek out my sheep, and will deliver them out of all places where they have been scattered in the cloudy and dark day. And I will bring them out from the people, and … feed them upon the mountains of Israel by the rivers … I will feed them in a good pasture, and upon the high mountains of Israel shall their fold be: there shall they lie in a good fold, and in a fat pasture shall they feed upon the mountains of Israel." This, blessed be his name, is just what the Lord is doing. He is seeking and finding the lost sheep, and bringing them into his fold, and blessing them, by the thousand and the ten thousand, with his own presence and infinite mercy.

Not only does a good shepherd once gather his sheep into his fold, but when they wander he brings them back: "He restoreth my soul," says David, (*Psalm 23:3*). This is according to the whole tenor of Scripture. (Compare *Psalm 89:30-33*). When Peter strayed, Jesus sought him. When Ephraim wandered, God said, "Is Ephraim a dear son?" (*Jeremiah 31:20*).

It was one branch of a shepherd's work to go before his flock, and thus be their leader. So the good shepherd "leadeth them out, and when he putteth forth his own sheep, he goeth before them." (*John 10:3, 4*). In like manner the psalmist cries: "Give ear, O Shepherd of Israel, thou that leadest Joseph like a flock." (*Psalm 80:1*). The shepherd went before the flock to keep the sheep from going into barren or dangerous places, to guide them into green pastures and to cooling fountains, and at evening to bring them safely to their fold. O how gently the Good Shepherd leads his flock? How abundantly he supplies all their wants. The science of mathematics affords no stronger reasoning than this: "The Lord is my Shepherd; I shall not want." It was an awful charge that God brought against some of old: "Woe be to the shepherds of Israel that do feed themselves! should not the shepherds feed the flocks?" (*Ezekiel 34:2*). Surely the good shepherd will not do thus. He provides food for the body. Not a sparrow is forgotten before God. Are ye not of more value than many sparrows, O ye of little faith! Thy bread and thy water is sure. When the last handful of meal was preparing, then was the prophet sent to supply the widow with plenty. Jesus also provides for the sustenance of our souls: "My grace is sufficient for thee." There is his blessed word. There are his precious ordinances. He has made provision that by his Spirit all the appointed means shall be efficacious. In short, God denies a Christian nothing, but to give him something better.

Jesus also keeps and defends his flock. If now and then wild beasts prowl about the fold and alarm the sheep, this makes them gather the more closely around their glorious Leader. Or if, in the way of persecution, Apollyon shall let loose his dogs upon the flock of Christ to worry them, it shall only make them the more willing to remain in the fold. God controls all that seek to do his people harm. Their mouths are holden. "Hear the word of the Lord, O ye nations … He that scattered Israel will gather him, and keep him, as a shepherd doth his flock." (*Jeremiah 31:10*). The Master said, "Behold, I send you forth as sheep in the midst of wolves." (*Matthew 10:16*). Yet he adds, "Let not your heart be troubled, neither let it be afraid." (*John 14:27*). If their enemies are mighty, he is almighty; if they are cunning, he knows all things; if they muster many, he marshals all the host of heaven, and devils are subject unto him. When Christ's sheep hear his voice and know it, it is to them most cheering. For the "words of the wise," which "are as goads, and as nails fastened by the masters of assemblies," are "given from one Shepherd." (*Ecclesiastes 12:11*). The true flock of Christ has a remarkable discernment, which makes it very difficult to lead them astray. "A stranger will they not follow." Jesus accustoms them to his voice. Its gentle tones and winning sweetness bind them close to the Redeemer. He is All-in-all to them.

III. Let us observe the effect of the Good Shepherd's care over his flock. They know his voice and they follow him. His Word is quick and powerful in their hearts. His example they love to imitate. Was he benevolent? So are they. Did he go about doing good? So do they. Was he meek and lowly? They are not proud and revengeful. Their great hope and aim are that they may be like him, and see him as he is. (*1 John 3:2*). They will be satisfied when they awake with his likeness. They learn to flee to him in times of danger. His name is a strong tower; the righteous run into it and are safe. Like the conies, God's people are a feeble folk, and like the conies, their defence is in the rock. On their Shepherd they depend for everything. In him they have strong confidence, yea, great boldness in the Lord. Yet they are far removed from self-confidence. They plead no merits of their own, but plead their title to membership in his flock. Hear them of old: "So we thy people and sheep of thy pasture will give thee thanks for ever." (*Psalm 79:13*). "O come, let us worship and bow down: let us kneel before the Lord our maker. For he is our God; and we are the people of his pasture, and the sheep of his hand." (*Psalm 95:6, 7*). Other places show how these timid ones come with boldness even to the throne of grace.

IV. But what are the *marks* which Christ puts on his sheep? These are much hidden from the eye of unregenerate men. Even the chief Shepherd was not known by the wise and prudent of his day; much less do such men see the image of God on the hearts of his people. Like their Master, they are often esteemed impostors, babblers, blasphemers, madmen, possessed of devils. But still they have their marks.

1. A sheep is gentle and quiet. It is not for war. A meek and quiet spirit is, in the sight of God, of great price. The difference between a saint and a sinner is the difference between a sheep and a goat, sometimes between a sheep and a wolf. "A sheep before her shearers is dumb," though losing her fleece. God's people have a law whose spirit they love: "If any man will sue thee at the law, and take away thy coat, let him have thy cloak also." (*Matthew 5:40*).

2. A sheep is free from guile. A fox is cunning and sly; but sheep have no craft. They are artless. Of each of Christ's flock it may be said with more or less exactness, "Behold an Israelite indeed, in whom is no guile." (*John 1:47*).

3. Sheep are tractable and not heady. From their nature they are governable. God loves the obedient, not the complaining; the submissive, not the murmuring.

4. A sheep is of a cleanly nature. Its habits are quite different from those of the swine. We expect to see the sow in the mire. She loves to be there. But if the sheep is there, it is not willingly. God's people are holy. If they were as holy as they desire, they never would sin any more.

*   *   *

1. All accounts of the Shepherd's life show us that there is much intercourse between him and his flock; and that as he loves them,

so they love him. This holds in a spiritual sense. Here is a delightful theme. Christ manifests himself to his people as he does not to the world. Many a time does he come unto them, and show them his covenant. Nor are these manifestations of his grace and glory lost upon them. Their souls learn to follow hard after him. They count all things but loss for the excellency of his knowledge. Consequently, the more intercourse between Christ and his people, the better do they love him.

2. Let us never forget that there is but one Shepherd and but one fold. How careful then ought we to be not to disown any whom Christ has received. It is better, through honest mistake, to receive him whom Christ rejects, than through uncharitableness to reject him whom Christ has received. How many wicked partition walls are set up in the fold of Christ! "Is Christ divided?" It is at our peril if we wound where Christ would heal.

3. Dear Christian brethren! sheep of Christ's pasture! often seek the guidance of your Leader. Go in quest of the green pastures and the still waters. Cry mightily to God. Ask him to lead you in paths of righteousness for his name's sake. Never lose sight of the Redeemer. Constantly petition him as did the spouse of old: "Tell me, O thou whom my soul loveth, where thou feedest, where thou makest thy flock to rest at noon: for why should I be as one that turneth aside by the flocks of thy companions?" (*Song of Solomon 1:7*).

How sweet and awful is the place, with Christ within the doors. It was communion with the Redeemer before his incarnation that made Jacob exclaim at Bethel, "This is none other but the house of God, and this is the gate of heaven." (*Genesis 28:17*).

Blest Jesus! What delicious fare. How sweet thine entertainments are! All must come humbly to the mercy-seat. Set your wants before the Lord as the widow set her empty vessels before the prophet, and he will supply them all; yea, there shall not be room enough to contain the blessing. A dear young Christian mother expiring three thousand miles from the Cape of Good Hope, in the interior of Africa, sent to her mother and sister in the capital of Virginia this message: "I never have regretted coming to this land of darkness. Heaven is as near to Mosika as to Richmond." She then kissed her babe and bade farewell to earth. So do his rod and his staff comfort those who walk through the valley of the shadow of death.

4. Here the sheep and the goats often mingle together; but it shall not be so always. The chief Shepherd will appear by-and-bye, "and before him shall be gathered all nations: and he shall separate them one from another, as a shepherd divideth his sheep from the goats; and he shall set the sheep on his right hand, but the goats on the left." (*Matthew 25:32, 33*). Solemn indeed will be that day. Final and fearful will be its separations. Nothing but that which infinite purity and omniscient rectitude shall approve will stand the test of the last day. I ask not, 'Are you a rare Christian?' but, 'Are you a *real* child of God?' You may not be a splendid worshipper, but are you sound at heart? What think you of Christ? Is he all your desire and all your salvation? Do you mark his footsteps? Do you exhibit his temper? Do you love his cause? Do you die unto the world? Are you alive unto God? Be honest with yourself; the day that is coming will strip off every disguise.

> "When thou, my righteous Judge, shalt come,
>   To take thy ransomed people home,
>   Shall I among them stand?
>   Shall such a worthless worm as I,
>   Who sometimes am afraid to die,
>   Be found at thy right hand?"

21
Christ a Physician

OFTEN in Scripture is sin spoken of as a disease, a sickness, a hurt; the plan of mercy as a remedy, a balm, a healing; and God, and particularly Christ, as a Physician. (*Psalm 38:7; Isaiah 1:6; Jeremiah 8:21, 22; Hosea 5:13; Matthew 4:23; 8:17; 9:12, 35; Mark 2:17; Luke 5:31*). More just or striking figurative language is nowhere found. Men's sins make them sick. The only remedy is sovereign grace. The Physician must be divine.

Let us look at the great doctrines of the gospel under this figure:

I. *Sin is a dreadful disease.* Yea, it is the very worst disease. It was the first, and so is the oldest malady. It infected man very soon after his creation. The devil was a murderer from the beginning. (*John 8:44*). For nearly six thousand years sin has committed its ravages and been gaining inveteracy. No other disease is so old.

Sin is also a universal disease: "All have sinned, and come short of the glory of God." "There is none righteous, no, not one: there is none that understandeth, there is none that seeketh after God. They are all gone out of the way." (*Romans 3:10-12, 23*). Other maladies have slain their thousands; this has slain its tens of thousands. The whole world is a graveyard, full of spiritual death and corruption. No mere man ever lived without sin. As soon as we begin to act we begin to transgress.

Not only is every man sick, but our whole nature is diseased. "The understanding is darkened;" the memory is polluted; the imagination of the thoughts of the heart is only evil continually; the throat is an open sepulchre; with their tongues men use deceit; the poison of asps is under their lips; their mouth is full of cursing and bitterness; their feet are swift to shed blood. The heart is deceitful above all things, and desperately wicked. Their hands are full of bribes and of blood. They love darkness rather than light. They put bitter for sweet and sweet for bitter. They call the proud happy and the humble miserable. They are utterly vain. Sin makes men blind, and deaf, and dumb, and lame, and lethargic. It is a terrible complication of diseases. It is a rottenness in the bones. It is a maddening fever, a wasting consumption, a paralysis of all the powers. Human nature is wholly corrupt. "From the sole of the foot even unto the head there is no soundness in it; but wounds, and bruises, and putrefying sores: they have not been closed, neither bound up, neither mollified with ointment." (*Isaiah 1:6*).

Sin is a perpetual disease. It rages day and night, on the sea and on the land, in the house of mirth and in the house of God. The wicked "sleep not, except they have done mischief." They devise mischief upon their beds. They "cannot cease from sin." Even in sleep their dreams are vain or vile. Sin has no rest. If for a season the evil spirit forsakes his house, it is only to bring with him seven other spirits more wicked than himself, and they enter in and dwell there, and the last state of that man is worse than the first.

Sin is a hereditary disease: "By one man's disobedience many were made sinners." We are conceived in sin and brought forth in iniquity. The child of a consumptive may die of old age, but the children of sinners must be sinful. "Who can bring a clean thing out of an unclean?"

Sin is also contagious. Sinners are enticers, seducers, corrupters. (*Isaiah 1:4*). Many are "factors for hell, studying to corrupt all about them." Men are often partakers of each other's sins. To the perpetual disgrace of Jeroboam and Manasseh, it is said that they "made Israel to sin." Some men strongly resemble the upas-tree, whose leaves and bloom and shade blighted all within its reach.

Sin is also the most deceitful and flattering disease. One of its strong delusions is, "Thou shalt not die." Paracelsus tells us of a disease "which made men die dancing." So with the wicked. When they cry, Peace and safety, lo, sudden destruction cometh upon them, and they shall not escape. See the throng of ungodly men marching to perdition, the slaves of Satan, the servants of corruption, the enemies of God. Their mirth would make an ignorant man think them the happiest of mortals, and not, as they are, condemned criminals, on their way to the eternal prison-house of inflexible justice. Just as the fool thought himself prepared for a long and merry life, his soul was required of him. Sin has its hectic flushes, its unnatural excitements, its delusive dreams, its strange ecstasies. The worse a man is, the better he thinks himself to be.

Sin is the worst disease, because it is the parent of all other diseases. In Paul's argument, "death by sin" is an axiom. But for sin, we should never have seen a human being faint, or sicken, or die. Suffering and agony have one parent – *transgression*.

Other diseases are calamities; this is a wickedness. Sin is not a misfortune; it is a crime. It is a wicked thing to be a sinner. Transgression brings guilt, God is angry with the wicked every day. The more sinful anyone is, the more is God displeased with him.

Sin is the most loathsome of all diseases. Pride is the worst kind of swelling. No heart is so vile as a hard heart. No vileness compares with an evil heart of unbelief. No sight is so appalling as a sight of vile affections. The physician of the body sees sights which try his nerves, but he who has right views of sin is sickened and frightened at the discovery. It is horrible and abominable to God and to all right-minded creatures.

Sin is also the most dolorous disease. They multiply their sorrows who hasten after transgression. The most bitter cries that ever were heard were extorted by sin. This is true of saints and of sinners, of earth and of hell.

Other diseases do but kill the body; this kills soul and body in hell for ever. They may pursue their victims to the grave; but "sin kills beyond the tomb." It will, if possible, rage more violently beyond the tomb than on earth. It will be followed by eternal regrets and reproaches, eternal weeping and wailing, eternal wrath and anguish.

Nor can this disease be cured by any means of human devising. If music did cure the bite of the tarantula, the music of the angelic choir, announcing the advent of Messias, will not of itself heal any soul. Nay, the melodies and harmonies of the skies, singing the song of Moses and the Lamb, would not save a soul. All reformations wrought by persuasion and the natural will never cure the heart. "If I wash myself with snow-water, and make my hands never so clean; yet shalt thou plunge me in the ditch, and mine own clothes shall abhor me." (*Job 9:30, 31*). "I fast twice in the week, I give tithes of all that I possess," said the Pharisee, while spiritual wickedness reigned within. Herod heard John gladly, and did many things, (*Mark 6:20*), but he sinned on. Saul lifted up his voice, and wept, and confessed his sin, but he was not turned from folly. Nor can any mortal "redeem his brother, nor give to God a ransom for him: for the redemption of their soul is precious." (*Psalm 49:7, 8*). We may weep and lament over our own sins or over the sins of others, but that will neither dethrone sin nor atone for it. God alone can do that work. Though conversion is not a miracle, as we now use that word, yet it is wrought by the almighty power of God, as truly as creation was the work of omnipotence.

II. *There is a remedy for sin.* This remedy is in Scripture sometimes called a healing, sometimes a recovery, and sometimes "the balm of Gilead." Let us carry out this figure. The balm or balsam here alluded to was an oily juice gathered from a tree about fourteen feet in height. It chiefly grew in Gilead. We know that this balm was very highly prized. It was famous as a remedy in many lands. The Ishmaelites who bought Joseph were going from Gilead to Egypt with, myrrh and spices and this balm. (*Genesis 37:25*). When Jacob sent presents down to Egypt, he forgot not to send balm. (*Genesis 43:11*). Ezekiel informs us it was part of the merchandise of Tyre. (*Ezekiel 27:17*). The best quality of balm sold for double its weight in silver. This celebrated medicine has long been mentioned as the best cure. Jeremiah says of Egypt: "Go up into Gilead and take balm, O virgin, the daughter of Egypt: in vain shalt thou use many medicines, for thou shalt not be cured." Again, of Babylon he says, she "is suddenly fallen and destroyed: howl for her; take balm for her pain, if so be she may be healed." (*Jeremiah 46:11; 51:8*). So that the general import of the phrase is clear and very striking. The remedy for sin, the gospel balm of Gilead, is found in the work and death of Christ. His blood cleanseth from all sin. (*1 John 1:7*). With his stripes we are healed. (*Isaiah 53:5*). His merits clothe our nakedness.

1. By the blood and righteousness of Christ we are justified. We have peace with God through our Lord Jesus Christ. He is the Lamb of God, that taketh away the sin of the world. He is all our salvation. The word *Jehovah,* commonly rendered LORD, is in Scripture variously combined with other words, and always much to the strengthening of our faith. Thus we have Jehovah-jireh, (*Genesis 22:14*), the Lord will provide; Jehovah-nissi, (*Exodus 17:15*), the Lord is my banner; Jehovah-shalom, (*Judges 6:24*), the Lord send peace; Jehovah-shammah, (*Ezekiel 48:35*), the Lord is there; Jehovah-rophi, (*Exodus 15:26*), the Lord that healeth thee; and Jehovah-tsidkenu, (*Jeremiah 23:6*), the Lord our righteousness. Which of all these could believers spare from the teachings of Scripture? Not one. But among them all, none are more precious than the two last cited. Well do our translators put that last cited in capital letters. The types all foretold that Christ should bear our sins. The prophecies did the same. Christ's death atones. By his sufferings we have remission. He is our ransom; and by his obedience we have acceptance, justifying righteousness, a right to the tree of life. Our blood is nothing, our tears are nothing, our works are nothing; all our righteousnesses are as filthy rags; they are of no avail. The first effect, therefore, of Christ's undertaking for us, is an effect external to us. It changes the state of things at the throne of God in reference to us. It reconciles God to the offer and grant of saving mercy to us sinners. It makes him willing and just to take into his favour us poor miserable outcasts and rebels. Thus by what Christ has done and suffered, all barriers to God's merciful communications to sinners are removed, and they are actually restored to the Divine favour. Eternal Justice is no longer against them, but for them. The sovereign Lord makes them his sons, his heirs, and joint-heirs with his Son to an inheritance incorruptible, undefiled, and that fadeth not away.

2. The same Jesus who reconciles God to sinners, reconciles sinners to God: Christ "is made unto us sanctification." If human hearts are ever overcome and brought sweetly to comply with the demands of God's law, it will be by looking on him that was pierced. When the Romans saw Caesar's bloody robes, they said, "His murderers shall die." And when by faith the sinner sees how his sins crucified the Lord of life, he says he will mortify his members, which are on the earth.

"Yes, my Redeemer, they shall die,
  My heart has so decreed;
  Nor will I spare the guilty things,
  That made my Saviour bleed."

Nothing but the cross will melt a hard heart, or bend a stubborn will, or give a death-blow to corruption. A sight of hell never frightened one out of the love of sin. The thunders of Sinai never made a rebellious heart submit to God. Pliny, the naturalist, says that blood readily extinguishes fire. It is sure that the blood of Christ not only quenches the flaming wrath around the throne of God, but it also extinguishes the fires of unhallowed desires in the soul. It begets hatred to sin, and love to holiness. In its application this remedy is often painful. The sinner is so accustomed to look to himself for righteousness and holiness, that when God is convincing him of his guilt and helplessness, he often fears that all is for ever lost. He supposes his exercises are but a foretaste of the wrath to come. Even renewed men, having a clear sight of their sins, are sometimes sore vexed. Luther in desertion was so overcome that he lay as one dead. But in all cases where it is applied, the gospel remedy is sovereign and efficacious. It availed for the dying thief, for the bloody Saul of Tarsus, for the cruel jailor, and for millions on millions who once esteemed themselves as vile and as worthy of everlasting death as any of us can possibly esteem himself. Christ came to save the chief of sinners, and if he failed in that, the whole object of his mission would not be attained.

III. *There is a great and good physician.* His name is Wonderful, Counsellor, The Mighty God, The everlasting Father, The Prince of peace, Jesus Christ the Righteous. He is the Physician of souls. None but he can cure a sin-sick soul.

He is a very tender Physician. He can be touched with a feeling of our infirmities. He was once hit by the archers himself. His compassions are without a parallel. The bruised reed he will not break; the smoking flax he will not quench. He died for his patients. His strength was dried up like a potsherd, that we might be strong in the Lord. His heart was melted in him like wax, that ours might be melted in penitence. By his stripes we are healed. He knows what temptation and sorrow mean. He is the most approachable being that ever walked the earth.

He will go wherever he is asked. He will go among rich or poor, old or young, captives or captors, if they really desire him. Never did he refuse to heal a sin-sick soul submitted to him. From the days of righteous Abel until now, he has graciously received every returning penitent. I was once asked, What is the most consolatory text in the Bible? I have never been able to answer the question, but I know of none sweeter than this: "Jesus Christ, the same yesterday, and today, and for ever." The Lord Jesus is still as ready to save as when he called Zacchaeus, poured his mercies on the dying thief, or granted the request of the Canaanitish woman.

Then he is always at hand. He is omnipresent. We need not wait a long time for him to come. He is a present help in time of trouble. (*Romans 10:6-10*).

He makes no charge for all his cures. He practises without money, without price. He utterly contemns all sordid proposals. The full soul he sends empty away, but he fills the hungry with good things, and gives grace to the humble. Grace is poured into his lips; the oil of grace is poured into every bleeding heart.

He seems most ready to go where he is most needed. When he sent forth his apostles to preach, he told them to begin at Jerusalem – to begin with his murderers – those who had taunted him, mocked him, and crucified him, crying, "His blood be on us and on our children." He knows that the whole need not a physician, but they that are sick.

And well does he love his work. Nothing could baulk his purpose. Having loved his own, he loved them to the end. His heart is set upon saving sinners, so as it is set upon nothing else. He delights in his work. He sees the travail of his soul, and is satisfied. His people are his crown. His redeemed are his diadem.

He is vastly skilful. He knows what is in man. He understands all the difficult and stubborn cases. His wisdom is more than equal to any demands we can make upon it. He has the tongue of the learned, that he should know how to speak a word in season to him that is weary. He knows the enormity of sin, the dreadful burden it brings upon the conscience, and its fearful obstinacy. He knows our frame and remembers that we are dust.

Never has he failed in any case that he undertook. One of his names is, Mighty to save. Manasseh and Paul and Bunyan are as holy and as happy as if sin had never defiled their souls. Whosoever believeth in him shall not perish, but have eternal life. Where sin abounded, grace hath much more abounded.

He is a famous Physician. His whole undertaking has been "to the intent that now unto the principalities and powers in heavenly places might be known by the church the manifold wisdom of God, according to the eternal purpose which he purposed in Christ Jesus our Lord." (*Ephesians 3:10, 11*). So famous is he that his name is above every name that is named in heaven and in earth. All heaven thinks itself well employed in singing, "Worthy is the Lamb that was slain to receive power, and riches, and wisdom, and strength, and honour, and glory, and blessing." (*Revelation 5:12*).

He will take his own time, use his own pleasure, and employ his own methods respecting the cure. He will have his own way or he will not do anything. He knows that his way is best. He admits no counsellor to teach him. The wisdom of creatures is folly.

His prescriptions are useless unless we confide in him implicitly. The whole efficacy of his remedies depends on our confidence in him. "According to your faith, be it unto you," is still the rule of distribution and admeasurement in his kingdom.

And now, poor, sin-sick, dying soul, repair to this Physician, submit your case to him, and seek for the healing remedy. If you stay away, you must die. "The wages of sin is death." There is balm in Gilead, and a Physician there. Why then is not your health recovered? Nothing but your unbelief hinders you from being a sharer in the infinite mercies of God. O come, and welcome to all the blessings of salvation.

22

The Gentleness of Christ

THE wants of men are such that any suitable relief brought to them must be marked by great kindness and gentleness. The wicked are often rough and boisterous. Towards God their conduct is insolent. They care not for a Redeemer. With the heirs of salvation it is different. They feel themselves to be feeble. They are grieved in spirit. They are often faint-hearted. They are poor and timid. A sense of sin bows them down. A sense of weakness destroys their self-confidence. Their boldness does not diminish their humility. Their confidence consists with contrition. Their adversaries are many, mighty, and malignant. Their understanding of divine things is often imperfect. The best of them have no confidence in the flesh.

Some of God's dear people are born with great weakness of intellect, which is not relieved either by education or by grace. They never take clear and strong views of any subject. They live and die children in understanding. They are often perplexed by things which are plain to others. Regeneration does not give new faculties, but a right direction to those we have.

Sometimes disease or an accident shatters the nervous system, and for life renders one incapable of vigorous exercise of mind or resolute purposes of heart. Divine grace does not restore health to the sickly, though it gives sweet submission in suffering. Many have a morbid tendency to dark views of their spiritual state. Nor have they learned to discriminate between exercises of mind which are the result of natural causes and those produced by religious truth.

Wrong teaching, especially in the earlier stages of religious experience, often sadly affects character. The truths of Scripture are presented out of proportion. The solemn and the terrible, the awful and the gloomy, sometimes take the place of the mild and gentle, the bright and cheering. Even in true piety there is often a sad mixture of superstition.

In some good men there is such a tendency to levity and inconstancy, that the Saviour sees it necessary often to make them smart for their transgressions, and to humble them in the dust. The terrors of the law are let loose upon them. The arrows of the Almighty stick fast in them. Some who now, by Divine grace, have a well-regulated temper, once had wild passions; but they have been tamed by severe discipline. Some of the most cheerful Christians once had months or years of dejection of mind and sharp anguish of spirit to cure their lightness and fickleness.

Besides, such are the infinite majesty and glory of divine things, such the unhappy effects of sin upon the mind, and such the unspeakable importance of salvation in the eyes of a renewed sinner, that the strongest among the saints often have the deepest sense of their weakness, and those who have the clearest views are the least satisfied with their attainments.

Consequently, many in the church are desponding, yet sincere. Their faith is weak, though unfeigned. They have many fears about themselves, while others have good hopes of them. Though they walk in darkness, they walk uprightly. If they do not go forward like some, yet they do not go backward. Their hearts cleave unto God. They stick to his ways.

There is not a more interesting subject than the treatment which Christ gives to the timid and feeble among his people. 1. All his people, at some time or other, have fears, and are conscious of feebleness. Their weakness and their leanness often constitute their song. 2 Any provision for such comprehends also the necessities of the strong. 3. It is delightful to the pious to know that their weakest brethren shall be cared for and upheld. 4. All sincere Christians love to contemplate the kindness of their Lord and Master, to whomsoever manifested.

We dare not tell such that a dim view of religious truth or a low state of religious enjoyment is the best. There may be a necessity for present distress, arising from some defect of character. But all Christians should seek for enlargement and establishment in truth, holiness, and comfort. Even the most perfect should be beckoned on to higher attainments.

Nor should we abate anything of the requirements of God's Word as a rule of life or of self-examination. If God is merciful, he is also holy. If he is condescending, he is also full of majesty. Presumption is a great foe to grace.

The great resources of God's people, whether comparatively weak or strong, must be found in the character, the covenant, and the grace of the Redeemer. In a review of their lives, the Lord's people ascribe their triumphs to no other cause. Like David, each of them says, "Thy gentleness hath made me great." (*2 Samuel 22:36; Psalm 18:35*).

*   *   *

1. The character of Christ, as given us both in prophecy and in history, is full of encouragement to all his people, even the feeblest. Thus said the evangelical prophet: "He shall not cry, nor lift up, nor cause his voice to be heard in the street. A bruised reed shall he not break, and the smoking flax shall he not quench: he shall bring forth judgment unto truth." (*Isaiah 42:2, 3*). Nothing in all the Scriptures is said contrary to this prediction. Our Lord's whole life upon earth was an illustration of its verity. In his righteous indignation, he has trodden blaspheming tyrants to hell; but never did he trample on a broken heart. Human ingenuity has never yet suggested anything expressive of kindness which he might have said or done, that he did not say or do, or something more loving. The shortest, but by no means the least instructive verse in his history is, "Jesus wept." This was at the grave of his friend Lazarus. At his last celebration of the Passover, he laid himself out to say the tenderest and most consolatory things to his mourning disciples. In his agony, he apologised for their drowsiness. To erring Peter he sends a personal message to meet him in Galilee. He bids unbelieving Thomas come and thrust his hand into his side, that he might no longer doubt. Often did he invite poor sinners to partake of the blessings of his salvation: "Come unto me, all ye that labour and are heavy laden, and I will give you rest." (*Matthew 11:28*). After his ascension to heaven, when one of his followers was pierced by a thorn in the flesh, and terribly buffeted by Satan, he

made this consolatory revelation: "My grace is sufficient for thee." (*2 Corinthians 12:9*).

2. The covenant, of which Christ is the surety and the head, abounds in provisions and promises made to the trembling and the feeble: "As thy days, so shall thy strength be;" "He that is feeble among them at that day shall be as David; and the house of David shall be as God, as the angel of the Lord;" "He giveth power to the faint; and to them that have no might he increaseth strength;" "Comfort ye, comfort ye my people, saith your God." These are mere samples of engagements made before the coming of Messiah. In the New Testament they are confirmed. Speaking of "him that is weak in the faith," Paul says: "He shall be holden up, for God is able to make him stand." (*Romans 14:4*). Similar promises abound in the gospels and in the epistles. The very last book of Scripture is full of the kindest things spoken to sincere believers. All these promises are yea and amen in Christ. Study them. Let them dwell in you richly.

3. In some stage of their experience all Christians have their fears and weaknesses. We must be babes before we are men. We must crawl before we can walk, and walk before we can run. The very best things come from small beginnings. The greatest rivers at their head are but little rills. The greatest oaks come from acorns no larger than a thimble. The greatest families and kingdoms had humble beginnings. The kingdom of heaven in the heart is like a grain of mustard-seed, which is the smallest of all seeds. Despise not the day of small things. We must take root downwards, and then bear fruit upwards. The finest picture on earth, when only the outlines were drawn, was a poor thing; not till it was finished was it fair to pronounce judgment upon it.

4. Some humble child of God may say, "I have made but poor progress; I am more and more out of conceit of myself. I have sore troubles, fears within, and fightings without." Let such remember, *a*. Whatever makes us lowly is good for us. Humility is the most excellent of graces. Without it there is no real progress heavenward. *b*. Paul speaks of it as the common experience of Christians in his day that they were sorely troubled: "We know not what we should pray for as we ought." (*Romans 8:26*). We are not sufficient, as of ourselves, to think anything. "O wretched man that I am! who

shall deliver me from the body of this death?" (*Romans 7:24*). Your troubles are not greater than these. *c.* God's plan is that our sanctification ordinarily should not be begun and finished in a day, as was that of the thief on the cross. Nature and grace are like the house of Saul and the house of David. The contest between them is long and deadly; but the house of Saul waxes weaker and weaker, and that of David stronger and stronger, finally getting full dominion. *d.* It is a precious token of God's regard to us that he so deals with us as to destroy our carnal security, mortify our pride, make us loathe and abhor ourselves, and yet gives us a relish for spiritual enjoyments, and leads us to seek them above all other things.

5. He is a real Christian and is making progress, to whom Christ is more and more precious. As our estimate of him rises, our estimate of ourselves necessarily becomes lower. To believers Christ is everything. He is all their salvation. But for the birth of Christ in Bethlehem, that would have been one of the least celebrated of all towns. But for his residence in Nazareth, the proverb might still have been true of it. But for his visit to the second temple, its glory would have remained every way inferior to that of the first. Christ dignifies everything with which he is connected. Union with him is life from the dead. If we are guilty, he has atoned; if we are vile, he is worthy; if we are nothing, he is All-in-all. And then he is so gracious to the needy and guilty and faint and trembling. See how he reasons with the desponding disciples on the way to Emmaus. During his ministry he granted great blessings even to those who approached him doubting and saying, "If thou wilt," or, "If thou canst." When the poor afflicted woman thought to steal a blessing from him and escape his notice, he stopped her, but only to deal kindly with her. Christ never puts new wine into old bottles. Some men begin their ministry with denunciations and threatenings of the law; but from the first, Christ pronounced blessings on the humble. The very last words in the Bible are: "The grace of our Lord Jesus Christ be with you all. Amen." There are heights, and depths, and lengths, and breadths of mercy in Christ beyond all human necessities, miseries, and sins. To be in Christ is heaven begun. To be with Christ and like Christ is heaven completed. His mercies are shoreless, fathomless, eternal, unchangeable. He has helped myriads to glory who were as weak, as unworthy, as desponding as any of us.

6. To his sincere followers Christ has a tender regard at all times and in all trials. His kind providence over them is constant, wise, and wonderful. With them, everything has a good issue. With them, all is for the best. Everything helps on the saints to glory. To the deeply afflicted, the Saviour says: "As many as I love, I rebuke and chasten;" "wherefore lift up the hands which hang down, and the feeble knees." Your brethren may cast you out under pretence of glorifying God; but he shall appear to your joy, and they shall be ashamed. (*Isaiah 66:5*).

7. Christ surely includes the case of even the feeblest and most desponding of his people when he speaks of them as his *little ones.* He will certainly avenge the wrongs of such. He regards them as the apple of his eye. He knows their sins, and errors, and follies, but he loves them still and tenderly. They may be babes and sucklings, yet out of their mouth he will ordain praise. Their weakness affords him a welcome opportunity to show pity and condescension. His are the compassions of a God. He is the express image of his Father, and his spirit is as loving as the Father's to the Son.

8. In his Word Christ fully authorises us to persuade all his people, even the humblest, to look at the quality rather than the quantity of their attainments. The stronger our graces the better. Christian character cannot be too vigorous. Nor should any sit down contented with small acquirements. But any real grace is a token for good. A shilling may be as good money as a pound. A dew-drop is as truly water as the ocean. A spark has the nature of fire no less than the glowings of a furnace. Kind is one thing; degree is another. To doubt the genuineness of our faith because we have not full assurance is not wise. He to whom Christ is precious, to whom the Word of God is sweeter than honey, to whom sin is odious, to whom secret devotion is a delight, who makes it the business of his life to honour his Master, and who regards the world as a broken idol, has the witness that he is passed from death unto life. "It is safer to be humble with one talent than proud with ten; yea, better to be a humble worm than a proud angel." (Flavel). "He that is contented with just grace enough to get to heaven and escape hell, and desires no more, may be sure he has none at all, and is far from being made partaker of the divine nature." (Janeway).

9. If the trembling and feeble would have the full comfort of Christ's salvation, let them do his will. In keeping the commandments there is great reward. "If ye know these things, happy are ye if ye do them." (*John 13:17*). Whenever we wander from the path of duty, we weaken our principles and wound our consciences. Let us carefully guard against censoriousness and severity of judgment. Let us forgive, as we hope to be forgiven. Let us love others as Christ has loved us. Let us wait upon the Lord in all his ordinances. If Paul could not do what he would, he would yet do what he could. "Prayer and pains, through faith that is in Christ Jesus, can do all things," says Eliot. No man ever sincerely did what he honestly believed to be his duty, and then solely relied on the infinite mercy of God in Christ, and yet came short of heaven. But we must obey as well as trust. We must do the will of God, as well as hope in his mercy. "Blessed are they that do his commandments, that they may have right to the tree of life, and may enter in through the gates into the city." (*Revelation 22:14*).

10. It would greatly comfort all God's people, if they would rely more upon the promise, covenant, and oath of God, and less on their own frames of mind and heart. Our feelings vary with a thousand influences; but the covenant of God is sure and unchangeable. "If we believe not, yet he abideth faithful: he cannot deny himself." (*2 Timothy 2:13*). The life of the believer is hid with Christ in God. He is like mount Zion, which cannot be moved. But how variable are his feelings; how easily discouraged is his heart. If left to himself, he must fail. But Jesus never changes. His mercy is from everlasting to everlasting upon them that fear him and keep his covenant. He pities like a God. He pours water upon him that is thirsty, and floods upon the dry ground.

11. Let all believers remember that they are not forbidden the nearest access to God. The covenant is as sure to the trembling and feeble as to any others. Christ's power is made perfect in man's weakness. If he accepted and saved none but the strong and resolute and unwavering, who would be saved? Did ever a good husband neglect a wife because she was weak and timid? and is not Christ the husband of all that put their trust in him? He says: "For a small moment have I forsaken thee; but with great mercies will I gather thee. In a little wrath I hid my face from thee for a moment; but with everlasting

kindness will I have mercy on thee, saith the Lord thy Redeemer." (*Isaiah 54:7, 8*). Jehovah, he is God. Let his people shout for joy. Let his ministers speak a word in season to him that is weary. Let all the saints comfort the feeble-minded. Let despondent, yet sincere believers, hope in God, for their redemption draweth nigh.

23
Christ Shall Yet Have a Glorious Reward

THERE is a general impression among Christians that true religion will yet pervade the earth. There is a difference among some good people as to the manner in which this work will be accomplished; but all agree as to the fact. Neither do we know the time when the inconceivable blessings of the gospel shall be made known to all men. "In giving us prophecies, God did not intend to make prophets of us." Yet we may modestly inquire what and what manner of time the Spirit of Christ did signify, when he foretold the latter-day glory. Much prophecy is yet to be fulfilled, and some prophecies are now in course of actual fulfilment.

I. *Let us take a brief view of the present moral state of the world.* It is admitted that appearances are often dark; and that the aspect of the world is discouraging.

Now and then Atheism proclaims its tenets, is confident that mankind are superstitious in their worship of Jehovah, makes its disciples of the drunkard, the licentious, the prostitute, and the blasphemer, and once in a while threatens a terrific eruption of its scalding lava on the face of society. Its latest form of development is in a wretched Pantheism.

Infidelity still uses great swelling words of vanity, makes hard and ungodly speeches respecting Jehovah and his saints, often spews out its venom against all that is pure and holy, asserts the sufficiency of human reason as a guide to heaven, betakes itself to the caves of sorcery, and can boast of nothing better than a death without hope, and a grave without a resurrection.

Gentilism still boasts her myriads of altars, purple with human gore and smoking with abominable incense. What heathenism once was, it still is. The pencil of inspiration has drawn a perfect portrait of it, (*Romans 1:21-32*). For nearly six thousand years the pagan world has been seeking an image of the invisible God, and the summit of its aspirings still reaches no higher than the sun, or moon, or stars, or devils, or crocodiles, or peacocks, or serpents, or images of gold, silver, wood, or stone. Its morals never mend. Under its sanctions every precept of the Decalogue is broken publicly and privately, ritually and legally. No marvel that when Satan is worshipped, there should be found habitations of cruelty. No nation without God's Word has in its language any term expressing what Christians mean by sanctification. Corruption is and ever has been the alpha and the omega of Gentilism. One of the greatest benefits derived from reading the early Christian fathers is the insight thus obtained into the abominations from which the gospel saved us. All that is stupid in the ass, silly in the dove, filthy in the swine, fierce in wild beasts, and venomous in serpents, is fitly ascribed to heathenism.

Although just now somewhat shorn of his power to persecute, the prophet of Mecca still practises his sorceries, maddens the passions of men, holds the cup of carnal delight to the lips of his besotted worshippers, and endeavours to light up the horrors of the grave by pointing to a Paradise of sin.

Notwithstanding all that has been done in blessing and in cursing, in fulfilling prophecy, and in setting up Messiah's kingdom, Judaism is still entrenched behind Targums, Paraphrasts, an oral law, endless traditions, and the most inveterate prejudices and enmity against the truth. Thus it is with things claiming no connection whatever with Christianity. When we come to nations professedly accepting the gospel, there is still much to dishearten.

The Oriental church still adheres to her ignorant priesthood, her sacraments of human invention, her apostolic supremacy, and her nearness to Messiah's sepulchre; but knows not that she is poor, and miserable, and blind, and naked, far from Christ's precepts, far from his example, far from his doctrines. In the pride of her apostolicity, she renounces every distinctive truth taught by apostles.

She, that has made the kings, merchants, and dwellers on earth drunk with the wine of her fornications, holds forth other goblets to the nations, saying: "I have perfumed my bed with myrrh, aloes, and cinnamon. Come, let us take our fill." (*Proverbs 7:17, 18*). Follow her footsteps to any region of the world, and you find that "the doctrine of the cross is least understood where crosses most abound." The lamp of God's Word is put under a bushel, waxen tapers are substituted, and darkness becomes visible.

Universalism still teaches that the wheat and the tares shall both be gathered into the garner, that the sheep and the goats shall be for ever in the same fold, that hell is a fiction, and damnation a chimera.

Pelagianism is not dead. It does not even sleep, but still preaches human ability, and boasts of the ease with which the Ethiopian can change his skin, and the leopard his spots. It boldly calls evil good, and bitter sweet. It denies the need of efficacious grace.

In its grossness Socinianism still talks about a created God, and speaks loudly in praise of virtue, though its rules and motives for a pious life are no better than those of Epictetus.

Unitarianism tells of the magnificent Jesus, philosophises into thin air the vital doctrines of the gospel, emblematises the blood of Christ, and raises its hideous voice against a vicarious atonement.

Arianism soars to its usual adventurous heights, and speaks of a grade above finite and below infinite. It discusses divinity as though by searching it could find out the Almighty to perfection.

Then, too, we meet fanaticism, presenting us a jumble of wild speculation, silly purpose and vicious practice. Break up its nest among the lawless, and presently you shall hear of it among the orthodox pretending to aid in a revival of religion.

And Antinomianism – that horror of all good men – still flourishes in many places. It boldly marches up to the cross of Christ, and from his precious blood draws arguments for living in sin. By its want of good fruit ye shall know it.

Besides, a low state of piety paralyses half the limbs of the body of Christ. Cold and selfish, many never aim high. A low estimate of evangelical doctrine makes many indifferent to the teachings of Christ himself. Often too do we hear unpleasant whisperings and buzzings in the camp of Israel. Some act as if they would rather make a proselyte from a sister church than a convert to Christ who would not follow with them. The standard of Christian manners and morals is low. Doubts of personal piety afflict many of Christ's professed followers. Sadly is the Christian profession compromised. Covetousness has fearful power. The lust of the flesh, the lust of the eye, and the pride of life terribly prevail. Fashion is the Juggernaut of Christendom. Christ and Belial are invited to the same feast. The Sabbath is in danger of being buried under railroads. Blasphemy vomits forth her poison. The church is a vassal often ingloriously chained to the car of state. The seed of the bondwoman lords it over the seed of the free woman. Tyranny, like the owl, loves darkness, and binds the masses in chains of ignorance. Often the shaking of the nations makes the loops of society fall from their ancient fastenings and introduces wild lawlessness. Yet there is no room for despair.

II. *Let us consider some of the encouragements to hope for the wide spread of truth and righteousness.* The promises of God and the prophecies of Scripture, like the udders of well-fed kine, are well distended and full of fatness. "All the promises do travail." Sixteen hundred and eighty-nine years before the Christian era, Jacob says, "Unto Shiloh shall the gathering of the people be." (*Genesis 49:10*). Six hundred and sixty-six years later, the prophet David speaking in the name of God to Messiah, says: "Ask of me, and I shall give thee the heathen for thine inheritance, and the uttermost parts of the earth for thy possession." (*Psalm 2:8*). Three hundred and eleven years later, by Isaiah, Jehovah says: "Behold, my servant shall deal prudently, he shall be exalted and extolled, and be very high … He shall see his seed, he shall prolong his days … He shall see of the travail of his soul, and shall be satisfied." (*Isaiah 52:13; 53:10, 11*). A hundred and fifty-seven years later, the great prophet of the captivity says: "I saw in the night visions, and, behold, one like the Son of man came with the clouds of heaven, and came to the Ancient of days, and they brought him near before him. And there was given him dominion, and glory, and a kingdom, that all people, nations, and languages, should serve him: his dominion is an everlasting dominion, which shall not pass away, and his kingdom that which shall not be destroyed." (*Daniel 7:13, 14*). In this passage, by the "Son of man" we are clearly to understand the incarnate Saviour; and by "the Ancient of days" the everlasting God, seated on the throne of the universe.

The coming of the Son of man with the clouds of heaven was his ascension to the right hand of God. This prediction was to begin to be fulfilled after the establishment of the Roman empire, spoken of in the same chapter as the fourth beast, dreadful and terrible, and strong exceedingly, having great iron teeth, devouring, breaking in pieces, and stamping the residue with the feet of it, diverse from all the other beasts that were before it, and having ten horns, (*verse 7*). The terms "dominion, and glory, and a kingdom," denote the extent, grandeur, and permanency of the possession purchased by Christ, and secured to him by covenant. What Daniel therefore saw was, "that in the vigour of the Roman empire Jesus Christ ascended to his God and Father, the Ancient of days, and took his seat at his right hand, and received a title to and entered on the possession of a kingdom, grand, glorious, and permanent." Other Scriptures declare that under the reign of Messiah "the earth shall be full of the knowledge of the Lord, as the waters cover the sea." "The light of the moon shall be as the light of the sun, and the light of the sun shall be sevenfold, as the light of seven days." (*Isaiah 11:9; 30:26*. With these texts compare *Psalm 22:27-31; 72:19; Habakkuk 2:14; Zechariah 14:9*). These passages clearly indicate a state of things not yet fulfilled in the history of the world. There is no method of interpreting language so as to confine these predictions to the past. Christ has not yet had his reward in the gathering of the nations. Great and glorious things may properly be expected in behalf of Zion.

Nor are pleasing indications entirely wanting. The present mode of studying the Bible in the original, so generally adopted by many of God's ministers, is favourable to a clear understanding of Scripture doctrine. It often looks as if Providence was erecting machinery that was to move the world. There is a blessed sisterhood of institutions, co-operating for the spread of the truth. All modern controversies have been handled to the advantage of sound Christianity. In no case has the enemy gained any decided or permanent victory. Modern inventions are generally capable of being turned to good account. Commonly they have had a good influence. Many great political changes have favoured freedom of inquiry, the reading of God's Word, and a sense of individual responsibility.

The general orderings of Providence in this age have favoured the church. Great success has attended many efforts to spread the gospel, especially among the most degraded tribes of men. The hope of better days powerfully animates the bosoms of many throughout the world. What has been done in the last *seventy* years is great compared with what was done for the same time preceding; yet much remains to be done; large portions of the world are still sunk in gross darkness.

III. *What can we do to promote the cause of Christ?* It should not discourage us that we can do nothing *efficiently*. The excellency of the power is of God. We may plant and water, but God alone can give the increase. This is, on many accounts, the best arrangement. If we depend on God, we shall not be disappointed. If he does the work, it will be well done, and to him, without dispute, will be all the glory. Yet we may do much *instrumentally*.

We may keep ourselves and those under our influence informed respecting the state of the world. It is a great thing to know and to make known how men are living in sin and dying in despair, having a dismal eternity before them, and their ruin being unnecessary, salvation having been provided, a ministry instituted, and a glorious gospel commanded to be preached.

We may cultivate an ardent love to the souls of men. Oh that there were a thousand times more of that godlike spirit which Shaftesbury scornfully called a "rage for saving souls." No man ever had too much love or pity for those that were perishing under the load of their guilt and in the horrors of their depravity. It is easy to over-estimate wealth, honour, station, but it is not possible to set too high a value on the salvation of a soul by Jesus Christ.

We may all encourage, and should never discourage, wise and practicable schemes of usefulness. Let us hinder nothing good. Let us do all we can to cheer the hearts and strengthen the hands of all faithful labourers, even if they follow not with us. Let us believe assuredly that all flesh shall see the salvation of God, for the mouth of the Lord hath spoken it. The decree has gone forth. Every knee shall bow, and every tongue confess that Jesus Christ is Lord, to the glory of God the Father. The whole work of evangelising the world is a work of faith. O have faith in God.

In particular, have faith in Christ, in his mediation, in his ability to execute all his offices. He has dominion over wicked men and devils. "All power in heaven and earth is given to" him. He saves, and he destroys. He kills, and he makes alive. He has the keys of death and of hell. He does all his pleasure in all worlds. For the good of his church he orders all things. He and his people are so far one, that in all their affliction he is afflicted, and in all his glory they rejoice. That which, in *Daniel 7:14,* is said to be given to Christ, is in the same chapter, *verse 27*, said to be given to the saints of the Most High. When Christ is glorified, his people shout for joy. When they are glorified, they enter into the joy of their Lord.

The desire to spread the gospel belongs to the very spirit of piety. "Let him that heareth say, Come." He who thinks he has escaped perdition, and has no desire to rescue others from wrath, does not know his own heart. He that is begotten of God loves his fellow-men. He longs for their salvation.

God's people can pray for the reign of grace over all the earth. Such supplications are agreeable to the will of God. (*Psalm 122:6*). The first three petitions of the Lord's Prayer embrace the same subject. There is too little united, hearty calling on God. All the progress hitherto made in bringing men to a saving knowledge of the Redeemer has been in answer to the fervent cries of the children of God. There is nothing more powerful for good than prayer.

Those who know somewhat the doleful case of the heathen, ought to plead their cause before all Christian people. Mankind are slow to believe how terribly the perishing nations have multiplied their sorrows by hastening after other gods than Jehovah.

Every member of the church should be trained and urged to do his full share of the great work. He should know his place, and keep it. He should love to do what he can for so blessed a cause.

All the churches should be trained to liberality in giving their worldly substance for spreading the gospel. Systematic benevolence is loudly called for. We must learn to carry our liberality to the extent of self-denial. We must remember the power of littles. The ocean consists of the aggregation of drops.

Our young men must freely give themselves to the work of the ministry at home and abroad. Parents must cheerfully give their sons to this service. It must come to be, in popular esteem, an honour to serve the Lord in any way his providence may permit. Why is the ministry so lightly esteemed? Why do we so seldom find a Hannah, a Eunice, or a Monica in the church of God? One well-qualified, laborious minister of the gospel is commonly far more useful than two men of equal talents in any other calling. It is enough to break the heart to see revival after revival without a host of young men rising up to publish salvation.

There should be a much deeper tone of piety in all the churches. Love is too cold. Faith too often staggers. Repentance sheds too few tears. Joy has but few feasts. Pity for the perishing too seldom stirs the soul to its depths. Adoring views of God have too little power over men's minds. Hope is too feeble to impart much animation. "In doing good," says Burke, "we are generally cold, and languid, and sluggish, and of all things, afraid of being too much in the right. But the works of malice and injustice are quite in another style. They are finished with a bold, masterly hand, touched as they are with the spirit of those vehement passions that call forth all our energies when we oppress and persecute." Oh that ministers and people, fathers and mothers, young men and maidens loved as they should a dying world, and laboured as they ought to turn many to righteousness.

PRAYER

Holy, holy, holy Lord God of hosts! The whole earth is full of thy glory. Blessed be the Lord for the precious things of heaven, for the dew, and for the deep that coucheth beneath, and for the precious fruits brought forth by the sun, and for the precious things put forth by the moon, and for the chief things of the ancient mountains, and for the precious things of the lasting hills, and for the precious things of the earth, and the fulness thereof. Still more would we bless thee for the good will of Him that dwelt in the bush, and for thy precious loving-kindness, and for the precious seed of gospel truth, and for the precious promises, and for precious faith to believe thy Word, and for the precious sons of Zion, comparable to fine gold, and for the precious death of thy saints, and for the precious name of Jesus, which is as ointment poured forth, and for the precious blood of the Son of God, through whom we have redemption.

Look in mercy on this dark world. Remember Zion. Make Joseph a fruitful bough, whose branches run over the wall. Oh that the salvation of Israel were come out of Zion. Bring back the captivity of thy people, that Jacob may rejoice and Israel be glad. Thou hast set thy Son on thy holy hill of Zion. Righteousness is the girdle of his loins, and faithfulness the girdle of his reins. Hasten the time when the wolf shall dwell with the lamb and the leopard shall lie down with the kid, the calf and the young lion and the fatling together, and a child shall lead them; and the cow and the bear shall feed, and their young ones lie down together, and the sucking child shall play on the hole of the asp, and the nations shall learn war no more, and thine ancient people the Jews and the fulness of the Gentiles shall be brought in; when the kingdoms of the world shall become the kingdoms of the Lord and of his Christ; when the Lord shall call them his people which are not now his people; when the angel shall fly in the midst of heaven, having the everlasting gospel to preach unto them that dwell on the earth, and to every nation, and kindred, and tongue, and people.

Lord God of hosts, cut short the work in righteousness. Let the ploughman overtake the reaper, and let a nation be born in a day.

> "Pity the nations, our God;
>   Constrain the earth to come;
>   Send thy victorious Word abroad,
>   And bring the strangers home."

We are indeed asking great things, but we do it at thy command. We ask no more than thou hast promised to thy Son, and no more than he has purchased by his most precious blood, and no more than he himself intercedes for in heaven. Amen.

24

The Gospel of Christ is Hid
from Some

"THE beauty of Scripture," says Luther, "consists in pronouns." It is sweet to find such Scriptures as these: "*I* am the Lord *thy* God;" "*I* have called *thee* by thy name;" "*I* am with *thee; I* will strengthen *thee; I* will uphold *thee* with the right hand of my righteousness."

The heart delights in fastening its affections on spiritual things, and calling them its own. This is laying hold on eternal life. Thus the soul tastes and sees that the Lord is gracious. What could the saints do were they never permitted to claim an interest in heavenly things? Wilkinson says: "All consolation in religion is connected with appropriation." Accordingly Job says, "I know that *my* Redeemer liveth." David: "Unto thee will I cry, O Lord *my* rock." In the *Song of Solomon* the church says, "*My* Beloved is *mine,* and *I* am *his.*" Thomas said, "*My* Lord and *my* God." Paul says, "He loved *me* and gave himself for *me;*" "*I* know whom *I* have believed."

Nor is there anything selfish or exclusive in this appropriation. The saints delight to have others joint partakers with them in the infinite benefits of salvation. The psalmist says: "O Lord *our* Lord, how excellent is thy name in all the earth;" "The Lord of hosts is with *us,* the God of Jacob is *our* refuge." John says, "Behold what manner of love the Father hath bestowed upon *us,* that *we* should be called the sons of God." In like manner Christians commonly speak of *our* Lord Jesus Christ, and of *our* brethren. If we are believers, to us pertain the adoption, and the glory, and the covenants, and the service of God, and the promises. Paul says, "Who shall separate *us* from the love of Christ?" He also says that those that call on Jesus Christ as Lord, own him as both *theirs* and *ours*. He further says to the Corinthians, "*We* are *your* rejoicing, even as *ye* also are *ours* in the day of the Lord Jesus." Jude speaks of the *common salvation,* that is, the salvation in which all believers have a joint interest, and are made fellow-heirs.

So also Paul speaks of "*our* gospel," as though he and his brethren were joint partakers of its benefits, as well as unitedly concerned to make it known. "*If our gospel be hid, it is hid to them that are lost.*" Very awful language is this, and the more so as the same thing is taught in other Scriptures: "The preaching of the cross is to them that perish foolishness;" "Behold, ye despisers, and wonder, and perish." (*2 Corinthians 4:3; 1 Corinthians 1:18; Acts 13:41*). Let us consider this solemn matter under the form of speech just cited: "If our gospel be hid, it is hid to them that are lost." We may inquire: –

I. *In what sense the gospel is not hid from any of us.*

1. The gospel is not hid from any of us in the same sense in which it is hid from the brutes. These have no natural capacities for understanding, receiving, or enjoying the gospel under any culture, however wisely or assiduously administered. The God who made them has given them neither minds nor hearts capable of grasping divine things. If their natures were so elevated as to lay hold of the gospel, they would no longer be brutes. With men it is far different. Their original capacity is such as to make it proper to address to them the gospel with all its doctrines, precepts, promises, requirements, and obligations. No man, therefore, can now truly plead incompetence of nature as a justification for a course of neglect or contempt towards the evangelical message. In this sense therefore the gospel is not hid from any of us.

2. Neither is the gospel hid from us in the sense in which truth is hid from unbalanced, disordered, deranged minds. From the force of his disease, the poor maniac connects ideas and facts most remote from each other, and groups together the most discordant assemblages of truth and fiction. He lays down false premises, and makes lawful deductions; or he lays down true premises, but infers something foreign and unnatural. Incoherence of thought is his disease, or flows directly from it. But these things cannot be

said of men in general. In the human mind as it came from the hands of God, there is nothing that would lead it thus to wander. Men have sense enough on all points on which an evil heart has no perverting tendency. There is not found in the human soul any disease unfitting it for receiving plain gospel truth, whenever it is rightly disposed.

3. Neither is the gospel hid from us in the sense in which the abstruse and difficult sciences are hid from the majority of men. It cannot be expected, it is not required, that men generally should become skilled in all the depths of mathematical or physiological inquiry. These things must remain very much confined to a few and hid from the many. And the many may be wholly excusable. But the gospel is a clear statement of plain facts and doctrines of such a nature as to require no profound argumentations, no brilliancy of wit, no scholastic acumen to know and apprehend its great essential truths. Thousands of unlettered men have understood its sublime mysteries of justification and sanctification by the blood and righteousness and Spirit of Jesus. The gospel is so plain that any right-minded person of common sense and an honest heart may understand enough of it to be saved by it. To such the Holy Ghost is given to enlighten the mind, take the veil from off the heart, and lift the soul up to God. Our gospel, therefore, is not hid from men in the sense in which the difficult sciences are hid from the multitude.

4. Nor is it hid from us by any act of prohibition from God forbidding us to inquire into its truths. There is no flaming sword turning every way, and warning us not to enter any book of Scripture. On the contrary, the Author of our religion says, "Search the Scriptures; for in them ye think ye have eternal life: and they are they which testify of me." (*John 5:39*). The great apostle to the Gentiles teaches the same when he says, "Prove all things; hold fast that which is good." (*1 Thessalonians 5:21*). It is a grand error of the Romish church to keep, contrary to God's will, the Holy Scriptures from the common people, thus taking away the key of knowledge. God has purposes and plans which he has concealed from us, some of them in part, and some of them wholly; but the very object of a revelation was that we might know his will. "Secret things belong unto the Lord our God: but those things which are revealed belong unto us and

to our children for ever, that we may do all the words of this law." (*Deuteronomy 29:29*). They are God's gift to us. Therefore they are not hid from us by any divine prohibition.

5. Nor is the gospel hid from us as it was from men who lived before the coming of Christ. Now the types and shadows have given way to the bright beams of light and truth issuing from the Sun of righteousness. So Paul says: "The word of God, even the mystery, which hath been hid from ages and from generations, but now is made manifest to his saints: to whom God would make known what is the riches of the glory of this mystery among the Gentiles; which is Christ in you, the hope of glory." (*Colossians 1:25-27*). The revelation is therefore made. We see the things which kings and prophets and righteous men desired to see but could not. We have them in our own language, in plain statements, easily read. We have the Bible, the clearest book ever written respecting so weighty matters. "He may run that readeth it." No honest inquirer after truth ever mistook its teachings on vital points. If we cannot read this book, we can hear its truths preached. It is in reference to this preaching especially that the apostle is speaking in *2 Corinthians 4:1-5*. He says that he and his fellow-labourers had not handled the Word of God deceitfully; but by manifestation of the truth commended themselves to every man's conscience in the sight of God; and immediately adds, "If our gospel be hid, it is hid to them that are lost." The fault was not in the preachers, for they told the truth, using great plainness of speech. In like manner, all of us do or may hear the gospel published in a way clear and decided. Who among us has not heard many sermons which faithfully presented the gospel? Christ is preached, and we all hear or can hear. The object of all good preaching is not to hide the gospel, but to make it known.

6. Nor is the gospel hid from us as it is from the heathen, who never heard its blessed truths. How shall men "call on him in whom they have not believed? and how shall they believe in him of whom they have not heard? and how shall they hear without a preacher? ... Faith cometh by hearing, and hearing by the Word of God." (*Romans 10:14, 15, 17*). There are millions on earth who never heard that Jesus Christ is the Lamb of God, that taketh away the sin of the world. The guilt of their transgression is not enhanced

by a knowledge of the glorious gospel. Its light has never shined on them. If men sin without law, they shall perish without law. But fearful beyond expression will be the doom of those who, knowing the way of life, turn from the holy commandments. To him that knoweth to do good and doeth it not, to him it is sin. In none of these senses is the gospel hid from us.

II. We may now show in *what sense the Gospel is hid from the unbelieving.*

This is truly an awful subject. It is so in its very nature; and it concerns many. The essence of this *hiding* consists in one's having eyes and not seeing, in having ears and not hearing, and in having a heart and not understanding. In some way, the truth reaches the intellect, and perhaps slightly moves the affections, but there it stops. It changes not the heart or the life. Thus one may be a learned critic, a clear expositor, or an apt teacher of many truths of the gospel, and yet never see its true force, nor apprehend its chief design. Pride and perverseness may hold him in such a state that he may not discern the real nature of the most glorious things. Sin hides the most precious truths from the mind, as clouds hide the rays of the sun from the earth. A benighted soul is a lost soul. A state of darkness is a state of guilt, depravity, and death. All sin produces blindness of mind. For their wicked rejection of known truth and duty, God, as a sovereign, hides the gospel from men. In sending so terrible spiritual judgments, God is not to blame. He is not bound to continue favours which are slighted and contemned. The pious and amiable John Newton says: "Let us suppose a person to have a curious cabinet, which is opened at his pleasure, and not exposed to common view. He invites all to come and see it, and offers to show it to anyone who asks him. It is hid, because he keeps the key; but none can complain, because he is ready to open it whenever he is desired. Some persons disdain the offer, and say, Why is it locked at all? Some think it not worth seeing, or amuse themselves with guessing at the contents. But those who are simply desirous for themselves leave others disputing, go according to appointment, and are gratified. These have reason to be thankful for the favour, and the others have no just cause to find fault. Thus the riches of divine grace may be compared to a richly-furnished cabinet, to which Christ is the door. The

Word of God likewise is a cabinet, generally locked up; but the key of prayer will open it. The Lord invites all, but he keeps the dispensation in his own hands. They cannot see these things except he shows them; but then he refuses none that sincerely ask him." So that God is clear in this matter. He hides not these things in any way that can impeach his justice or his wisdom; yet he hides them effectually. Left to themselves, men seek to become wise and become fools. This is a punishment for their pride or other sins. We read of some on whom God sent strong delusion, and gave them up to believe a lie, that they might be damned, because they had pleasure in unrighteousness. They delighted not in the truth. They cared neither to know nor to do God's will. Surely God was at liberty to hide from them that which they so much disliked. Their ignorance proves the truth of the words, "If our gospel be hid, it is hid to them that are lost." All the treasures of wisdom and knowledge are hid in Christ. He who despises the Saviour, despises all the lessons we can learn from him. The truth is also hidden in the letter of Scripture. As the time of the day is hid in the figures of the sundial, but cannot be read unless the sun shines and reveals the truth, so is saving truth hid in the letter.

The instrumentality employed in hiding the gospel from the minds of men is various. Sometimes the work is done by Satan. So says the apostle: "If our gospel be hid, it is hid to them that are lost: in whom the god of this world hath blinded the minds of them which believe not, lest the light of the glorious gospel of Christ, who is the image of God, should shine unto them." (*2 Corinthians 4:3, 4*). The great adversary darkens and confuses the mind of unbelievers. For this they are to blame, because they are in league with the wicked one. Let them resist and renounce the devil, and he shall have no power to hide the gospel from them.

Men blind one another. Many seducers and deceivers are entered into the world. They operate "with all deceivableness of unrighteousness in them that perish; because they received not the love of the truth, that they might be saved." (*2 Thessalonians 2:10*). Many lie in wait to deceive, beguiling unstable souls, and employing cunning craftiness and sleight of men. Such cannot succeed but with those who do not wish to know the truths of the gospel. The deceiver and the deceived are both guilty. Men hide the gospel from themselves. They love darkness rather than light. They love to be deceived. They shut their eyes against the truth. Its light is painful to them. They seek darkness. They extinguish the lamp of truth. They corrupt their own minds. They obliterate good impressions. They resist the Spirit. They seek to hide the gospel, and it is hidden.

Thus is God righteous in all cases, even where the blindness is most dreadful. God is not responsible for this darkness. Man is the author of his own blindness. Were it not for the sun, we should have perpetual darkness; and were it not for God, we should never have any divine light. Were the sun never to shine on the world, and were God to withhold all his beams from us, neither the one nor the other would be chargeable with the darkness that should follow.

When the sun shines in his strength, and all nature rejoices in his light, the blind cannot behold his beauty. Were there ten thousand suns, the blind, would be no better off. The fault is in their vision. So if, instead of one, there were ten thousand gospels, each giving the brightest light to lead the soul to God, the unbelieving would continue in their present unhappy state. The very light that is in them is darkness, and they love to have it so. When Lord Nelson put the telescope to his blind eye, we do not wonder that he could not see the concerted signals. If our gospel be hid, it is hid to them that are lost.

This subject has a solemn bearing on persons who were once somewhat enlightened, but are now in deeper darkness than ever. So was it with Jerusalem, over which Christ wept and said: "If thou hadst known, even thou, at least in this thy day, the things which belong unto thy peace! but now they are hid from thine eyes." (*Luke 19:42*). There are set times, chosen seasons, precious harvests, when, if people are rightly disposed, they may know. But if these are neglected, awful darkness ensues. The gospel, once made to shine into the mind, but then rejected, may be hid from the eyes for ever. Such are undone. Their day is past. Their doom is sealed.

Some complain that the Bible is so mysterious that it is like a sealed book, and when they read it, they become bewildered. They see nothing in it plain or intelligible. Ought not such honestly to inquire into their spiritual condition? Does not their bewilderment prove that they are *lost?*

Others apprehend somewhat of the truth, but presently "stumble at the Word, being disobedient." Their stumbling makes them disobedient, and their disobedience makes them stumble. This is the grand error of many. They refuse submission to what they do know, and so they learn nothing aright. The light is hid from such, because they are *lost*.

To some, Christ crucified is foolishness. The idea of salvation by the righteousness of another is opposite to all their conceptions. They deride the doctrine of life to sinners by the death of the Saviour. Speak to them of their own merits as the ground of their acceptance, and they approve such boasting. A gratuitous salvation they scorn. Their present temper continuing, they are lost for ever.

Some think that by their own natural wit they can arrive at saving knowledge. Such often exclude themselves from heaven by a jest or a trifle. Many are damned for a quibble. They judge all things by some fantastic rule, perhaps in their view quite philosophical. When will men learn that the world by wisdom never knew God? Persisting in this self-conceit, such are hopelessly lost.

God always hides saving knowledge from the "wise and prudent." That which we learn by our unaided faculties puffs up and blinds the mind. "Seest thou a man wise in his own conceit? there is more hope of a fool than of him." (*Proverbs 26:12*). The lifting up of the soul unto vanity does itself exclude the light of truth. This is its natural tendency. Such a state of mind spurns the aid of the Spirit of God. And flesh and blood can never reveal the great truths of the Bible. It is only by an unction from the Holy One that any man is ever able to see divine things aright. They are spiritually discerned. He that is not led by the Spirit of God must err. Often do we see men stumbling at straws, making difficulties where a child sees its way clear, insisting upon understanding things of no immediate practical utility, and yet refusing to bow their necks to the plainest and most practical precepts. Such are lost.

No marvel that the careless never come to the knowledge of the truth. If men would be wise unto salvation, they must cry after knowledge, and lift up their voice for understanding; they must seek her as silver, and search for her as for hid treasure. The whole plan of God requires care, candour, attention, earnestness. Some are so heedless that they do not know what the gospel is. They dream or guess at the contents of the Bible. They are deaf to the proclamations of mercy. O they are *lost*.

Cavilling, prejudice, cherished error, a halting mind, an unforgiving temper, any sin wilfully indulged may work the same ruin to the soul.

Thus we see that the work of destroying the soul is a work done in this life. One says, "When men perish *under* the gospel, they are benighted at noon. They have created to themselves a horrid darkness in the midst of a bright and clear day. They are lost in a day of salvation. *Lost,* not only *under* the means of salvation, but *by* them. Gospel light strikes them blind. The sweet, vital savours of the gospel strike them dead. Invited, yet lost! Warned, exhorted, besought, reproved, yet lost! *Lost,* not as to anything which is theirs, but as to themselves. Not a part lost, but the whole. *Lost contrary to expectations.*" The darkness, the errors, the ignorance, the folly of unregenerate men, are as sure and certain tokens of what is to be their state hereafter, as are the faith, and hope, and love of Christians respecting their eternal well-being. As the work of saving the soul is a work of time, and not of eternity; so the work of destroying the soul is also done in this world, and not in the next. And the evidences of this work being done or in process are often clear and decisive. If men would reason as fairly about their standing in God's esteem as they do respecting temporal matters, they would soon be convinced of their lost estate. The smoke of the bottomless pit issuing forth in ungodliness surely proves that the fires of perdition are burning within. One wanders up and down in a forest and finds no safe path. He knows that he is lost. But when one errs from the truth and follows the mazes of iniquity, he often infers that he is in a safe way.

Remember that men are lost in this world. On a lost soul in the Day of Judgment will be found no sign of perdition that is not found upon it on earth. Whatever may be men's apprehensions, but few of the unregenerate learn the truth that they are already lost. In two ways men are convinced of their miserable state. One is in time, and leads to salvation. The other is when the day of grace is over.

T___ was very sick. Her physician was sent for. He came and kindly watched by her bed. The day before her death she seemed calm and tranquil, and inquired if she should probably recover. She was answered in the negative. "How long can I live?" said she. The answer was, "Possibly until tomorrow morning." "Then," she said, "I am lost, lost, lost!" At short intervals until she breathed her last, her piteous cry pierced the ears of attendants: "I am lost, I am lost, lost, lost, lost!" O why will unbelievers keep on in sin, and go to eternity for ever to mourn heaven lost, a crown of glory lost, an eternity of bliss lost, the means of grace lost, the day of salvation lost, all opportunity to make peace with God lost, and lost for ever?

Though the unregenerate are at present lost, yet they are not lost beyond recovery. By God's command Christians still pray, ministers still preach, and offers of mercy are still given; and by God's grace sinners are still converted. What a glorious truth that Jesus Christ came to seek and to save that which was lost. Almost the only true thing Christ's enemies ever said against him was, "This man receiveth sinners." He admitted the charge, and spake three parables in vindication of his matchless mercy.

25

The Sin and Danger of Not Believing in Christ

IN both Testaments God expresses his displeasure against unbelief. By Moses he says to Israel: "Ye did not believe the Lord your God;" "Ye rebelled against the commandment of the Lord your God, and ye believed him not, nor hearkened to his voice." (*Deuteronomy 1:32; 9:23*). Again, God complains of Israel: "They would not hear, but hardened their necks, like to the neck of their fathers, that did not believe in the Lord their God." (*2 Kings 17:14*). By the psalmist he says, "They believed not in God, and trusted not in his salvation." (*Psalm 78:22*). By another prophet he thus threatens them: "If ye will not believe, surely ye shall not be established." (*Isaiah 7:9*). The New Testament is no less clear. The great sin of the Jews under the ministry of John the Baptist was their unbelief. (*Matthew 21:32*). The Son of God marvelled at the unbelief of his own disciples, and sharply rebuked it. (*Mark 6:6; Luke 24:25*). Our Lord himself expressly says: "He that believeth not is condemned already;" "He that believeth not the Son shall not see life; but the wrath of God abideth on him." (*John 3:18, 36*). Paul says, by unbelief the natural branches were broken off. (*Romans 11:20*). Unbelief hinders prayer: "How then shall they call on him in whom they have not believed?" (*Romans 10:14*). "The god of this world hath blinded the minds of them which believe not." (*2 Corinthians 4:4*). "God shall send them strong delusion, that they should believe a lie: that they all might be damned who believed not the truth, but had pleasure in unrighteousness." (*2 Thessalonians 2:11, 12*). "But the fearful, and unbelieving, and the abominable, and murderers, and whoremongers, and sorcerers, and idolaters, and all liars, shall have their part in the lake which burneth with fire and brimstone: which is the second death." (*Revelation 21:8*). Unbelief may relate to any doctrine, or promise, or threatening of God. It commonly has special reference to the person, work, offices, and sufferings of the Saviour. Then it is a rejection of him as he is offered in the gospel. He demands our affectionate confidence, and we withhold it.

Unbelievers are of two classes, *speculative* and *practical*. All speculative unbelievers are also practical unbelievers; but some practical unbelievers have no intellectual doubts of the truths of the Bible. Speculative unbelievers are of two sorts. Some rage and rail and blaspheme. Others doubt, hesitate, are sceptical. This latter class alternately hope that the Bible is not true, and fear that it is true. Meantime they live as if it were not true, and so are practical unbelievers. If they do not deny, they suspect. This is truly unbelief. Not to credit is to disbelieve. Not to receive is to reject. A refusal to *obey* the gospel is as truly dangerous as a scornful denial of its claims.

The object of this chapter is to show the sin of unbelief. It is a great offence against God in many ways. It is very wicked and deserves God's hot displeasure.

1. Unbelief is a very heinous sin, because it is an impeachment of the divine veracity. God's Word is his testimony. It is the highest testimony ever given. When a judge gives a decision or a jury gives a verdict contrary to good evidence, all right thinkers have but one opinion. We take the testimony of men. We act wisely in so doing. But "if we receive the witness of men, the witness of God is greater." (*1 John 5:9*). Man is fallible, man is corrupt, man often deceives, man is often deceived. Yet in some cases man is and must be believed. Under certain circumstances everyone gives credit to the word of man. Much more then should we believe God, who is infallible, and who cannot lie. From the days of Moses until now the best governments on earth have held that two or three witnesses were sufficient to prove any fact. If so, shall we not believe the Trinity of persons in the Godhead? Jesus adopts this kind of argument when he says: "I am not alone, but I and the Father that sent me. It is also written in your law, that the testimony of two men is

true. I am one that bear witness of myself, and the Father that sent me beareth witness of me." (*John 8:16-18*).

The testimony of Christ confirming all the doctrines taught by the prophets and by himself was open, clear, decisive. The very highest proofs of his knowledge, veracity, and sincerity, were amply given. The testimony of his Father was given in an audible voice from heaven. It was repeated in the many stupendous miracles wrought by Almighty power. In these the third person of the adorable Trinity also bore testimony in a manner both striking and convincing. In *Hebrews 2:3, 4*, Paul argues thus: "How shall we escape, if we neglect so great salvation; which at the first began to be spoken by the Lord, [that is, Christ,] and was confirmed unto us by them that heard him; God also [that is, the Father] bearing them witness, both with signs and wonders, and with divers miracles, and gifts of the Holy Ghost." So that the three that bear record in heaven have given testimony upon earth. Their witness is harmonious, unequivocal, often repeated, and accompanied by infallible signs. He, therefore, who lives in unbelief, discredits and impeaches the testimony of the Father, Son, and Holy Ghost. That this is a heinous sin cannot be doubted.

Well do the Scriptures say, he that believeth "hath set to his seal that God is true." They as distinctly say, "He that believeth not God hath made him a liar; because he believeth not the record that God gave of his Son." (*1 John 5:10*). This language is indeed awful, but it is just. God's honour in regard to his veracity is dear to him. He never will part with it. He says: "My glory will I not give to another." The heavens and the earth shall pass away, but his Word shall not pass away. Every jot and tittle shall be fulfilled. Because God is perfect, he is jealous of the honour of his name. An evil being may be reckless of his reputation for veracity, but a good being, never. To man you can offer no greater indignity than to say that he lies. How dreadful then the sin of making God a liar.

Besides, God has made his Word the chief means by which to test the confidence of his creatures in his truth: "Thou hast exalted thy Word above all thy name," (*Psalm 138:2*); that is, above all by which thou hast made thyself known. And the chief burden of God's Word is, redemption by his Son, together with histories, laws, doctrines, promises, and threatenings. His Word is truth selected from the boundless field of omniscience. It is more precious than gold, yea, than much fine gold. His words are fitly spoken. They are like apples of gold in a network of silver. They are more precious than rubies. To disbelieve them is to trample pearls under our feet. It is to take the covenant of God and treat it with contempt. Unbelief, therefore, is of the nature of sacrilege. It puts the holiest things to base uses. Moreover, God has not only pledged his word, but he has added to it the awful solemnity of an oath. He who disbelieves his Word charges him with falsehood. He who discredits his oath charges him with perjury. A witness may give his testimony upon oath, and we may decide in the teeth of all he swears, but in so doing we declare our utter want of confidence in his statements. If God is displeased at anything, it must be at this atrocious insult.

Nor is this all. To disbelieve God is to believe his enemies, and especially his great adversary, the father of lies. Eve believed the devil rather than her Maker. When Ahab rejected the testimony of the man of God, he was ready to believe the lying prophets of Baal. Chateaubriand says: "Men are ready to believe anything when they believe nothing. They have diviners when they cease to have prophets; witchcraft when they cease to have religious ceremonies; they open the caves of sorcery when they shut the temples of the Lord." He who does not believe God surely believes the great deceiver. Such impiety is shocking to all right-minded persons. Its wickedness is manifest to all whose consciences are not seared as with a hot iron.

2. He who by unbelief rejects the Word of God and his well-beloved Son, impugns the Divine wisdom. If we say that we do not need the salvation of the gospel, we charge God with making a needless sacrifice, and needless provision for our souls. When one says he is well, he declares that he needs no remedy. When one says he is good enough, and justifies himself, he cannot but look upon redemption by atoning blood as either a fable or a folly – a vast expenditure to no wise purpose. God's wisdom determined that Christ's work and death were necessary for our salvation. Unbelief says, "We can do without a Saviour." Or if the sense of guilt is strong, then our unbelief, tending to despair, impeaches God's wisdom by saying that the death of Christ is insufficient, and his blood inefficacious to wash away our sins. We say the remedy is not adequate. We say that sin stains too deeply and guilt presses too heavily for us to hope in the

atonement of God's dear Son. In this view the scheme of redemption is a failure. It lacks virtue. It meets not men's wants. Could a more heinous impeachment of God's wisdom be made? Shall man be wiser than God, who charges his angels with folly? Is it surprising that the Judge of all the earth should be offended, yea, incensed, when men reject his Son and his gospel, which is both the wisdom of God and the power of God unto our salvation?

3. Unbelief is a rejection of kindness, a slighting of unspeakable mercy offered to us by the Lord. The refusal of Jesus Christ has no parallel for ingratitude, stubbornness, and daring impiety. Sovereign Love holds to our lips the cup of salvation. Unbelief puts it away, and says, "Let thy gifts be to thyself, and thy rewards to another; I need them not; I trust them not; I accept them not." In unbelief, the debtor in prison refuses to let Jesus be his Surety. By unbelief, the poor naked soul refuses the spotless righteousness of Christ, and cleaves to the filthy rags of its own righteousness. Unbelief refuses to permit the great Deliverer to come in and knock off the chains of fiery condemnation. It spurns the balm of Gilead, although the soul is all diseased. God expostulates with the wicked, and says, "How shall I give thee up? As I live, I have no pleasure in the death of the sinner. My repentings are kindled together." The Father of mercy calls them. The Son of his love cries, "Come unto me, all ye that labour and are heavy laden." The Holy Spirit woos. The church of God says, "Come." Surely it cannot be safe, it must be perilous, lightly to esteem such love and pity, mercy bought with blood – the blood of propitiation; mercy offered to us by the Lord himself; mercy so much needed by us all; mercy rejected by none but the perverse. God's love to us is amazing; Christ's love to us far exceeds any love the best man bears to him; the love of the Holy Spirit is unsurpassed. How, how can we slight such kindness?

4. Unbelief is a denial and refusal of the grace of God in the gospel of his Son. And we need all the grace proffered to us. We are sinful, guilty, justly condemned, blind, ignorant, wretched, impotent. We are without strength, without holiness, without righteousness, without saving knowledge, without healing medicines, without hope, without God in the world. This is and must continue to be our state till we are made partakers of that grace which is rich, free, unmerited, abundant, treasured up in Christ, and proclaimed in

the glorious gospel. But unbelief says, Christ has died in vain, his intercession is of no value or importance, his gospel is a fable. In robbing our own souls of this mercy, we rob God of the glory of his grace. In a word, if a man should choose to set himself in a universal opposition unto God, he can think of no more compendious way than this, of unbelief.

5. Unbelief is a slighting of God's power both to save and to destroy, and of his authority as a Lawgiver and Governor. He has brought all his sovereignty to bear on the duty of faith in Christ: "This is his commandment, that we should believe on the name of his Son." (*1 John 3:23*). To disregard this command is to contemn all his power over us, for he requires faith in his Son under the sanction of the most awful threatenings, many of which have been already recited.

6. The sin of unbelief is in most cases terribly aggravated. It is commonly a sin that has been long persisted in. If men are now unbelievers, they have been committing that sin all their days. Their lives have been lives of unbelief. For one act of unbelief Moses was denied admission into Canaan. For one act of unbelief Zacharias was struck dumb. But our acts of unbelief have been as numerous as the calls of mercy which we have resisted. And our unbelief has been indulged against much instruction and knowledge. Often has the light shone as clear as day. Often have we heard appeals as solemn as death, and as tender as the compassions of a dying Saviour. If we are now in unbelief we know, indeed we have long known, it was a sin. For unbelief indulged under a much darker dispensation, the carcases of six hundred thousand men fell in the wilderness. Again, we have seen great sinners turn from sin to the Saviour, and find mercy. In their renovated lives we had the proof of the power of Christ to save. We must be guilty for disregarding the lessons of such examples. Hear the Son of God himself on this matter: "The publicans and the harlots believed John; and ye, when ye had seen it, repented not afterward, that ye might believe." (*Matthew 21:32*). Yea more, the salvation of the gospel is God's last offer to man. Christ's atonement rejected by unbelief, there remains no more sacrifice for sins. God will never send another Saviour into the world. Christ himself said: "If ye believe not that I am he, ye shall die in your sins." (*John 8:24*). Indeed, unbelief is

by pre-eminence the damning sin of all who hear the gospel and perish. It is of the nature of *all* sin to work death; but unbelief is a sin without which no other sin that we in a gospel land commit renders damnation inevitable. It is the act of a poor condemned criminal on his way to execution refusing a pardon. It is the act of Esau taking the pottage, eating it, and giving up the birthright for ever. And unbelief is a sin always wilfully committed. So charges Christ himself: "Ye will not come to me, that ye might have life." So charge the apostles: "Ye judge yourselves unworthy of everlasting life." Unbelief persisted in, seals our perdition. It closes every door of hope, and leaves us enshrouded in the darkness of despair for ever and ever. It does all this by grieving the Holy Ghost, by vexing him to depart from us.

7. Indeed, how can unbelief be other than an enormous sin, when it has its seat in pride, self-will, self-righteousness, love of riches, love of human honours, and hardness of heart? "The wicked, through the pride of his countenance, will not seek after God," (*Psalm 10:4*); "How can ye believe, which receive honour one of another, and seek not the honour that cometh from God only?" (*John 5:44*). "Ye cannot serve God and mammon," (*Matthew 6:24*); "If any man love the world, the love of the Father is not in him," (*1 John 2:15*); "Ye do always resist the Holy Ghost." (*Acts 7:51*). These are but samples of the manner in which God speaks of the causes of unbelief. All unbelief has its seat in dreadful depravity.

8. We may judge of the heinousness of the sin of unbelief from the dreadful sentence resting on all in whom it reigns. The Bible says they are "condemned already." They are condemned by the first covenant, which says: "Cursed is every one that continueth not in all things which are written in the book of the law to do them," (*Galatians 3:10*); "The soul that sinneth, it shall die" – *it* shall die – it *shall* die – it shall *die*. And O what a death! But to this condemnation is added that of the gospel: "He that believeth not is condemned already ... This is the condemnation, that light is come into the world, and men loved darkness rather than light." (*John 3:18, 19*). O this double condemnation, how terrible! It is a condemnation from God, the Lawgiver, the Judge of all. His sentence is irreversible. And it "*already*" rests on unbelievers. The Day of Judgment will declare and enforce it, but it will not alter it.

He who lives and dies condemned, will awake to shame and everlasting contempt on the morning of the last day, and will stand self-condemned as well as God-condemned at the tribunal of Christ. Beware, unbeliever, beware. "Forsaking truth and embracing error, angels shrunk into devils. Forsaking error and grasping truth, sinners rise to the dignity of saints, and to the companionship of angels."

*   *   *

1. What a dreadful thing is sin! It is so daring, so stubborn, so mischievous, so ruinous to man, so dishonouring to God.

2. What mercy is found in God in providing a Saviour, in offering him to our acceptance, in waiting on ungrateful and rebellious men so long, and in actually leading many to the Saviour.

3. What a dreadful doom awaits those who will not be reclaimed! "It shall be more tolerable for … Sodom and Gomorrah in the day of judgment than for" such. "Unbelief brings greater guilt" and sorer punishment "than the sins of the worst of heathens, who never heard of these glorious things, nor have had this Saviour offered to them." … "The moth shall eat them up like a garment, and the worm shall eat them like wool," says God; "but my righteousness shall be for ever, and my salvation from generation to generation." (*Isaiah 51:8*).

4. Let us carefully guard against that great parent of unbelief, a self-righteous temper, which says, "I am holy, I am clean, I am pure." "If righteousness come by the law, then Christ is dead in vain." (*Galatians 2:21*). To expect heaven on the ground of your own merit is, says Edwards, to "arrogate to yourself the honour of the greatest thing that ever God himself did." … "To take on yourself to work out redemption is a greater thing than if you had taken it upon you to create a world." A self-righteous spirit is fatal to the soul.

5. "Take heed, brethren, lest there be in any of you an evil heart of unbelief, in departing from the living God." (*Hebrews 3:12*). It dishonours and provokes God. It grieves the Saviour. (*Mark 3:5*). It grieves the Holy Spirit of promise. An attack of fever is not so bad as an assault of unbelief.

6. The great business assigned us on earth by God himself is, believing – believing on the Lord Jesus Christ. When the multitude said to Jesus, "What shall we do, that we might work the works

of God? Jesus answered and said unto them, This is the work of God, that ye believe on him whom he hath sent." (*John 6:28, 29*). So when the jailor cried, "Sirs, what must I do to be saved?" Paul and Silas said, "Believe on the Lord Jesus Christ, and thou shalt be saved, and thy house." (*Acts 16:30, 31*). This is the tenor of all the Scripture. It is only by faith that we enter into rest. Be sure you truly believe: "Without faith it is impossible to please God." "Till you have this faith, you have no special interest in Christ. It is only believers that are united to him, and are his living members. And it is by faith that he dwells in our hearts, and that we live in him. (*Ephesians 3:17; Galatians 2:20*). In vain do you boast of Christ, if you are not true believers. You have no part or portion in him. None of his special benefits are yours till you have this living, working faith." (Baxter). The law presses until we believe. Forgiveness and acceptance come not till we close in with Christ: "He that believeth on him is not condemned: but he that believeth not is condemned already." (*John 3:18*). Why, O why do not all perishing sinners flee to Christ? Why will men involve their souls in deeper sin and more alarming danger by persisting even for an hour in the rejection of Christ?

26

The Reproach of Christ

REPROACH is shame, opprobrium, infamy, disgrace, exposing men to scornful derision.

Nothing has rendered men so liable to taunt, reviling, and malignity as love to Jesus Christ. The Lord himself told his people that it should be so: "Ye shall be hated of all men for my name's sake;" "If the world hate you, ye know that it hated me before it hated you." The reproach of the cross has not ceased. (*Matthew 10:22; John 15:18; Galatians 5:11*). Whoever would be a true Christian must obey the summons: "Let us go forth therefore unto him without the camp, bearing his reproach." (*Hebrews 13:13*). The great scandal of Christianity is the cross and the Crucified. It has long been so. The very expectation of a Redeemer, thousands of years before his coming, was an offence to men, and exposed them to virulent scorn.

It is mentioned by the apostle to the Gentiles as worthy of special notice, that "by faith Moses, when he was come to years, refused to be called the son of Pharaoh's daughter; choosing rather to suffer affliction with the people of God, than to enjoy the pleasures of sin for a season; esteeming *the reproach of Christ* greater riches than the treasures in Egypt: for he had respect unto the recompence of the reward." (*Hebrews 11:24-26*). This is an illustrious example of faith, and full of instruction. Let us look at it in some of its more important bearings.

Ancient Egypt was a wonderful country. The Hebrews called it Mizraim, from the son of Ham, who bore that name. To this day the Arabs call it Mizr. By the Greeks and Latins it was called Egypt, the origin of which word we do not know. To its great river, the

Nile, was first given the name of *the Father of waters*. To the over-flowings of this river the land of Egypt owes its extraordinary fertility. Egypt is about four hundred and fifty miles in length. It is commonly divided into Upper Egypt, Lower Egypt, and the Delta. Anciently it was subdivided into forty-two provinces. In Upper Egypt was one of the most remarkable cities known to antiquity; and the whole land was sufficiently supplied with cities and towns. The Egyptians were greatly averse to the life of shepherds or herdsmen. They gave great attention to the culture of grain. Not less than twenty million bushels of corn were for a long time annually sent from Egypt to Rome. The land generally afforded two crops every year – one before and one after the overflowing of the Nile. The Egyptians were a people remarkable for their skill in the arts. No contemporary nation equalled them. To this effect ancient history speaks clearly. The productions of the soil were very various. Different species of wood and varieties of marble in Egypt induced men to become skilful manufacturers. The monuments of ancient art among this people are amazing. For thousands of years the pyramids have been the wonder of the world. One of these covers an area of thirteen acres, and is still four hundred and seventy-four feet above ground. In Upper Egypt, the sphinxes, obelisks and temples still amaze the beholder. Wonderful statuary and paintings are still found in that region. The ancient Egyptians were to a great extent the fathers of science and of literature. Philosophy, astronomy and geometry early found favour among them. There too the practice of making permanent and intelligible records seems first to have extensively prevailed. In their acquirements, the priests of Egypt excelled the savants of all nations; yet the superstitions of the country were strange, mighty, and numerous; there were gods by the thousand; religious worship was addressed to men, to stars, to domestic animals, and even to plants; thus proving that mere science can save no people from debasement, and that "those who are most delicate as to the decencies of life are often the most gross as to the decencies of religion."

For a long time this country was governed by a race of kings known to us as the Pharaohs. The word Pharaoh signifies sovereign power, and is not very different from our word emperor or autocrat. Each of the Pharaohs probably had a proper name; but none of these names are preserved to us in Scripture until the time of Rehoboam, when Pharaoh Shishak lived. We do not, therefore, know which of the Pharaohs was on the throne at the birth of Moses.

But we are well-informed that he had an only child, a daughter, whom he greatly loved, and who was herself childless. According to the Egyptian laws, she was at liberty to adopt whom she would as her son, and on his adoption he became the heir expectant and apparent of the throne of Egypt. The name of Pharaoh's daughter, according to Josephus, was Thermutis. This woman was led to adopt Moses under the following circumstances. For some time a cruel decree had been in force that all the male children of the Hebrews, who had now for a long time been in abject slavery, but who yet rapidly increased in numbers, should be put to death as soon as they were born.

In *Hebrews 11:23*, the apostle says: "By faith Moses, when he was born, was hid three months of his parents, because they saw he was a proper child; and they were not afraid of the king's commandment." What it was that made them regard him with unusual interest, we know not; but they risked their lives to save his. Having kept him concealed for three months, and finding further secrecy impracticable, they put him into a small vessel, or watertight basket, and exposed him on the banks of the Nile. Thermutis, the king's daughter, coming thither to bathe, and perceiving the basket, ordered it to be brought. She opened it, and found a weeping infant. There was watching, at a little distance, a Hebrew girl, about ten years old. It was Miriam, the only sister of Moses. She came to Thermutis, and asked if she would have a Hebrew nurse. God led her to assent, and soon the delighted little sister brought Jochebed, the wife of Amram, and the mother of the babe. The princess gave to the child the name of Moses, which is a compound Egyptian word signifying *drawn out of the water.*

Thermutis had her adopted child taught in all such matters as the vast science and literature of the country could afford. He was also instructed in more important matters. His pious parents taught him the religion of Abraham, Isaac, and Jacob, and early imbued his mind with excellent precepts of wisdom, virtue, and godliness. At what precise age his education was considered complete, is not certain; but it is probable that it was not until he was at least thirty years old, perhaps nearer forty than thirty.

The Scriptures do not inform us as to the circumstances attending the first open act whereby Moses disowned any connection with the royal family. Whether it was done in words and actions, or by actions only, is not known; nor is it necessary that it should be. His forsaking of the court was a matter which could not be misunderstood. Soon after, he fled the country, and went to Midian, and allied himself to Jethro, and remained for forty years longer, until he was called of God to return to Egypt. But it is his conduct in retiring from court that is specially noticed by the apostle: "By faith Moses, when he was come to years, refused to be called the son of Pharaoh's daughter; choosing rather to suffer affliction with the people of God, than to enjoy the pleasures of sin for a season; esteeming the reproach of Christ greater riches than the treasures in Egypt; for he had respect unto the recompence of the reward." (*Hebrews 11:24-26*).

In contemplating the reproach of Christ, and the manner of overcoming it, let us consider:

I. *The choice which Moses made.* It consisted of two parts: something forsaken, and something embraced; something refused, and something received; something relinquished, and something laid hold of. What did he give up?

1. The highest *honours* which earth had to bestow. Egypt was at this time, in an important sense, the mistress of the world. She had more resources, more character, more national glory, than any of the nations of antiquity. Her glory had been filling the world with wonder for ages, and at no time more than within the last eighty years. No crown on earth glittered with such dazzling brightness as the crown of Egypt. More foreigners came to that land to seek wisdom and to wonder than were then going to all the world besides. Priests of other lands came here to study theology. The magi of remote nations visited its schools to study astrology. Whatever was supposed to be useful or ornamental in life, could be found or learned in Egypt. By leaving the court, Moses lost all opportunity of conversing with learned men, and of being an object of admiration as the great light of science and literature in his generation; for although he was not an eloquent man, yet the Bible tells us he was a man "mighty in words." The meaning is that he had not any great fluency, nor did he seek meretricious ornament in speech; yet his great learning and

wisdom were remarkable. That Moses could write with sublimity hardly equalled by any of the ancients, has been confessed by sober critics since the days of Longinus. That in sentiment and style, if not in delivery, he was a sublime preacher and poet, requires no proof beyond that given us in the last two chapters of the Pentateuch. As a historian and a lawgiver, he has no equal. His fitness to govern, and his power to command, have never been surpassed. Moses, then, relinquished all the honour which, as a scholar, a man of science, a military commander, and king of the most enlightened and powerful nation under heaven, he might have enjoyed. Converse with the polite and the great, even as their Mentor or Apollo, he gave up for the life of a shepherd in Midian. The crown of Egypt grew dim, and its glory faded before his eye of faith.

2. He also relinquished all the *pleasures* which the absolute monarchy of ancient Egypt might have afforded. The Scripture says he cared not to enjoy "the pleasures of sin for a season." How many wondrous arts for gratifying our carnal nature are known at courts of great kings, is no secret.

3. He also gave up *great wealth.* There is much force in that phrase, "the treasures in Egypt." Many ancient thrones had vast treasures. It was so with the Jewish throne in the days of Hezekiah, and with that of Babylon in the days of Belshazzar. It was unquestionably so in Egypt in the time of Moses. During the long famine in the days of Jacob, Joseph had bought up all the land in Egypt, and brought it into the possession of the crown.

We have seen what he *relinquished;* let us see what he *embraced.* The apostle uses two phrases, neither of which sounds sweetly in the ears of a carnal man. The first is, "affliction with the people of God;" the other is, "the reproach of Christ."

The afflictions of the people of God at this time were very great. They were in the most abject bondage. They were the slaves of slaves. Servants ruled over them. The Egyptians themselves now for a long time had been nothing but tenants at will of the land under their sovereign. They were at the mercy of their monarch for a home, for food, for raiment, and even for life. These were the degraded people who were the masters of the Hebrews. Over them they had the power of life and death. They had actually murdered many of them, and had made all of them to groan and sigh with the enormous burdens of labour and toil which had been placed upon them. Joseph, who had been dead one hundred and four years, was forgotten. Gratitude for his eminent services was nowhere found. For Moses to make common lot with such a people was an act of great humiliation. The rest of their condition can easily be conjectured. It was exceedingly dark. No one of us has ever witnessed such scenes of misery and degradation. Abject poverty had wrought its usual effects. The Hebrews were far from being highly virtuous, as we might have hoped from their possessing the knowledge of the true God. Only a few of them were truly pious. The great mass of them were gross and sensual unbelievers, who, for their outbreaking sins, perished in the wilderness. When Moses first appeared among them, about the time of his forsaking the court, "he supposed his brethren would have understood how that God by his hand would deliver them: but they understood not." (*Acts 7:25*). Yet they were the people of God by promise and by profession. What little piety there was on earth was chiefly among them. They, too, had the traditions of the patriarchs. They were beloved for the fathers' sakes. To them pertained the covenant, and the promise, and the ordinance of circumcision.

Then their pretended expectation of the Messiah rendered them even more hated than otherwise they would have been. To the Egyptians it looked like a mark of special stupidity, stubbornness, and arrogance for a people thus sunk down in the deepest degradation to be talking about a great king that should arise from among them, be the King of kings and Lord of lords, and establish a government that should have no end and no limit – a kingdom that should rule over all. Hence "the reproach of Christ" mentioned by Paul as coming on Moses at the making of his choice.

II. Let us consider *the elements of his choice.*

1. It was a *choice*, a firm and decided purpose of the *will,* a hearty and voluntary preference of one thing, a cordial and controlling refusal of another thing. Paul speaks both of choosing and refusing. What Moses did he did not by compulsion, nor by over-persuasion, but of choice.

2. It was a choice made at the most critical period of life, when he was about to enter on a splendid career; "at an age when the heart

is most devoted to the pursuit of pleasure, most susceptible of the allurements of ambition."

3. It was a deliberate and intelligent choice. Nothing in the existing state of things around him led to his decision. The popular current was quite the other way. It was also the choice of a man, and not of a child who could not understand what he was doing. The Bible says "he was come to years." In the Greek it is "when he was become great." It is manifest from the Bible chronology that Moses was not less than forty years old. Nor was it the choice of a man who knew not the sweets of a palace. He had been brought up in ease and affluence. He was not a rude boor, incapable of enjoying the refinements and elegancies which encircled the throne of Egypt. Nor was it the choice of a man whose mind was soured by unsuccessful intercourse with the world. So far his relations, public and private, had been as pleasant as possible. The whole history of Moses shows him to have been a man of uncommon tenderness of sensibility, fitting him for intercourse with refined society. He was no ascetic. Nor did he expect by voluntary humility to merit the favour of God. Nor was his choice that of an old man who knew that he could not much longer enjoy the world. Eighty years later "his eye was not dim, nor his natural force abated." He was no dotard. His choice was that of a full-grown man with a sound, mature mind, just as he was about to enter on a course for life – a life in which he had been led to expect stirring events.

4. The choice of Moses cannot be properly estimated without remembering that it was not the pursuit and prospect of great earthly advantages which he relinquished with the probability that affliction and reproach would come in their room. No: he gave up the actual possession of these good things with the entire certainty that the evil things would come. He was not merely in the high road to honour and wealth and power, but he could lay his hand on them all. He had "become great," "mighty in words and deeds;" he was eminent among the Egyptians.

5. Nor could Moses have failed to remember that in refusing to be called the son of Pharaoh's daughter he was exposing himself to the charge of base ingratitude towards his royal benefactress. Moses was not a man whose feelings were so blunted that he was not alive to any just reproach that might be cast upon him. Indeed, *Exodus 4*

shows that he was a man peculiarly modest, diffident, and sensitive to the opinions of mankind. Yet he chose as he did.

6. The choice of Moses was an unreserved, an unconditional, and a final choice. The royal displeasure once incurred, and the royal confidence once forfeited, there was no hope of return. He indeed had no desire to win back the favour of the Pharaohs. He gave up all to the cause he espoused. He did not even look back.

7. His choice was a gracious choice. Without the aid of God's Spirit on his heart he never would have made it. Flesh and blood did not reveal to him the great things that lay at the foundation of his decision.

III. Let us now consider *the wisdom of his choice.* It was wise then. Moses *believed* it to be so. His history since has demonstrated its wisdom. True, he was forced to flee his country. Soon he was away in Midian. But God visited him there, and spoke to him in the burning bush, and in due time called him to be leader to his people. In the majesty of a mighty man of God, he appeared the august ambassador from heaven at the court of Pharaoh; there he wrought great wonders; then in a marvellous manner he led forth God's afflicted people; became the historiographer of the world; gave laws to the most renowned nation whose history has reached us; in an important sense he became the lawgiver of all nations; he inscribed his name on the pinnacle of fame above that of any of his countrymen or contemporaries; he beheld God and knew him face to face; he had so much honour paid him that to hinder his tomb from becoming the scene of superstitious devotions, no man knows the place of his burial unto this day. When he died, God stood by him; when he was buried, Jehovah buried him – an honour conferred on no other. Ages after his death he appeared in great glory on the mount of transfiguration. Since that time his splendid career has been becoming still more brilliant; and yet it doth not appear what he shall be, only when Christ shall appear he shall be like unto the glorified Lamb of God. It is now (1867) nearly three thousand four hundred years since Moses made his choice. Eighty of these were spent in affliction and reproach, yet not without comforts, joys, and supports which none of Egypt's monarchs ever tasted. The remaining more than three thousand years have all been spent in heaven. Yet eternity is hardly begun, and the work of redemption is not consummated either in regard to Moses or his race. The glories of salvation have but begun to be revealed. Already in heaven they sing the song of Moses and the Lamb; yet what is that song compared to the hosannas and hallelujahs which shall fill the upper temple when the fulness of the Gentiles, the abundance of the seas, and the nation of the Jews shall return to God; and when the work of redemption shall be concluded by the sublimities and splendours of the resurrection morning, of the judgment day, and of the marriage supper of the Lamb! Could we ask Moses what he now thinks of his choice, does any doubt what his answer would be? When Peter, James, and John saw him on the holy mount, did they see anything in his appearance that argued sorrow or relenting of choice? Was his countenance way-worn or gloomy? Rather, was it not cheered with light like the sun, and glory like unto that of the angels of God?

IV. *The cause of his choice* next claims our attention. The cause of his choice was his faith. So we are distinctly told: "By faith Moses, when he was come to years, refused to be called the son of Pharaoh's daughter." (*Hebrews 11:24*). The great object of *Hebrews 11*, where the choice of Moses is stated, is to celebrate the grand achievements of this illustrious grace. The faith of Moses was not a blind credulity; it was not a sottish superstition; it was a reliance on the divine testimony given to the fathers, and through them to their posterity. His faith looked at things which could be seen neither by sense nor reason. He "had regard to the recompence of reward" – the reward of eternal life. He looked back to former ages, and he looked forward to coming ages. The chief excellency of his faith was, the respect which it had to the Messiah. He believed all that God had said respecting the Deliverer which should arise. The coming of Christ was no secret among the Jews. It was always a pillar of their faith. Moses bore the reproach of Christ. He "esteemed the scoffs cast on the Israelites for expecting the Messiah to arise from among them, in whom all the nations of the earth should be blessed, 'greater riches than the treasures of Egypt.'" Wonderful indeed have been the effects of true faith, wherever it has existed.

*   *   *

1. True religion is the same in all ages. It is based on the same principles: it produces the same effects. Whoever properly believes God has the same religion that Moses had, and under fair trial will prove it.

2. Let every man examine himself, and see what manner of spirit he is of. It is a great mercy when God so deals with us here as to furnish us a real test of our true character.

3. The apostle speaks well when he tells us of "precious faith." What could we do without it? "Faith makes all evil good to us, and all good better; unbelief makes all good evil to us, and all evil worse. Faith laughs at the shaking of the spear; unbelief trembles at the shaking of a leaf. Faith finds food in famine and a table in the wilderness. In greatest danger faith answers, I have a great God. When outward strength is broken, faith answers, The promises are strong still. Then faith pulls the sting out of trouble, and draws out the wormwood of every affliction." O let us have faith in God. O Lord, increase our faith.

4. Let us not be discouraged, however much our condition may differ from our wishes. "The life of a man does not consist in what he has, but in what he is and hopes to be." The same God that led Moses into Midian can bring us out of any depths into which affliction may have cast us. The strong arm with which God saved Moses and his people is as mighty as ever.

5. The wicked one gives his servants a treatment very different from that received by God's people. "The wages that sin bargains to give the sinner are, life, pleasure, and profit; but the wages it pays him are, death, torment, and destruction. He that would understand the falsehood and deceit of sin must compare its promises and its payments together." But the Lord gives good measure, pressed together and running over. In death he gives victory.

> "How often has the gloom which spread
> Above the Christian pilgrim's head,
> And darkened all his earthly way,
> Like Israel's beacon, cloud by day,
> Changed, as the hour of death drew nigh,
> To flame that streamed along the sky,
> And lit his footsteps through the night
> With holy fire and heavenly light."

Where is your treasure? Where are your affections? If the earth should be burned up, have you anything left?

6. Let us receive the word of exhortation. Like Moses, we all are passing through scenes which are manifesting our preferences. Had he chosen this world, how different his history, how sad his destiny. We *must* choose this world or the next. The present is near, urgent, and flattering; but it is vain, fleeting, and full of disappointment. "Our love to creatures is like the running of a stream in a channel that is too narrow for it, where stops and banks do make it go on with roaring violence. Our love to God is like the brook that slideth into the ocean, where it is insensibly swallowed up."

7. Let us not be cast down by the reproach of Christ. Others have borne it, and even triumphed in it. All will come right at last. The Son of man has been here in weakness and suffering; but in due time he shall come in his glory, and all the holy angels with him, and before him shall be gathered all nations. Then it will be found an immortal honour to have borne shame and spitting for him: "If ye be reproached for the name of Christ, happy are ye; for the Spirit of glory and of God resteth upon you." (*1 Peter 4:14*). All this will be manifest in the last day. For the King shall say unto them on his right hand, "Come, ye blessed of my Father, inherit the kingdom prepared for you from the foundation of the world." (*Matthew 25:34*). One smile from the eternal Judge will for ever obliterate all painful impressions made upon us by the scorn of men who have despised us for Christ's sake.

> "Under sorrows and reproaches,
>   Let this thought our courage raise:
>   Swiftly God's great day approaches;
>   Sighs shall then be changed to praise.
>   We shall triumph
>   When the world is in a blaze."

27
Conclusion

GREAT and glorious is our theme when we speak of Christ. He will occupy our thoughts for ever. The preceding chapters have discussed several weighty points. The pious reader will allow some brief remarks on kindred topics in conclusion.

I. *Union with Christ.* The New Testament abounds with teaching respecting the union between Christ and believers. Our Lord himself dwelt much on it, especially near the close of his life. In his intercession he prays "that they all may be one; as thou, Father, art in me, and I in thee, that they also may be one in us: that the world may believe that thou hast sent me. And the glory which thou gavest me I have given them; that they may be one, even as we are one: I in them, and thou in me, that they may be made perfect in one." (*John 17:21-23*). The union between Christ and believers is variously set forth in holy Scripture.

1. Inspired writers compare it to the union between the stones in an edifice and the foundation. By one of the prophets Jehovah says: "Behold, I lay in Zion a chief Corner-stone, elect, precious; and he that believeth on him shall not be confounded." The apostle of the circumcision takes up the figure, and refers it to Christ: "To whom coming, as unto a living stone, disallowed indeed of men, but chosen of God, and precious, ye also, as lively stones, are built up a spiritual house." (*1 Peter 2:4, 5*). The apostle of the Gentiles employs like language: "Ye are built upon the foundation of the apostles and prophets, Jesus Christ himself being the chief Corner-stone; in whom all the building fitly framed together groweth unto

an holy temple in the Lord: in whom ye also are builded together for an habitation of God through the Spirit." (*Ephesians 2:20-22*). Believers rest their whole weight on Christ. This foundation can never fail. The conflagration of the last day shall in no wise disturb the Rock on which they rest. It shall stand for ever. They are not dead, but lively stones, and are an habitation of God through the Spirit.

2. Union with Christ is compared to the union of the members in the human body: "Know ye not that your bodies are the members of Christ? ... He that is joined unto the Lord is one spirit; ... ye are the body of Christ, and members in particular ... For as the body is one, and hath many members, and all the members of that one body, being many, are one body: so also is Christ." (*1 Corinthians 6:15, 17;12:12, 27*). Let not the hand say to the foot, "I have no need of thee;" nor the eye to the hand, "I have no need of thee." Christ is the head of the body, the church. So she is sure of his sympathy. No man ever yet hated his own flesh; neither did Christ ever hate one of his own members. He regarded the cruelties of Saul of Tarsus as directed against himself. He loved his church of old; he loved her unto death; he loves her still; he shall love her for ever.

3. Christ is the Husband of his church, and she is his spouse, his love, his dove, his undefiled. "The husband is the head of the wife, even as Christ is the head of the church ... Husbands, love your wives, even as Christ also loved the church, and gave himself for it." (*Ephesians 5:23, 25*). No husband ever loved his wife as Christ loved the church. His love is infinite, eternal, unchangeable. Feeble as she may be, she comes up safely "from the wilderness, leaning upon her Beloved." (*Song of Solomon 8:5*).

4. Union with Christ is sometimes compared to the union of the branches with the stock: "I am the true vine, and my Father is the husbandman ... Every branch in me that beareth fruit, he purgeth it, that it may bring forth more fruit ... I am the vine, ye are the branches ... As the branch cannot bear fruit of itself, except it abide in the vine; no more can ye, except ye abide in me ... Abide in me, and I in you." (*John 15:1-5*). Thus believers get sap and nourishment and fruitfulness from Christ, and from Christ alone. In the same connection, the Saviour says: "Without me ye can do nothing." No wonder that the branch severed from the trunk withers and dies.

By this union with Christ his people enjoy all spiritual blessings. In particular, they have pardon by his blood, acceptance by his righteousness, renewal by his Spirit, increase of grace, divine sympathy in their sorrows, victory in temptation, support in death, a glorious resurrection, a public acquittal in the Day of Judgment, and everlasting life. Severed from Christ, no man is strong, or wise, or righteous, or holy, or safe. United to Christ, all that is included in a great salvation belongs to the believer.

So that the real child of God ought not to faint, nor be discouraged. He may have the same temptations and afflictions as his Lord; but "if we suffer, we shall also reign with him: if we deny him, he also will deny us." Therefore, "if any man suffer as a Christian, let him not be ashamed; but let him glorify God on this behalf." (*2 Timothy 2:12; 1 Peter 4:16*).

Thus also the feeblest child of God shall be tenderly beloved and cared for. The weak in faith shall be holden up, for God is able to make him stand.

If these things are so, it is not surprising that God's people have so fervent love one to another. Their union among themselves arises from their union with Christ. The closer they are drawn to him, the nearer they are to one another.

II. *Admiration of Christ.* The people of God do greatly admire and wonder at the excellence and glory of Christ. In proportion to their faith, they delight in thinking of his all-sufficiency, and are carried away with their pious thoughts, their souls being made like the chariots of Amminadib. This shall be a part of their employment in the last day and for ever.

When Christ shall come to be glorified in his saints, he shall also come to be admired in all them that believe. Even in this world, the people of God often forget their trials by the way, and are lost in admiration of Christ. When a young man, for seventeen days I watched by the dying-bed of a dear Christian friend. Shortly before his death, thinking of the Redeemer, he wrote:

"What Christian has not sometimes given expression to the feelings of his heart in some such language as this: 'What a Saviour!' That there should be to us, lost and ruined sinners, any Saviour, is marvellous mercy, is worthy of our highest admiration; but that there should be to us such a Saviour, is still more astonishing. I have thought that we might have had a Saviour, who should have been able to save us, and should have actually saved many, and yet not have been such a Saviour. Less tender, less condescending, less forbearing, I have thought, he might have been, and yet have been a Saviour. It seems as if Jesus had said more kind things and done more kind acts than were absolutely necessary to have been said and done by him. Need he have made that apology for his disciples, who could sleep when he was in his agony – 'the spirit indeed is willing, but the flesh is weak?' I wonder how they could have slept in such an hour but I wonder more at the apology their Master made for them. Need he have uttered that prayer on the cross, 'Father, forgive them; for they know not what they do'? We don't expect such things from the innocent when dying by the hand of violence. If he had maintained silence during these hours of inconceivable anguish, we should have been satisfied. But oh, think of his forgetting himself, and when they were deriding, and in every way insulting him, hear him meekly addressing his Father on their behalf, asking him to forgive them, and pleading for them that they knew not what they did. It was not necessary that he should have paid any visible attention to the supplication of the thief. It could not have been expected of him. But that he should have turned his head, and looked such forgiveness and love while he said, 'Today shalt thou be with me in paradise,' is a strange mystery of love. O 'what a Saviour!' Why, he knows from experience what pain is; he has had the trials I have; he has been through the vale of tears; he knows how I am tried; he remembers how he was tried. If he never smiled, yet he wept – even over the very city and people whose soil and hands were about to be stained with his blood. I wonder that I love him so little; I wonder he is not more precious to me; I wonder any should be offended in him. How can he appear a root out of a dry ground? Why don't all see his form and comeliness?"

Such admiration of the Saviour naturally leads to: –

III. *The imitation of Christ.* It is with great authority over the conscience that the Scripture says: "Let this mind be in you which was also in Christ Jesus;" and "Consider him that endured such contradiction of sinners against himself, lest ye be wearied and faint in your minds." (*Philippians 2:5; Hebrews 12:3*). Christ's example shows us what the Christian graces are, and how far they are to be carried. It is sometimes said that there is a point beyond which forbearance ceases to be a virtue. If there be such a point, surely it would have been reached in the life of Christ. But where is it? He hath left us an example that we should follow his steps. It is true Christian love to sing:

> "Such was thy truth, and such thy zeal,
> Such deference to thy Father's will,
> Such love, and meekness so divine,
> I would transcribe and make them mine.
>
> "Be thou my pattern; make me bear
> More of thy gracious image here!
> Then God the Judge shall own my name
> Amongst the followers of the Lamb."

That this is not overstraining the matter is evident from Scripture. John says that every man who hopes to see Jesus as he is, purifies himself even as He is pure. (*1 John 3:3*). Paul says: "I am crucified with Christ: nevertheless I live; yet not I, but Christ liveth in me." (*Galatians 2:20*). It is therefore a great fault in professors of religion that they do not more earnestly strive to imitate Christ in love, and gentleness, in tenderness of heart, in submission to the will of God, in zeal for the divine glory, in self-abnegation, in silence under unjust reproaches, and in all his imitable virtues. The highest honour we can render to the Lord Jesus is honestly and earnestly to pray and labour to be like him.

Of course nothing distresses the people of God so much as to find themselves full of imperfection, even after they have long been followers of the Lamb. They still daily cry: "Forgive us our debts, as we forgive our debtors." (*Matthew 6:12*).

Philip Henry says: "If my prayers were written down, and my vain thoughts interlined, what incoherent nonsense would there be! I am ashamed, Lord, I am ashamed! Oh pity and pardon! ... These following sins were set home with power upon my conscience: 1. Omissions innumerable. I fall short of duty in every relation. 2. Much frowardness upon every occasion, which fills my way with thorns and snares. 3. Pride; a vein of it runs through all my conversation. 4. Self-seeking; corrupt ends in all I do. Applause of men often regarded more than the glory of God. 5. My own iniquity. Many bubblings up of heart-corruption, and breakings forth too. Lord, shame hath covered my face."

Indeed, the best men weep day and night over their unbelief, hardness of heart, pride, vanity, ingratitude, discontent, self-will, self-righteousness, irritability, envy, censoriousness, carnal security, spiritual deadness, lack of fervour, and other sins and short-comings. This has been the case with men of every age. Job says, "I abhor myself, and repent in dust and ashes." (*Job 42:6*). David cries, "Mine iniquities have taken hold upon me, so that I am not able to look up; they are more than the hairs of mine head: therefore my heart faileth me." (*Psalm 40:12*). Isaiah said, "Woe is me! for I am undone; because I am a man of unclean lips, and I dwell in the midst of a people of unclean lips." (*Isaiah 6:5*). Peter "fell down at Jesus' knees, saying, Depart from me; for I am a sinful man, O Lord." (*Luke 5:8*). The bitterest cry ever heard on earth was that of the Saviour on the cross, "My God, my God, why hast thou forsaken me?" (*Matthew 27:46*). Next to this in bitterness was the cry of Paul: "O wretched man that I am! who shall deliver me from the body of this death?" (*Romans 7:24*). The *body of this death* is a Hebrew form of expression, signifying *this dead body*. The language is supposed by some to have been derived from the mode of punishing murderers adopted by certain ancient tribes, who fastened the several parts of the body of the murdered to the corresponding parts of the murderer, then confining his hands so that he could not effect his own release. In his distress, the poor criminal would cry, "Who shall deliver me from this dead body? Oh that I had some relief. Will no one help me?"

So Paul cried for deliverance. He loathed sin. He hated nothing so much. Whenever he contemplated it, it filled him with terror and detestation. He consented to the law that it was good: yea, he delighted in the law of God after the inward man. With his mind he served the law of God. He loved holiness, yet so annoyed was he by indwelling sin, and so violent were its assaults upon him, that he pronounces himself carnal, sold under sin. The contest was dreadful, the war fearful. Nothing was to him so offensive as his own corruptions. In the jail at Philippi, his flesh torn with the scourges, his feet fast in the stocks, surrounded by the gloom of midnight, he prayed, and sang praises to God, and the prisoners heard him. He was in stripes above measure, in prisons more frequent, in deaths oft. Of the Jews five times he received forty stripes save one. Thrice was he beaten with rods, once was he stoned, thrice he suffered shipwreck, a night and a day had he been in the deep; in journeyings often, in perils of waters, in perils of robbers, in perils by his own countrymen, in perils by the heathen, in perils in the city, in perils in the wilderness, in perils in the sea, in perils amongst false brethren; in weariness and painfulness, in watchings often, in hunger and thirst, in fastings often, in cold and nakedness. Yea, the Holy Ghost witnessed that in every city bonds and afflictions awaited him. Yet of all these he said, "None of these things move me." But when sin pierces him he cries, "O wretched man that I am!" O, it is a good sign to mourn for sin, and to long for holiness. How sweet heaven will be to all weary pilgrims. There we shall be for ever done with temptation. There we shall never, never sin. There we shall be like him, for we shall see him as he is. Even now a view of him by faith has a transforming power, as Paul teaches: "We all, with open face beholding as in a glass [mirror] the glory of the Lord, are changed into the same image from glory to glory, even as by the Spirit of the Lord." (*2 Corinthians 3:18*). And Paul himself follows his cry with the triumphant shout: "I thank God through Jesus Christ our Lord." (*Romans 7:25*).

IV. *Glorifying Christ.* If the views previously presented are correct, then it is true that all the saints do greatly desire to put the highest honour upon Christ – they glorify him. In receiving honour from his people, Christ and the Father are not separated. When we in heart honour one person of the Godhead, we virtually honour all. And it is the will of God that "all men should honour the Son, even as they honour the Father." (*John 5:23*). How full the Scriptures are of this matter, the pious reader will easily remember.

This truth is often and delightfully illustrated in the *Life of David Brainerd.* Under date of November 22, 1744, he writes:

> "Came on my way from Rockciticus to the Delaware. Was very much disordered with a cold and pain in my head. About six at night I lost my way in the wilderness, and wandered over rocks and mountains, down hideous steeps, through swamps, and most dreadful and dangerous places; and the night being dark, so that few stars could be seen, I was greatly exposed. I was much pinched with cold, and distressed with an extreme pain in my head, attended with sickness

at my stomach; so that every step I took was distressing to me. I had little hope for several hours together, but that I must lie out in the woods all night in this distressed case. But about nine o'clock I found a house through the abundant goodness of God, and was kindly entertained. Thus I have frequently been exposed, and sometimes lain out the whole night; but God has hitherto preserved me, and blessed be his name. Such fatigues and hardships as these serve to wean me from the earth; and, I trust, will make heaven the sweeter. Formerly when I was thus exposed to the cold and rain, I was ready to please myself with the thoughts of enjoying a comfortable house, warm fire, and other outward comforts; but now these have less place in my heart, through the grace of God, and my eye is more to God for comfort. In this world I expect tribulation; and it does not now, as formerly, appear strange to me. I do not in such seasons of difficulty flatter myself that it will be better hereafter; but rather think *how much worse it might be,* how much greater trials *others* of God's children have endured, and how much greater are yet *perhaps reserved for me.* Blessed be God, that he makes the thought of my journey's end and of my dissolution a great comfort to me under my sharpest trials, and scarce ever lets these thoughts be attended with terror or melancholy; but they are attended frequently with great joy."

The secret of this remarkable calmness and heroism is elsewhere clearly expressed by the pious sufferer. Under date of July 26, 1747, he says:

"This day I saw clearly that I should never be *happy* – yea, that God himself could not make me happy – unless I could be in a capacity to please and glorify him for ever."

Again, September 19, of the same year:

"Oh how I longed that God should be glorified *on earth!* … Bodily pains I cared not for; though I was then in extremity, I never felt easier. I felt willing to *glorify God* in that state of bodily distress, as long as he pleased I should continue in it." Again, September 27, of the same year, he says: "I am almost in eternity. I long to be there. My work is done; I have done with all my friends; all the world is nothing to me. I long to be in heaven, praising and glorifying God with the holy angels. All my desire is to glorify God."

The last recorded words taken from his lips are:

"I shall soon glorify God with the angels."

Thus felt also inspired men of old: "I will glorify thy name for evermore." (*Psalm 86:12*). Thus the prophet enjoined: "Glorify ye the Lord in the fires." (*Isaiah 24:15*). Thus the Saviour taught: "Let your light so shine before men, that they may see your good works, and glorify your Father which is in heaven." (*Matthew 5:16*). The sickness of Lazarus was "not unto death, but for the glory of God, that the Son of God might be glorified thereby." (*John 11:4*). Christ and the Father are one. Whoever glorifies the Father, glorifies the Son; and whoever glorifies the Son, glorifies the Father.

V. *Reigning with Christ.* Many saints have left the world crying, "Come, Lord Jesus, come quickly." The Master had come, and was calling for them. The last words of Robert Bruce were: "Now God be with you, my children; I have breakfasted with you, and shall sup with my Lord Jesus Christ this night." Grimshaw said: "I shall have my greatest grief and my greatest joy when I die. My greatest grief, that I have done so *little* for Christ; my greatest joy, that Christ has done so *much* for me." Felix Neff's last words were: "Victory! victory! victory! by Jesus Christ." Dr Marshman's were: "Can you think of anything I am yet to do for the kingdom of Christ?" Dr W J Hoge: "I could tell of Jonathan Edwards, and of many wonderful authors and poets, but they are all comparatively low down. Christ! Christ! the glory of Christ."

Though Christ's people know their Lord, the best is that they are known of him.

It was probably a part of a hymn in use in the primitive church, and is certainly a part of Scripture: "If we suffer [with him], we shall also reign with him." (*2 Timothy 2:12*). More than half a century after our Lord's ascension to glory, he sends to the angel of the church at Laodicea this message: "*To him that overcometh will I grant to sit with me in my throne, even as I also overcame, and am set down with my Father in his throne.*" (*Revelation 3:21*). Doddridge's paraphrase of this promise is: "For your further encouragement, hear the last promise which I make to all who exert themselves in that holy warfare to which I am calling you, with becoming vigour and resolution. As for the valiant conqueror, I will give him to sit down with me upon my glorious and exalted throne in the heavenly world; as I also myself have conquered the enemies which violently assaulted me in the days of my flesh, and am set down with my Father upon his throne; my faithful servants shall partake with me of this honour in the great day of my appearing, and shall live and reign with me for ever."

Poole explains the promise thus: "I will give him great honour, dignity, and power; he shall judge the world in the day of judgment, (*1 Corinthians 6:3*), and the twelve tribes of Israel, (*Matthew 19:28*); he shall be made partaker of my glory, (*John 17:22, 24*). But such must come to my throne as I came to it. I overcame the world, sin, death, the devil, and then ascended, and sat down with my Father in his throne: so they that will sit down with me in my throne of glory must fight the same fight, and overcome, and then be crowned."

What is meant by this glorious promise is, and must remain, very much a secret, until we go and see for ourselves, and by a blessed experience find out what it is to enter into the joy of the Lord. Even Paul, who had often been rapt in visions of the third heavens, could tell us no more than this: "I heard unspeakable words, which it is not lawful for a man to utter." (*2 Corinthians 12:4*). The ancient artist drew Helen with a veil over her face, thus confessing that to paint her was impossible. It is far more impossible for us to picture the glories of the celestial state. We must wait till we behold it with our eyes. Then we shall say, "The half was not told us."

> "On wings of faith mount up, my soul, and rise;
> View thine inheritance beyond the skies.
> Nor heart can think, nor mortal tongue can tell,
> What endless pleasures in those mansions dwell.
> Here my Redeemer lives, all bright and glorious;
> O'er sin, and death, and hell he reigns victorious.
>
> "No gnawing grief, no sad, heart-rending pain,
> In that blest country can admission gain.
> No sorrow there, no soul-tormenting fear,
> For God's own hand shall wipe the falling tear.
> Here my Redeemer lives, all bright and glorious;
> O'er sin, and death, and hell he reigns victorious.
>
> "No rising sun his needless beams displays,
> No sickly moon emits her feeble rays.
> The Godhead here celestial glory sheds;
> Th'exalted Lamb eternal radiance spreads.
> Here my Redeemer lives, all bright and glorious;
> O'er sin, and death, and hell he reigns victorious.

Conclusion

"One distant glimpse my eager passion fires,
Jesus, to thee my longing soul aspires.
When shall I at my heavenly home arrive?
When leave this earth, and when begin to live?
For here my Saviour is, all bright and glorious;
O'er sin, and death, and hell he reigns victorious."

Printed in Great Britain
by Amazon

11361652R00160